Klaus Weyerstraß

A tool for supporting economic policy-making in the former Yugoslavia

Osteuropa

Geschichte, Wirtschaft, Politik

begründet von

Wolfgang Eichwede, Frank Golczewski
und Günter Trautmann †

herausgegeben von

Wolfgang Eichwede, Frank Golczewski,
Friedbert Rüb und Monica Rüthers

Band 49

LIT

Klaus Weyerstraß

A tool for supporting economic policy-making in the former Yugoslavia

Documentation and applications of a macroeconomic multi-country model

LIT

Financial Support by the Österreichische Forschungsgemeinschaft (ÖFG) for the publication of this book is gratefully acknowledged.

Bibliographic information published by the Deutsche Nationalbibliothek
The Deutsche Nationalbibliothek lists this publication in the Deutsche Nationalbibliografie; detailed bibliographic data are available on the Internet at http://dnb.d-nb.de.

ISBN 978-3-643-90771-4

A catalogue record for this book is available from the British Library

Klosbachstr. 107
CH-8032 Zürich
Tel. +41 (0) 44-251 75 05 Fax +41 (0) 44-251 75 06
E-Mail: zuerich@lit-verlag.ch http://www.lit-verlag.ch

Distribution:

In the UK: Global Book Marketing, e-mail: mo@centralbooks.com
In North America: International Specialized Book Services, e-mail: orders@isbs.com
In Germany: LIT Verlag Fresnostr. 2, D-48159 Münster
Tel. +49 (0) 2 51-620 32 22, Fax +49 (0) 2 51-922 60 99, e-mail: vertrieb@lit-verlag.de

In Austria: Medienlogistik Pichler-ÖBZ, e-mail: mlo@medien-logistik.at
e-books are available at www.litwebshop.de

PREFACE

In this book, a quarterly macroeconometric multi-country model for Bosnia and Herzegovina, Slovenia, Serbia and Croatia is described in detail. The multi-country model is then tested by evaluating its ability to reproduce the endogenous variables in an ex post simulation. Furthermore, some of the constituting models of the individual countries are used to evaluate economic policies.

The development of the constituting single-country models has been a continuous process which began in 1998 with the model for Slovenia as part of a collaboration between the Slovenian Ministry of Economic Affairs, Verbundplan (an energy consulting company based in Klagenfurt), the University of Klagenfurt and the Institute of Macroeconomic Analysis and Development (IMAD) in Ljubljana.[1] The model developed within this project was called SMEEM (Slovenian Macro Economic Energy Model) and it combined a macroeconomic model and an energy-system model for carrying out energy-sector related analyses. Based upon this initial model, a structural macroeconometric model of the Slovenian economy was built, called SLOPOL (SLOvenian economic POLicy model).

The development of the model for Serbia was initiated within the international research project "Strategic Partnership in Support of the Integrated Regional Development Plan (IRDP) of the Autonomous Province of Vojvodina", financed by the Austrian Development Agency ADA. The project was jointly carried out by the Institute for Advanced Studies, Vienna, and ECONOMICA Institute of Economic Research, Vienna, in close cooperation with the Centre for Strategic Economic Studies "Vojvodina CESS", Novi Sad, Serbia.

The model for Bosnia and Herzegovina was created within a research project supported financially by the *Jubiläumsfonds* of the Austrian National Bank (project no. 12823). Further improvements on this model were inspired during different research projects in Bosnia and Herzegovina.[2]

---

1 Contract "Integriertes Energieprogramm – Makroökonomisches Modell für Slowenien (Austrian-Slovenian Co-operation for an Integrated Energy Program – Development and Implementation of a Macroeconomic Model)" between the Slovenian Ministry of Economic Affairs and Verbundplan GmbH, financed by the Austrian Federal Chancellery (Bundeskanzleramt).

2 "Strengthening the National Planning Process in Bosnia and Herzegovina". EU Twinning Project, 2013 – 2014. Short-term Macroeconomic Expert in the project "EU Fiscal Policy Support to Bosnia and Herzegovina", an EU funded project, 2008.

The development of the Croatian model as well as the integration of the individual single-country models into a multi-country model was supported financially by the *Jubiläumsfonds* of the Austrian National Bank (project no. 13363).

The individual models for Bosnia and Herzegovina, Slovenia and Serbia have been described in Berrer et al. 2009, Weyerstrass and Neck 2007, and Weyerstrass 2009, respectively. A description of the model for Croatia and the first version of the multi-country model can be found in Behrens, Haber and Weyerstrass (2011).

This book is based on my Habilitation thesis, submitted at the Klagenfurt University, Department of Economics. For wide-ranging support and critical discussions during the process of developing the model and writing this book, I would like to extend grateful thanks to Prof. Dr. Reinhard Neck from Klagenfurt University. Dr. Dmitri Blueschke, also from Klagenfurt University, deserves gratitude for his great support in implementing the Slovenian model into the optimisation algorithm OPTCON, implemented in MATLAB, and in conducting the optimisations.

Special thank is due to my parents and to my wife Andrea, who always supported me in an optimal way, even without an optimisation algorithm.

Wals near Salzburg, April 2016 Klaus Weyerstrass

CONTENTS

INTRODUCTION

Economic policy decisions should be based on a sound assessment of their potential costs and benefits rather than on intuition alone. The qualitative impacts of fiscal and monetary policy measures or of external events like sudden oil price hikes on the domestic economy can be derived from economic theory but only a comprehensive representation of the economic interdependencies enables the quantification of these effects. Furthermore, policy-makers as well as private economic agents like planners in companies require forecasts of economic developments in the short and medium-term future. Hence, it is desirable to have a tool at hand that facilitates the evaluation of different economic policy measures as well as the generation of economic forecasts. As for any other country, this also applies to the successor states of the former Yugoslavia.

A macroeconomic model is such a tool, especially if it is an econometric model based on sound theoretical foundations and estimated with actual data from the economy under consideration. The construction of such a model requires a dataset with sufficiently long time series to provide reliable estimates of the relations between the economic variables. For the countries which were part of Yugoslavia until 1991 or even longer, this poses a major problem. For some of the countries, Serbian resistance to independence resulted in wars, leading to major destruction. This applies in particular to Bosnia and Herzegovina and, to a lesser extent, to Croatia. In addition to the war-related damage which some countries in the region had to face, all successor states of the former Yugoslavia had to engage in a transformation process towards market economies. Many data, especially those from national income accounting, are therefore of dubious quality, in particular for the first few years of the transition process. In addition to data problems relating to this transformation process, the countries of the former Yugoslavia are continuously adopting European Union (EU) standards regarding macroeconomic data definitions and classifications, resulting in frequent revisions of previously released data.

For these reasons, estimations of behavioural equations for macroeconometric models for the countries under consideration have to rely on data starting between 1995 and 2000, depending on the country. This book describes the data situation and the construction of macroeconometric models for Bosnia and Herzegovina, Slovenia, Serbia and Croatia. The shortness of the time which has elapsed since their declarations of independence is still impeding the creation of macroeconometric models for Montenegro and Kosovo. Neither has a macroeconometric model been constructed for Macedonia for the multi-country model described here due to the lack of sufficiently long time series of data of reliable quality, especially in a higher than annual frequency.

FROM YUGOSLAVIAN DISINTEGRATION TO EUROPEAN INTEGRATION

From 1991 onwards, the Socialist Federal Republic of Yugoslavia (SFRY) disintegrated into several independent states. For some of the Yugoslav republic's constituent Entities, the secession resulted in armed conflicts, known as the Yugoslav Wars. Finally, the following states were created from the former Yugoslavia: Bosnia and Herzegovina, Croatia, Kosovo, Macedonia, Montenegro, Serbia and Slovenia.

On 25 June 1991, Croatia and Slovenia were the first countries to declare their independence. In January 1992, both countries were internationally recognised by most countries. In September 1991, the Republic of Macedonia declared its independence, Bosnia and Herzegovina following in April 1992. The remaining countries formed the newly created Federal Republic of Yugoslavia. In June 2006, after a referendum in Montenegro, Serbia and Montenegro declared their independence. Finally, in February 2008 Kosovo unilaterally declared its independence from Serbia. Most European countries officially recognised Kosovo as an independent state, but its status is still in dispute.

Among the former Yugoslav republics, the separation of Bosnia and Herzegovina from Serbia was the most problematic one, largely due to its greater ethnic heterogeneity, while the other former Yugoslav republics are by and large more homogenous. Bosnia and Herzegovina (BiH) is home to three ethnic "constituent peoples", Bosniaks, Serbs and Croats. Bosnia and Herzegovina was recognised internationally in April 1992, after its proclamation of independence from the Federal Socialist Republic of Yugoslavia. Concomitantly the Serbs in Bosnia proclaimed the "Republika Srpska of Bosnia and Herzegovina" and withdrew from national government bodies. Subsequently war broke out in BiH. Peace was achieved only in 1995 following pressure from the international community. On 21 November 1995 a peace agreement was reached in Dayton (USA) that put an end to the war. The final agreement was signed in Paris on 14 December 1995. The Dayton peace agreement created a Bosnian state with two Entities and weak centralised institutions. The Federation of Bosnia and Herzegovina (FBiH) is mainly inhabited by Bosnian Muslims and Croats and covers 51 percent of Bosnia and Herzegovina's total territory, while the Republika Srpska (RS) is inhabited by ethnic Serbs and covers around 49 percent of the territory. By recognising the Republika Srpska and the FBiH, the Dayton Agreement consolidated the divisions which had arisen as a consequence of the Bosnian war. Since 1996 the power of the Entities relative to the federal government has decreased significantly. Nevertheless the Entities still have numerous powers themselves. The Brčko District in the north of the country was created in 2000 out of land from both Entities. It officially belongs to both, but it is governed by neither and functions under a decentralized system of local government. The Brčko District has a multi-ethnic population and an above average level of prosperity. The Federation of Bosnia and Herzegovina is divided into ten cantons, representing the third level of Bosnia and Herzegovina´s political subdivision. All of them have their own cantonal government, which is under the law of the Federation as a whole. Some cantons are ethnically mixed and have implemented special laws to ensure the equality of all constituent peoples. The fourth level of political division in Bosnia and Herzegovina is represented by the municipalities.

The European Union's policy towards the countries of the Western Balkans[3] has taken the form of the Stabilisation and Association Process (SAP) launched at the Zagreb Summit in November 2000.[4] Any country aiming at membership of the European Union must conform to the conditions set out by Article 49 and the principles laid down in Article 6(1) of the Treaty on the European Union. The relevant criteria were established by the Copenhagen European Council in 1993 and strengthened by the Madrid European Council in 1995. At the Copenhagen European Council, the following criteria for EU accession were concluded:[5]

- Political criteria: the stability of institutions guaranteeing democracy, the rule of law, human rights, and respect for and protection of minorities.
- Economic criteria: the existence of a functioning market economy as well as the capacity to cope with competitive pressure and market forces within the European Union.
- Criterion for adoption of the acquis commaunitaire: the ability to take on the obligations of membership, including adherence to the aims of political, economic and monetary union.
- For the European Council to decide to open negotiations, at least the political criteria must be satisfied. At the Madrid European Council in

3 The Western Balkans comprises Albania, Bosnia and Herzegovina, Croatia, Kosovo, the former Yugoslav Republic of Macedonia, Montenegro and Serbia

4 See http://europa.eu/scadplus/glossary/stabilisation_association_process_en.htm

5 See http://ec.europa.eu/enlargement/the-policy/conditions-for-enlargement/index_en.htm

1995, the membership criteria were amended by the following requirements:

- The candidate country must have created the conditions for its integration through the adjustment of its administrative structures.
- European Community legislation must be transposed into national legislation.
- More importantly, legislation must be implemented effectively through appropriate administrative and judicial structures.

The requirement that candidate countries fulfil these criteria is meant to ensure that accession will only take place if an associated country is able to assume the obligations of membership. The process is intended to ensure peace and stability in the region by providing support for the strengthening of democracy as well as the development of a market economy. It emphasises the development of regional cooperation, e.g. by a free trade area and political dialogue. The main purpose of the Stabilisation and Association Process is to establish special relations between the countries concerned and the European Union in exchange for reforms with a view to accession, which involves aligning their legislation more closely with that of the EU.

The Stabilisation and Association Process was strengthened at the Thessaloniki Summit in 2003, taking over elements of the accession process. It rests on:

- Contractual relationships by means of bilateral Stabilisation and Association Agreements (SAA), the conclusion of which depends on the progress made by the countries within the process; their application for membership is evaluated based on the results of their compliance with the provisions, particularly concerning trade.
- Trade relations at regional level and with the EU; the EU grants trade preferences to the Western Balkans countries.
- A financial instrument, the Instrument for Pre-Accession Assistance (IPA).

The Western Balkan countries that have acquired candidate country status continue to benefit from certain aspects of the Stabilisation and Association process although they are engaged in the process of accession. As part of this process, they already enjoy free access to the EU single market for practically all their exports, as well as EU financial support for their reform efforts. The centrepiece of the process is a Stabilisation and Association Agreement (SAA) which represents a contractual relationship between the EU and each Western Balkan country, entailing mutual rights and obligations.

The first former Yugoslav republic to join the European Union was Slovenia. The country applied for membership in 1996 and became part of the EU in 2004. Slovenia was also the first – and so far only – country of the former Yugoslavia and the first country from Central and Eastern Europe (CEE) to join the euro area at the beginning of 2007. Croatia applied for EU membership in 2003, Macedonia in 2004, and Serbia at the end of 2009. Croatia was recognised as an EU candidate country in June 2004. Accession negotiations started in June 2006 and were finished in June 2011. In October of the same year, the European Commission endorsed the country's EU accession, which was formally approved by the European Council in December 2011. Following a positive referendum held in January 2012, it was finally decided that Croatia should join the European Union on 1 July 2013. In December 2005, Macedonia was granted the status of a candidate country. However, since Greece is blocking accession negotiations, these have not yet begun. The reason for this is a dispute about the name of the country. Since Greece claims the name "Macedonia" for one of its provinces, the official name for the country is the "Former Yugoslav Republic of Macedonia" (FYROM). Montenegro applied for EU membership in December 2008 and was recognised as a candidate country two years later. Accession negotiations started in December 2012. In March 2012, Serbia was granted the status of an EU candidate country. Accession negotiations started in January 2014. In economic terms, high fiscal deficits and debt, which are largely caused by a great number of inefficient public companies, are the main issues to be solved before accession. Bosnia and Herzegovina and Kosovo are still "potential candidate countries".[6] As part of the EU accession process, Macedonia and Croatia signed Stabilisation and Association Agreements in 2004 and 2005, respectively. Montenegro followed in 2007, and the SAAs between the EU and Bosnia and Herzegovina and Serbia were both signed in 2008. As part of the SAAs, trade barriers are gradually removed and the rules of law in the associated countries are gradually brought in line with EU regulations. Hence, some of the economic benefits of European integration can be reaped by the countries well before actual accession.

European integration of the former Yugoslav republics leads to an intensification of international trade and increasing foreign direct investment. As the latter involves the transfer of knowledge and technology, productivity

---

[6] Details on the statuses of the Western Balkan countries in the EU accession process are to be found on the website of the European Commission, DG Enlargement: http://ec.europa.eu/enlargement/index_en.htm

growth can be expected to speed up. Hence, the capital stock is growing faster, pushing the production possibility frontier outwards, i.e. yielding higher economic growth without additional inflationary pressure. On the other hand, the gradual opening-up of EU labour markets might result in net emigration from the accession countries. However, as the recent EU enlargement rounds have shown, in most cases such international migration was rather limited. Nevertheless, for some Western Balkan countries, in particular for Bosnia and Herzegovina, Macedonia and Serbia, net emigration can be significant, in particular in times of recession or very low economic growth with high unemployment. Such net emigration might put considerable strain on their growth potential, especially if highly qualified and young people leave the country.

MACROECONOMIC MODELLING

When creating a macroeconomic model, different approaches are possible. One class of models is based on general equilibrium theory. The parameters of these models are based primarily on national accounts data from one particular year. Another method is the creation of econometric models. The notion behind these models is to reproduce the data-generating process as accurately as possible (Granger 1997). This data-generating process consists of the realisation of a multidimensional stochastic process. Econometric models can be further subdivided. Firstly, there are models in which the division into endogenous and explanatory variables is based on economic theory. The resulting models are referred to as structural. This contrasts with theory-free models in which the variables of interest are investigated with time-series methods.

From Tinbergen's (1939) work on macroeconomic models up to and including the 1960s, the "Cowles Commission" approach was the predominant strategy in the development of macroeconomic models. Structural econometric models were specified, estimated and then rigorously tested (Fair 1992). The development of these models is closely related to Keynesian theory. In the 1950s and 1960s, such structural models were widely used for economic forecasting. In the late 1960s and early 1970s, critical objections to these models began to be raised, directed especially against the core of Keynesian theory. One response to these concerns was to work on a microeconomic foundation of Keynesian theory, in particular its central elements of sticky wages and prices. Objections to structural models were also based on growing scepticism about the assumption of adaptive expectation formation. It was argued that economic agents build rational expectations, implying that they know the true economic model and use all available information. Another reason for the criticism of Keynesian theory was rooted in the stagflation of the 1970s, which put the trade-off between inflation and unemployment which is inherent to these models into question.

In 1976, Robert E. Lucas argued against the use of structural models for the purpose of policy simulations (Lucas 1976). The gist of his argumentation, which has since been known as the Lucas critique, is that the parameters of a structural econometric model vary when the policy regime changes. Sargent (1981) argues that the Lucas critique is largely based on the notion that parameters of observed decision rules should not be viewed as structural. Instead, according to Sargent, only "deep parameters" such as preferences and technologies can be viewed as structural parameters. These parameters would be invariant to changes in policy regimes. Providing for such "deep parameters" requires a different class of macroeconomic models, namely Computable General Equilibrium (CGE) models.

An approach emerged which took the Lucas critique into account in structural models like the ones described in this book in the so-called London School of Economics tradition, initiated by Sargan (1964). According to this approach, the underlying long-run specification is derived from economic theory, while the dynamic adjustment process is based on the time series properties of the data. Error correction models involving cointegrated variables combine the long-run equilibrium and the short-run adjustment mechanism. More details on error correction models can be found below in the following section.

One response to criticism of the adaptive expectations which are inherent in structural Keynesian models consisted in an attempt to implement rational expectations into these models. An example for this procedure can be found in Taylor (1993). Another response to the objections was the complete abandonment of structural models. Sims (1980) argued that these models should be replaced with vector autoregressive (VAR) models. In a VAR model, all variables are endogenised and each variable is explained by its own past values as well as the development of the other variables in the past. While the Lucas critique is an argument against the use of structural models for forecasting, VAR models can also be criticised. Since they are purely data driven, the signs of some coefficients might conflict with economic theory and cannot, therefore, be interpreted meaningfully. In addition, it has been shown that unrestricted VAR models have poor forecasting properties, since some coefficients represent inefficient estimators. The solution to this problem is to restrict certain parameters of the model in such a way that they lie in a predetermined range or have a particular sign. These models are referred to as structural or Bayesian VAR models. However, these a priori restrictions are often theoretically less justified than the restrictions in structural models because the latter are based on a fully formulated economic theory (Hall 1995). Another objection to the use of VAR models arises from the fact that often a large number of lags are necessary to map the behaviour of a time series adequately. This is particularly true when the data used have a seasonal pattern. In addition, unrestricted vector autoregressive models are not capable of reproducing the long-term behaviour of a time series.

While one route of circumventing the problems associated with structural, Keynesian-style macroeconometric models was the development of purely data-driven models, another route was the creation of models more in line with neoclassical theory, or models with "deep" structural parameters. One strand of such structural macroeconomic modelling was the development of Real Business Cycle (RBC) models. These circumvent the Lucas critique since deep structural parameters are calibrated. RBC models are structural models in which "real" (particularly technology) shocks are the predominant source of economic fluctuations. The seminal contribution to this literature comes from Kydland and Prescott (1982). However, these models do not fit the actual data very well (Fair 1992). The RBC literature requires that a particular functional form is chosen for, the utility function of households, for example. Any error in the specification of this functional form translates directly into errors in the reproduction of the endogenous model variables.

Finally, attempts have been made to integrate neoclassical features like rational expectations with Keynesian elements such as rigidities. Early contributions to this New Keynesian theory can be found in Mankiw and Romer (1991). The papers in these volumes focused mostly on microfoundations that could produce Keynesian macroeconomic effects. More recently, New Keynesian macroeconomics have found their way into macroeconomic models. This class of models is called Dynamic Stochastic General Equilibrium (DSGE) models and their methodology is explained in Woodford (2003). Economists in international organisations are are now actively estimating quantitative models of this type and using them to analyse optimal monetary and fiscal policies. As one prominent example, the New Area-Wide Model (NAWM) of the Europen Central Bank is neoclassical in nature, with intertemporal decisions of households and companies maximising expected life-time utility and the expected stream of profits, respectively (Christoffel et al. 2008). Forward-looking expectations play a key role in influencing the adjustment of quantities and prices, and changes in supply-side factors have a pronounced impact in the short run as well. On the other hand, the NAWM includes nominal and real frictions that have been identified as empirically important, such as sticky prices and wages (so that some Keynesian features prevail in the short run), habit persistence in consumption and adjustment costs in investment. In addition, this model incorporates frictions prevalent in an open economy, including local-currency pricing (giving rise to imperfect exchange-rate pass-through in the short run), and the costs of adjusting trade flows.

Although New Keynesian models are used widely by international organisations nowadays, the multi-country model for the former Yugoslavia described in this book follows more the Keynesian tradition, augmented by some neoclassical features like the determination of potential GDP. The reason for abstaining from general equilibirum assumptions and rational expectations is mainly that the economies in the former Yugoslavia are far from being in an equilibirum. Persistently high unemployment and external deficits are clear indications that these economies are not characterised by only temporary deviations from clearly defined long-run equilibria, but instead the equilibria themselves are changing due to the ongoing transformation process. During this transformation, it is also unlikely that households or companies are able to form rational expectations reaching far into the future.

MODELLING AND ESTIMATION PROCEDURE

The macroeconomic model for the former Yugoslavia described in this book takes the form of a multi-country model. Single-country models for Bosnia and Herzegovina, Slovenia, Serbia and Croatia have been developed and linked via trade and exchange rates to form a multi-country model. In this chapter, technical details are given on the modelling approach. The following chapter describes the way in which the individual country models have been linked to form a multi-country model while the constituting country models are described in detail afterwards.

UNIT ROOT TESTS

Before starting with the modelling, the variables to be used have to be tested for their order of integration. For this purpose, the Augmented Dickey Fuller (ADF) Test (Dickey and Fuller 1979), the Phillips-Perron (PP) Test (Phillips and Perron 1988) and the KPSS test (Kwiatkowski et al. 1992) were performed. The detailed results of these tests can be found in Table 15 for the levels and in Table 16 for the first differences in the variables, both in the appendix. In the tables, the cells with the values of the test statistics have been marked dark grey if the respective test statistic indicates that the variable is non-stationary, while a light grey cell indicates stationarity. The variables are classified as stationary or non-stationary, respectively, if this is indicated by at least two of the three unit root tests.

In some cases the variables are classified as integrated of an order larger than one. This means that neither the level nor the first difference of the respective variable is stationary. This problem is caused by the shortness of the time series and by the fact that many quarterly time series had to be derived from the respective annual values. The unit root tests were developed for long time series, i.e. the shorter the time series the less reliable the results of these tests. For Slovenia, this problem is less prevalent than for the other countries as the time series for Slovenia are longer and more original quarterly data are available.

Bearing these caveats in mind, the unit root tests identify most variables as integrated of order one, i.e. the variables are non-stationary in levels but the first differences are stationary. If two variables are of the same order *d* of integration, i.e. *I(d),* and they are cointegrated, then a linear combination of these variables is integrated of order *d-1*. In the case of variables with a unit root, i.e. if the variables are integrated of order one, as is the case for the majority of the variables included in the macroeconometric models described in this book, and if two or more of these variables are cointegrated, then a linear combination of them is stationary, i.e. integrated of order zero (Engle and Granger 1987). In this case, the variables may be used in error correction models.

ERROR CORRECTION MODELS

Since at least the vast majority of the macroeconomic variables used in the models for the former Yugoslavia can be classified as being integrated of order one, for almost all behavioural equations, error correction models (ECM) were chosen as the most appropriate modelling approach. An ECM combines the long-run, cointegrating relationship between the levels of the included variables and the short-run relationship between the changes (differences) of these variables. The ECM approach has the advantage that all variables in the estimated equation are stationary; hence there is no problem with the occurrence of spurious correlations.

An ECM may be estimated in two ways: the short-run and the long-run relationship may be estimated in one step or in two steps. The latter was proposed by Engle and Granger (1987). In their method, first the long-run, cointegrating relationship is estimated, containing all variables in levels without lags. In a second step, the model in differences is estimated. In this model of the differences, the residuals of the cointegrating relationship are included with a lag. For the equations in the multi-country model, both approaches have been employed, depending on the properties of the equations. In general, an error correction model has the following form:

$$\Delta y_t = \alpha \Delta y_{t-1} + \sum_{i=0}^{p} \left(\beta_1 \Delta x_{1,t-i} + \ldots + \beta_r \Delta x_{r,t-i} \right)$$
$$+ \gamma \left[y_{t-1} - c - \delta_1 x_{1,t-1} - \ldots - \delta_r x_{r,t-1} \right] + \varepsilon_t$$

In this specification, y is the endogenous variable, x_r are the r explanatory variables, ε denotes the error term and t is the time period. The number i of lagged differences to be included in the equation depends on their significance. The term in square brackets contains the cointegrating relationship, which depicts the long-run relation between the endogenous and the exogenous variables. In the long run, all adjustments towards the equilibrium have been completed. Hence the difference terms in the equation are zero in the long run, and only the relationship between the levels persists.

As the specification shows, the short-run dynamic behaviour of the endogenous, i.e. the left-hand variable, is driven by short-run movements of the right-hand side variables, as well as by past deviations from the long-run equilibrium.

In the models for the countries of the former Yugoslavia which are included in the multi-country model, almost all equations have been specified in logarithmic differences, i.e. the endogenous variables are defined as growth rates. The growth rate is generally defined with respect to the same quarter of the previous year (i.e., t-4). In some rare cases, instead of the change from one year earlier (t-4), growth over the previous quarter (t-1) had to be used due to the significance and/or sign of the coefficients.

LINKING THE INDIVIDUAL COUNTRY MODELS TO A MULTI-COUNTY MODEL

The sub-models for Bosnia and Herzegovina, Slovenia, Serbia and Croatia are linked via their bilateral trade relations and bilateral exchange rates. In this chapter, the theoretical foundations of the trade and exchange rate equations are elaborated. The exact specifications for each country can be found in the following chapter.

Data on exports and imports are available by country for trade in goods at current prices, but not for trade in services or measured at constant prices. Hence, the bilateral trade relations between the countries included in the multi-country model were based on nominal export and import data from balance of payments statistics. These data were used to divide total exports and imports into trade between Croatia, Bosnia and Herzegovina, Serbia and Slovenia and trade by these countries with the rest of the world. The resulting shares were applied to exports and imports according to national accounts, both at current and at constant prices.

Due to statistical problems related to the timing and recording of foreign trade, published data on exports from country i to country j differ from data on imports from country j from country i. In order to mitigate this problem, the export and import shares between the countries included in the model for the former Yugoslavia were based on the average of exports and imports between each pair of countries. Exports are recorded free on board (f.o.b.), while imports are measured including cost, insurance and freight (c.i.f.). This ensures that the value of exports from each country to another is identical to the respective imports to the recipient country from the sender, except for the previously mentioned measurement problems.

For modelling the trade relations between the countries of the former Yugoslavia, behavioural equations for bilateral exports between each country pair were estimated, while by definition the imports of country i from j are identical (aside from the above-mentioned measurement errors) to the corresponding exports in the other direction, transferred into the domestic currency of the recipient country. In each sub-model, real exports from country i to country j ($i \neq j$, $i,j =$ Croatia, Bosnia and Herzegovina, Serbia and Slovenia) depend on real demand in the recipient country and on the real bilateral exchange rate. The real bilateral exchange rate is composed of the nominal bilateral exchange rate and the ratio of the price levels in the two countries. A real depreciation of the domestic currency positively influences exports from country *i* to country *j*, as in this case country *i*'s goods and services become relatively cheaper compared to country *j*'s products. A real depreciation of the domestic currency occurs either as the result of a nominal depreciation (i.e. the domestic currency becomes relatively cheaper on the foreign exchange market) or when prices in the recipient country rise faster than in the originating country. Exports are also positively influenced when domestic demand and hence import demand increases in the recipient country.

Trade between Bosnia and Herzegovina and Slovenia depends on domestic demand in the recipient country and on the ratio between the price levels in these countries, but not on the bilateral nominal exchange rate. The reason for omitting the latter variable in these export equations is the fact that Bosnia and Herzegovina runs a currency board with the euro as the anchor currency. Hence there is a fixed parity between the Bosnian convertible mark and the euro (1 euro equals 1.95583 marks). Exports from each former Yugoslav country to the rest of the world depend on the real effective exchange rate of the respective country and on world trade. The real effective exchange rate takes the real exchange rates into account, i.e. the nominal exchange rates and the price ratios, vis-à-vis the currencies of the most important trading partners, weighted with their respective shares of a country's foreign trade.

Besides bilateral exports and imports, the four country models are linked via their bilateral exchange rates. The exchange rates between the currencies of the countries (the Bosnian convertible mark KM, the Croatian kuna, the Serbian dinar and the euro in the case of Slovenia) are explained by the interest differential and the ratio of the price levels between each country pair. For Slovenia, which has been a member of the euro area since 2007, the euro series was extended backwards for the period prior to 2007 using the conversion rate between the Slovenian tolar and the euro.

Including the interest differential is based on the theory of interest rate parity. The (uncovered) interest rate parity states that an appreciation or depreciation of one currency against another currency might be neutralised by a change in the interest rate differential. If, for example, interest rates in Serbia increase while Croatian interest rates remain unchanged, then the Serbian dinar appreciates against the Croatian kuna by an amount that makes further arbitrage unattractive. The inclusion of the ratio of price levels between each pair of countries in the relevant bilateral exchange rate equation is based on the theory of purchasing power. Purchasing power parity (PPP) is a theory of long-term equilibrium exchange rates based on the relative price levels of two countries. The concept is founded on the law of one price, according to which – in the absence of transaction costs and official barriers to trade – identical goods will have the same price in different markets when the prices are expressed in terms of one currency. In its 'absolute' version, the purchasing power of different currencies is equalised for a given basket of goods. In the 'relative' version, the difference in the rate of exchange in prices at home and abroad, i.e. the inflation differential, is equal to the percentage depreciation or appreciation of the currency. Due to Bosnia and Herzegovina's currency board arrangement, the model contains no bilateral exchange rate equation between the Bosnian KM and the euro.

In the export and import equations of the former Yugoslav republics with respect to the rest of world, international price competitiveness is represented by the real effective exchange rates between the countries concerned.

The nominal effective exchange rate of the Serbian dinar is determined by important bilateral exchange rates. Since Serbia's most important trading partners are the countries of the euro area, the nominal effective exchange rate of the Serbian dinar is mainly determined by the exchange rate vis-à-vis the euro. When including both the euro and the US dollar, the latter has the wrong sign. Hence, only the euro is considered as a determinant of the nominal effective exchange rate of the dinar in the Serbia model. The real effective exchange rate is influenced by the nominal effective exchange rate and by price developments. In the model, the latter are approximated by the inflation rate in Serbia. In theory, it is the inflation differential rather than pure inflation in Serbia that matters. However, it would have been difficult to construct an international inflation rate consistent with the regional pattern of Serbia's external trade as reflected in the effective exchange rate. Therefore, in the real effective exchange rate equation only inflation in Serbia has been included in addition to the nominal effective exchange rate.

The real effective exchange rate of the Croatian kuna is determined by the nominal exchange rates between the kuna, the Serbian dinar, the euro and the US dollar. By including the Serbian dinar and the euro (for Slovenia and, via its currency board arrangement, Bosnia and Herzegovina), bilateral trade is captured with the other former Yugoslav republics contained in the multi-country model. Furthermore, the aggregated euro area is Croatia's most important trading partner while the US dollar represents all other trading partners. In addition to these nominal exchange rates, in the equation the real effective exchange rate is influenced by inflation in Croatia. While the real effective exchange rate which represents Croatia's trade with a wide range of countries should be influenced by the inflation differential between Croatia and these other countries, it would be difficult to construct a weighted average of inflation in these countries. Furthermore, in forecasts, these international inflation rates would have to be predicted, since they would be exogenous in the model for the former Yugoslavia. Hence, only inflation in Croatia was considered in addition to the bilateral nominal exchange rates in the real effective exchange rate equation.

For Slovenia, its real effective exchange rate is modelled against a group of 41 countries. Since the time series on which the estimations of the behavioural equations are based include the period before Slovenia's euro area accession in 2007, the bilateral exchange rate between the Slovenian tolar and the euro is included as one of the explanatory variables in the effective exchange rate equation. In addition, the exchange rate between the euro and the US dollar is considered. As the real exchange rate takes the nominal exchange rate and price developments into account, the consumer price index (CPI) in Slovenia (in the long-run relationship between the levels of the variables) and the inflation rate (in the part of the equation capturing the short-run dynamics) are included as further explanatory variables.

Bosnia and Herzegovina runs a currency board with the euro as the reference currency. Therefore, except for a risk premium, the short-term interest rate in Bosnia and Herzegovina is essentially determined by its counterpart in the euro area. Hence, the short-term interest rate is exogenous in the model. In a term structure equation, the long-term interest rate depends on the short-term rate of interest. Due to the currency board arrangement operated by the Central Bank of Bosnia and Herzegovina, the nominal effective exchange rate of the Bosnian mark is determined by important bilateral exchange rates other than that with the euro. Since the other countries of the former Yugoslavia still account for a substantial share of Bosnia and Herzegovina's external trade, the exchange rates vis-à-vis the Croatian kuna and the Serbian dinar determine the nominal effective exchange rate of the Bosnian mark. In addition, the exchange rate vis-à-vis the US dollar is included in the equation to approximate all other currencies. The real effective exchange rate is influenced by the nominal effective exchange rate and by price developments. In the model, the latter are approximated by the inflation rate in Bosnia and Herzegovina. In theory, as already mentioned above, it is the inflation differential rather than inflation in Bosnia and Herzegovina exclusively that matters. However, as for the other sub-models it would have been difficult to construct an international inflation rate consistent with the regional pattern of Bosnia's foreign trade as reflected in the effective exchange rate. Therefore, in the real effective exchange rate equation only inflation in Bosnia and Herzegovina was included in addition to the nominal effective exchange rate.

Macroeconomic policy analysis and risk management require taking account of the increasing interdependencies that exist across markets and countries. This invariably means that many different channels of transmission must be taken into consideration. These increased interdependencies could be due to common observed global shocks (such as changes in oil prices), they could arise as a result of global unobserved factors (such as the diffusion of technological progress), or could be due to specific national or sectoral shocks. It is also likely that even when all "common" factors are allowed for, there can be important residual interdependencies due to policy and trade spillover effects that remain to be explained. Therefore, a fairly detailed global framework is needed if we are to investigate the relative importance of such diverse sources of comovements in the world economy.

The rest of the world is regarded as one entity, and is represented by world trade. Alternatively, the rest of the world could have been modelled in more details by applying the Global Vector Autoregressive (GVAR) methodology which has recently been developed. The GVAR methodology provides a general global modelling framework for the quantitative analysis of the relative importance of different shocks and channels of transmission mechanisms. In particular, the GVAR comprises a compact model of the world economy designed to explicitly model the economic and financial interdependencies at national and international levels. It combines individual country/regional vector error-corrcction models, where the domestic variables are related to corresponding foreign variables constructed exclusively to match the international trade, financial or other patterns of the country under consideration. The individual country models are linked in a consistent manner so that the GVAR model is solved for the world as a whole. It can then be used to investigate the degree of regional interdependencies via impulse response analysis. The framework relies exclusively on observables, which typically include macroeconomic aggregates and financial variables, with the country-specific foreign variables serving as a proxy for common unobserved factors.[7]

The GVAR model was originally introduced in Pesaran, Schuermann and Weiner (2004), where 11 country/region models were estimated over the period 1979Q1-1999Q4. The GVAR framework was subsequently extended in a number of ways in Dees, di Mauro, Pesaran and Smith (2007), in collaboration with the European Central Bank.

For the multi-country model for the former Yugoslavia it was decided to abstain from such a detailed modelling of the world economy, since the focus lay of modelling the interdependencies between the four countries contained in the model. However, future model extensions could involve an augmenting of the multi-country model by a GVAR model for the rest of the world.

---

7 This information was extracted from the following websit on 11 May 2015: https://sites.google.com/site/gvarmodelling/gvar

THE INDIVIDUAL COUNTRY MODELS

Following on from the description of the way in which the individual country models are linked to form the multi-county model, this chapter describes the four constituting parts of the multi-country model in detail. The models are based on the conventional aggregate supply / aggregate demand (AS-AD) framework, where the long-run relationships have mainly been chosen on the basis of theoretical considerations.

PREVIOUS WORK

Most data for the individual country models were taken from national sources. These will be specified in the relevant chapters below. Some time series of exogenous variables are common to all four sub-models, principally the price of oil and world trade. The oil price comes from a database provided by the Energy Information Administration (EIA) of the US Department of Energy, and world trade comes from the OECD Main Economic Indicators database. In addition, some euro area aggregates were used in some of the sub-models, such as short and long-term interest rates for the euro area average, taken from the Eurostat database.

Within the framework of a funded research project[8] running from 1998 to 1999, a quarterly macroeconometric model of *Slovenia's* economy was implemented and applied to evaluate a number of energy policy strategies and their effects on the most important macroeconomic indicators. In the following years, the model was constantly updated and extended to address several issues related to Slovenia's accession to the EU and to the euro area. Publications on the various applications of the model include Haber et al. (2002), Neck and Weyerstrass (2003), Neck, Weyerstrass and Haber (2004, 2005), Weyerstrass et al. (2000, 2001, 2002), Weyerstrass and Neck (2007, 2008, 2013).

---

[8] Contract "Integriertes Energieprogramm – Makroökonomisches Modell für Slowenien (Austrian-Slovenian Co-operation for an Integrated Energy Program – Development and Implementation of a Macroeconomic Model)" between the Slovenian Ministry of Economic Affairs and Verbundplan GmbH, financed by the Austrian Federal Chancellery (Bundeskanzleramt).

The macroeconometric model for *Bosnia and Herzegovina* was developed as part of a research project that was financially supported by the Jubiläumsfonds of the Austrian National Bank (project no. 12823). A description of the model developed within this research project was documented in Weyerstrass (2009) as well as Weyerstrass et al. (2009).

The model for *Serbia* was created within an international co-operation, partly funded by the Austrian Development Agency (ADA) (Berrer et al. 2009). The research project was carried out in cooperation with the Centre for Strategic Economic Studies of the Autonomous Province of Vojvodina ("Vojvodina-CESS"), Novi Sad, Serbia. Starting in autumn 2009, the model was continuously applied to generate macroeconomic forecasts for Serbia by Vojvodina-CESS (Grozea-Helmenstein et al. 2009, 2010, 2011). More recent model documentation can be found in Weyerstrass and Grozea-Helmenstein (2013a).

More academic applications of the models for Bosnia and Herzegovina and for Serbia consisted in tentative estimations of the macroeconomic effects of euro area membership of these countries (Weyerstrass and Neck 2011a, 2011b). Applying the models for Bosnia and Herzegovina and for Slovenia, Weyerstrass and Grozea-Helmenstein (2013b) analyse the macroeconomic effects of different euro area scenarios on these two economies.

The model for *Croatia* was developed within a research project funded by the Jubiläumsfonds of the Austrian National Bank (project no. 13363). Within this project, the individual country models were linked to a first version of the multi-country model for the former Yugoslavia. Both the Croatian part and the multi-country model are described in Behrens, Haber and Weyerstrass (2011).

In the following subsections, the equations for the individual country models will be documented. For each behavioural equation, t-statistics are provided in parentheses below the estimated coefficients. In addition, the adjusted R^2 and the Breusch-Godfrey test for serial correlation are provided.

In the equations, some coefficients are statistically insignificant or the Breusch-Godfrey test signals problems with the serial correlation of the residuals. However, in some cases the specification of the equations has not been adapted with the aim of removing the serial correlation or retaining only significant coefficients since the equations are based on economic theory, and theoretical consistency was given priority over excellent statistical results. One important reason for giving statistical properties lower priority is the limited data quality, with the exception of data for Slovenia, which joined the EU and the euro area at an early point in time and therefore had to comply with European standards regarding the definition and quality of statistical data from a much earlier time.

THE MODEL FOR BOSNIA AND HERZEGOVINA[9]

Introduction and data issues

Data availability and sources

The development of a macroeconometric model for Bosnia and Herzegovina (BiH) has to take the effects of the war in the 1990s into account, since the war aggravated the economic consequences originating from its secession from the former Yugoslavia. After the 1992 to 1995 war in Bosnia and Herzegovina, economic activity had dropped to less than 20 percent of its pre-war level. By the time hostilities broke out in 1992, Bosnia's inflation rate was already at 120 percent; during the war, it rose to over 1,000 percent. Unemployment was about 30 percent at the start of the war, and by 1995 it had risen to 75 percent. All sectors of the economy were hit hard by the conflict. About 45 percent of industrial plants, including about 75 percent of the oil refineries, were destroyed, damaged or plundered. After the signing of the Dayton peace agreement in 1995, which marked the end of the war, it took some time for the Bosnian economy to stabilise and to enter a path of high economic growth.

When constructing a macroeconomic model, which relies on stable econometric relations, only data for the period after the war-related economic crisis should be taken. Hence, it was decided to use data starting in 1999. For some variables, covering the public sector in particular, data for Bosnia and Herzegovina are only available from 2000 onwards or even later. Because of the short time series, a higher than annual frequency was needed so as to increase the degrees of freedom. At the time of developing the model for Bosnia and Herzegovina, the full set of data was available until the end of 2010. Some variables, in particular those that are calculated on a monthly basis (in particular the labour market as well as financial and fiscal data), were also available for 2011. On the other hand, GDP data are published with a considerable time lag, and there is a sizable delay between the publication of the production and the expenditure sides of GDP. As an example, first estimates of GDP by production in 2010 were released in July 2011, while preliminary data on GDP by expenditure in 2010 did not appear until September 2011.

9 Earlier versions of this chapter were published in Weyerstrass (2009) and Weyerstrass et al. (2009).

For some macroeconomic variables, monthly figures are available. This applies in particular to labour market indicators, prices and wages. Monthly interest rates have been available since 2002. Regarding the public sector, quarterly time series reach back to the second half of 2004.

Taking the availability of data for all the variables at the different frequencies into account, it was decided to base the macroeconometric model for Bosnia and Herzegovina on quarterly data, starting in 1999, i.e. after the first significant restructuring and rebuilding activities following the war had been completed. For some aggregates, notably for the expenditure side of GDP and the public sector, quarterly data had to be constructed. For these variables, at least some annual figures were available for the entire period from which the quarterly time series could be derived. For other variables, notably interest rates and effective exchange rates, no additional information was available to extend the (quarterly) data. Hence, these time series do not start until 2002. Furthermore, data on capital stock had to be constructed since no official capital stock figures are available for Bosnia and Herzegovina. The relevant data were provided by the National Bank of Bosnia and Herzegovina (CBBH) and the Statistical Office of Bosnia and Herzegovina while fiscal data are released by the Ministries of Finance at the different levels of government (state and Entities).

Data transformations

In the following, the construction of quarterly time series on GDP by expenditure, public finances and capital stock is elaborated.

Nominal GDP by expenditure

In Bosnia and Herzegovina, official GDP data for the production and expenditure side are only published on an annual basis. There is still a sizable gap between the production and expenditure approaches of GDP. In 2007, the Central Bank of Bosnia and Herzegovina released estimates of the quarterly GDP during the period 2000 to 2006. This estimate refers to total GDP based on production as quarterly data on GDP is only published for the production side of total GDP, but not for the expenditure components. Furthermore, data on the expenditure side only covers the short period since 2004. Hence, annual GDP expenditure data for the years 1999 to 2003 had to be constructed, and for the entire period since 1999 quarterly time series of these aggregates had to be determined.

The calculation of total GDP by expenditure for the years 1999 to 2003 was based on the growth rates of GDP by production. Then, after subtracting net trade, for which annual data are available from the balance of payments statistics for the entire period (see below), the remaining expenditure components were derived by assuming the same shares in total GDP as observed in 2004. Regarding the quarterly time series of GDP expenditure components at current prices, the following computations were made:

Exports and imports: the Central Bank of Bosnia and Herzegovina has published annual balance of payments data going back to 1998 and quarterly data back to 2001. The balance of payments data on international trade in goods and services were used to derive the quarterly profile of national accounts data on exports and imports. These calculations were performed in two steps. First, the quarterly balance of payments data were extrapolated backwards to 1999 by assuming the same quarterly profile as observed in 2001. In a second step, the sub-annual behaviour of the balance of payments data was transferred to the annual national accounts data on the exports and imports of goods and services.

Public consumption: the quarterly division of public consumption according to national accounts statistics was based on public finance data. The sum of the items "compensation of employees" and "purchases of goods and services" was used as an indicator for public consumption according to national accounts. Public finance data are available on an annual basis from 2000 onwards, and quarterly time series start in the third quarter of 2004. Hence, before resorting to the quarterly profile of public finance data for the sub-annual division of public consumption, the quarterly time series had to be extrapolated backwards to 2000. Details on this can be found below in the subsection on the treatment of public finance data. Once the quarterly time series of government outlays on the compensation of employees and the purchase of goods and services had been constructed, the sub-annual profile of the sum of these expenditure items was taken to divide the annual values of public consumption according to national accounts statistics. Finally, for 1999, the quarterly profile of the year 2000 was assumed.

Consumption of private households: as an indicator for the expenditures of private households, value added tax (VAT) (since 2006, sales tax before) revenues were used. These figures were provided by the CBBH. As mentioned above, annual public finance data cover the period from 2000 onwards, while quarterly time series start in the third quarter of 2004. Hence, the first quarterly time series of VAT/sales tax revenues had to be extrapolated back to 2000. Details on this can be found below in the subsection on public finances. Using annual data on VAT/sales tax revenues and private household consumption, a behavioural equation of the following form was estimated with private consumption as the dependent variable and VAT/sales tax revenues as the explanatory variable.

$$\text{Consumption}_t = c + \beta\ \text{VAT}_t + €_t.$$

The constant *c* and coefficient *β* were estimated with annual data on consumption and VAT revenues in the period *t*. *€* denotes the residuals. By dividing the constant *c* by four, adding quarterly VAT/sales tax revenues multiplied by the coefficient β, and adding a quarter of the annual residuals of the estimation, a quarterly series for private consumption adding up to the actual annual figures was calculated for the period starting in 2000. The average of the resulting quarterly profile in 2000 and 2001 was then used to derive the quarterly private consumption series for 1999, i.e. the year for which constructed annual private consumption data but no data on VAT revenues were available.

Gross fixed capital formation: lacking any indicator for the sub-annual development of fixed investment, the same quarterly profile as for total GDP was taken.

Changes in inventories: the quarterly time series was calculated as the difference between total GDP and the sum of the final demand components, i.e. private and public consumption, gross fixed capital formation and net exports.

Real GDP by expenditure

For real GDP by production from 2000 onwards, growth rates have been published by the Agency for Statistics of Bosnia and Herzegovina. Concerning the expenditure components, the CBBH publication containing estimates for the 2004 to 2006 period covering GDP both at current and at the previous year's prices. Thus, for the missing years, annual figures had to be derived, and quarterly time series needed to be constructed for the entire period.

The 1999 level of real GDP by production was constructed by taking the growth rate for 2000. Regarding the expenditure side, total GDP from 1999 to 2003 and from 2007 onwards was constructed by resorting to the growth rates of real GDP according to the production approach in the same periods. The quarterly profile of the real expenditure aggregates was then assumed to be the same as the quarterly pattern of the respective nominal aggregates. In this way, deflators of total GDP and of the expenditure components could also be derived.

Public finances

The Central Bank of Bosnia and Herzegovina collects and publishes public finance data from the Ministries of Finance and Funds at all level of governments in Bosnia and Herzegovina (state, Federation of Bosnia and Herzegovina, Republika Srpska, Brčko District, local governments, social security funds, and PE [Public Enterprise] for road reconstruction and maintenance). For the macroeconometric model, the following revenue and expenditure items were distinguished:

- Revenues
- Total revenues
- Taxes on income and profit
- Payroll taxes
- Value added tax
- Social security contributions
- Grants and other revenues
- Other revenues
- Expenditures
- Total expenditures
- Compensation of employees
- Purchases of goods and services
- Social benefits
- Subsidies
- Interest payments
- Public investment (net acquisition of non-financial assets)
- Other expenditures

Annual time series of public finance data go back to 2000, and quarterly time series start in the second half of 2004. Hence, in a first step the quarterly series of the various revenue and expenditure items had to be extrapolated back to 2000. It has to be observed that government data for the local level (municipalities) are not compiled on a quarterly basis. Therefore, the annual figures are a bit higher since they include the local level. To correct for this bias, annual data were distributed to quarters according to the sub-annual profile of original quarterly data so as to make the annual sums compatible.

For tax revenues, quarterly time series are only published for total taxes but not for the detailed breakdown as it is available on an annual basis. Furthermore, for the period 2000 to 2002 tax revenues are only broken down into direct and indirect taxes. For the construction of the model database it was assumed that in these years the shares of taxes on income and profit and of payroll taxes were the same as in 2003 in relation to direct taxes.

In relation to the division of the annual figures of the different tax categories, it was assumed that in each quarter the shares of the respective tax categories in total taxes were equal to the corresponding shares in the annual figures. Hence, the quarterly division of income taxes, payroll taxes and VAT was based on the quarterly profile of total tax revenues. The quarterly division of total tax revenues before 2005 was based on the sub-annual pattern observed in 2005.

On the expenditure side, no detailed data are available for the compensation of employees, purchases of goods and services, social benefits and subsidies in the period prior to 2003. Hence, for the period 2000 to 2002 annual time series for these aggregates were constructed according to the respective shares of these items in total expenditures in 2003. The division of quarters from 2000 to the second quarter of 2004, i.e. the period for which no quarterly public finance data are available, was based on the quarterly profile observed in 2005.

Capital stock

For Bosnia and Herzegovina, no official capital stock data is available. Hence, a capital stock series was constructed by applying the Perpetual Inventory Method (PIM). According to the PIM, the net capital stock at the end of the current year (K_t) is equal to the capital stock at the end of the previous year (K_{t-1}) plus gross fixed capital formation (I_t) minus depreciation (DEP_t) in the current year:

$$K_t = K_{t-1} + I_t - DEP_t.$$

In addition to this net capital stock, a gross capital stock can be defined. The gross capital stock at the end of each year is given by the aggregation of previous fixed capital formation, without taking depreciation into account. However, since the capital stock is reduced in the production process, it makes more sense to use the net capital stock in macroeconomic models.

The application of the Perpetual Inventory Method requires an initial capital stock to be determined in the starting year t_0. One option would be to assume that after the war, the capital stock in Bosnia and Herzegovina was totally demolished or outdated, implying an initial value of zero in 1995. However, it seems reasonable to assume that not the entire capital stock was destroyed. In addition, investment data is only available from 1999 onwards; thus there remains a gap of four years between the end of the war and the starting year of the investment data.

For these reasons, it was decided to base the starting value of the capital stock on international data. Capital stock estimates exist for Macedonia (Roberts 2002). Since Macedonia is also a small successor state of the former Yugoslavia, it is particularly suited as a benchmark for Bosnia and Herzegovina. An important distinction between Macedonia and Bosnia and Herzegovina is that the former gained its independence in 1991 without a war. Hence, its capital stock might have been outdated after the socialist Yugoslav era, but it was not destroyed by acts of war. Therefore, the starting value of the capital stock in Bosnia and Herzegovina at the beginning of 1999 was based on a slightly lower capital-output ratio than the value of 1.6 found by Roberts (2002) for Macedonia. The starting capital-output ratio for Bosnia and Herzegovina was set at 1.5. This value refers to the net capital stock, i.e. cumulative gross investment net of depreciation.

Capital stock data refer to the stock at a certain point in time while GDP and investment data are flows during a certain period. The first year for which GDP data for Bosnia and Herzegovina are available is 1999; hence the starting value of the capital stock was determined by multiplying the annual GDP figure for 1999 by the assumed capital-output ratio of 1.5. This figure was then taken as the initial value of the capital stock at the end of 1999 or the beginning of 2000, respectively. From the first quarter of 2000 onwards, the capital stock was then extrapolated by applying the Perpetual Inventory Method, i.e. by adding quarterly gross fixed capital formation and subtracting depreciation.

Depreciation could take different patterns. With straight-line depreciation, the market value of an asset in constant prices is assumed to decline by the same amount each period. This amount is equal to *1/Tth* of the initial value of the asset, where T is the service life of that particular asset. With geometric depreciation, the market value in constant prices is assumed to decline at a constant rate in each period (e.g. OECD 2001). The latter will normally be a good approximation of the former; hence a constant depreciation rate was assumed. The above equation for calculating the capital stock can thus be rewritten in the following form (δ is the depreciation rate):

$$K_t = (1-\delta)\ K_{t-1} + I_t.$$

Although depreciation is published as part of the GDP income side, this series is not suitable for the capital stock extrapolation, since depreciation according to national accounts statistics deviates from the consumption of fixed capital. The physical depletion of the capital stock is therefore typically not identical to economic depreciation as accounted for in the national accounts statistics. If capital stock data were available, depreciation could be calculated by re-arranging the above equation for the PIM accordingly. However, as already mentioned, capital stock data are not available for Bosnia and Herzegovina; hence the depreciation rate could not be derived in this way.

Since no information is available on the depreciation of the capital stock in Bosnia and Herzegovina, the depreciation rate for the calculation of the capital stock according to the Perpetual Inventory Method was based on data for other countries. The OECD publishes data on gross and net capital stocks, gross fixed capital formation and consumption of fixed capital (depreciation) for 14 countries (OECD 1997). Since some of these aggregates are missing for some countries, a complete set of relevant data is only available for ten countries[10]. The unweighted average of the depreciation rate (current year consumption of fixed capital as a percentage of the capital stock at the end of the previous year) amounts to 5 percent. The value ranges between 2.7 percent in Greece and 8.7 percent in Canada. However, these extreme values are outliers; the depreciation rate generally lies between 4.6 percent and 5.7 percent. Hence, at least for developed industrialised countries, a depreciation rate of about 5 to 6 percent per year seems a reasonable assumption.

When the Perpetual Inventory Method is applied to Bosnia and Herzegovina with an annual depreciation rate of 6 percent (1.47 percent per quarter), the capital-output ratio rises from 1.5 in 1999 to slightly above 2 in 2010. Due to the legacy of the former Yugoslav era and, more importantly, the impacts of the war, physical capital in Bosnia and Herzegovina needs to be rebuilt and modernised considerably. Hence, a rising capital-output ratio should also be expected in the future. In the OECD countries, this value lies in the range of about 2.5 to 3.

---

[10] These are Canada, USA, Australia, Belgium, Finland, France, Germany, Greece, Italy and Sweden.

Model equations

The model consists of behavioural equations for all the relevant markets of the economy of Bosnia and Herzegovina. The following list gives an overview of the endogenous variables of these model blocks:

- market for goods and services: consumption of private households, gross fixed capital formation;
- external sector: exports and imports of goods and services;
- labour market: labour demand by companies, labour supply by households;
- financial market: long-term interest rate, nominal and real effective exchange rate;
- public sector: the most important revenue and expenditure items of the consolidated general government;
- supply block: potential GDP, non-accelerating inflation rate of unemployment (NAIRU), total factor productivity (TFP).

In this section, the behavioural equations of these model blocks are described. In addition to the explanatory variables derived from economic theory, many equations contain dummy variables. These account either for outliers in certain periods or for seasonal effects, since the data on which the model is based have not been seasonally adjusted, mainly due to the brevity of the time series.

In the following, t-statistics are provided in parentheses below the estimated coefficients. The adjusted R^2 is the coefficient of determination, adjusted for the degrees of freedom. The adjusted R^2 penalises for the addition of regressors which do not contribute to the explanatory power of the model. LM denotes the Breusch-Godfrey test for serial correlation. Unlike the Durbin-Watson statistic for AR(1) errors, the LM test may be used to test for higher order ARMA errors, and it is applicable whether or not there are lagged dependent variables. The null hypothesis of the LM test is that there is no serial correlation up to lag order p, where p is a pre-specified integer. The local alternative is ARMA(r,q) errors, where the number of lag terms $p = \max(r,q)$. This LM statistic is computed as the number of observations times the (uncentered) R^2 from the test regression. Under quite general conditions, the LM test statistic is asymptotically distributed as $\chi^2(p)$. In all cases, p was determined as 2. *, **, *** means that the null hypothesis of no serial correlation has to be rejected at the 10, 5 and 1 percent level of significance, respectively. The suffix _BiH in the variable name indicates the sub-model for Bosnia.

Supply side

In the supply block, potential GDP is determined. The calculation of potential output is based on a Cobb-Douglas production function with constant returns to scale. In addition to the production factors of labour and capital, autonomous technical progress is considered. Since potential GDP is a measure of the long-run production possibilities of an economy, it is the long-run trends rather than the actual realisations of the production factors that enter the production function. An exception is the capital stock, where it is assumed that it is normally fully utilised. Autonomous technical progress is defined as total factor productivity (TFP). Under these assumptions, trend employment, the capital stock and trend total factor productivity are considered for calculating potential output. Except for the capital stock, neither of these variables is observable. For countries not in a transition process, capital stock data are published officially. Since this is not the case for Bosnia and Herzegovina, this variable had to be constructed. Trend employment is defined as the labour force minus natural unemployment. The inflation-stable unemployment rate NAIRU (non-accelerating inflation rate of unemployment) is modelled by first applying a Hodrick-Prescott (HP) filter to the actual unemployment rate in order to extract the trend. To be able to extrapolate the NAIRU in model simulations, the NAIRU is then modelled as an auto regressive process.

The production function has the following form:

$$\log(\text{YPOT\_BiH}) = 0.65 \log(\text{TRENDEMP\_BiH}) + 0.35 \log(\text{CAPR\_BiH}) + \text{TRENDTFP\_BiH}.$$

In this equation, YPOT_BiH is potential GDP, TRENDEMP_BiH is the labour force adjusted for structural unemployment, CAPR_BiH is the real capital stock, and TRENDTFP_BiH is the long-run trend of total factor productivity (TFP). Since for the time being, no income data for the national account exist for Bosnia and Herzegovina, the production elasticities of the employment (0.65) and capital (0.35) factors were based on international empirical evidence. In industrialised economies, the wage share of total income is about 65 percent. Under the assumption of constant returns to scale, all income is distributed to the production factors. According to the marginal productivity theory of distribution, in competitive market economies the production factors are paid according to the value of their respective marginal product. Hence, in the production function the weight of labour input is set to 0.65 and, based on the assumed constant returns to scale, the weight of capital input is set to 0.35. These are also the production elasticities taken by the European Commission in its potential output estimations for EU Member States (D'Auria et al. 2010).

Before calculating potential GDP according to the above equation, trend employment and trend total factor productivity have to be determined. Trend employment is calculated by subtracting natural or structural unemployment from the labour force. Since structural unemployment is non-observable, this variable has to be estimated. In the model for Bosnia and Herzegovina, this is done by applying a Hodrick-Prescott (HP) filter to the actual unemployment rate in order to extract the trend. Structural unemployment is then defined as the long-run trend in actual unemployment. Estimating the NAIRU with the Hodrick-Prescott filter has certain drawbacks. The filter is only "optimal" in special cases and may produce extreme second order properties of detrended data. However, none of these shortcomings and undesirable properties seems to be overly problematic, since the HP filter has withstood the test of the time and is widely used in empirical studies. In addition to some possible undesirable statistical properties, the HP filter is a mechanistic tool. Therefore, it cannot take structural factors affecting the NAIRU such as labour market reforms or increased education of the labour force into account. However, this drawback is not very serious since such factors would in any case be difficult to implement in an aggregated macroeconometric model.

In order to endogenise the NAIRU, it is modelled as an auto regressive (AR) process, and the following estimated equation is included in the model:

$$\log(NAIRU\_BiH/NAIRU\_BiH_{-4}) = \underset{(38.926)}{4.517}\,AR(1) - \underset{(-18.714)}{8.331}\,AR(2) + \underset{(11.978)}{7.859}\,AR(3) - \underset{(-8.626)}{3.797}\,AR(4) + \underset{(6.636)}{0.752}\,AR(5)$$

Adjusted R^2: 0.999 LM(2): 0.090

Applying growth accounting, total factor productivity (TFP) is calculated as that part of real GDP that is not due to labour and capital input, where both production factors are weighted with their production elasticities:

$$\log(TFP\_BiH) = \log(GDPR\_BiH) - 0.65 \log(EMP\_BiH) - 0.35 \log(CAPR\_BiH)$$

In this equation, TFP_BiH denotes actual (i.e. not trend) total factor productivity, GDPR_BiH is real GDP (expenditure approach), EMP_BiH stands for actual employment, and CAPR_BiH is, as before, the real capital stock.

For the production possibilities, the long-run trend rather than the current level of total factor productivity is relevant. Therefore, the actual TFP series is smoothed by applying the Hodrick-Prescott filter so as to remove short-run fluctuations, which are caused by the business cycle or by any short-run shocks. Trend TFP has been endogenised by estimating the following equation and implementing it in the model.

$$\log(TRENDTFP\_BiH/TRENDTFP\_BiH_{-4}) = \underset{(7.568)}{0.016} + \underset{(35.925)}{3.749}\, AR(1) - \underset{(-16.618)}{5.362}\, AR(2) + \underset{(10.184)}{3.471}\, AR(3) - \underset{(-6.994)}{0.860}\, AR(4)$$

Adjusted R^2: 0.999 LM(2): 2.729

Demand side

As mentioned above, there is still a sizeable gap between the expenditure and production sides of GDP data in Bosnia and Herzegovina. Therefore, in those equations in which GDP is used as a proxy for final demand, real GDP from the expenditure side (GDPR_EXP_BiH) has been used.

Consumption of private households

According to the Keynesian view, consumption of private households depends on their current disposable income. Following an alternative theory, the permanent income hypothesis stipulates that households base their consumption decisions on expected income over their lifetime. Accordingly, it is wealth rather than current income that determines consumption. In reality, a certain proportion of households can be expected to be credit constrained. These households do not have the opportunity to borrow on expected future income; thus they can only consume using their current income. Therefore, in the model for Bosnia and Herzegovina both consumption theories are combined, implying that private household consumption depends on both current disposable income and wealth. Wealth effects are approximated by the real long-term interest rate. The interest rate as a determinant of consumption accounts both for the fact that some households finance part of their consumption via bank loans and for intertemporal decisions on the allocation of income to consumption in the present period and in the future. The higher the interest rate, the higher the opportunity costs are of spending income for current consumption. The income effect would indicate a positive relationship with the interest rate since rising interest rates generate higher income from assets. On the other hand, the substitution effect suggests a negative relationship due to the opportunity costs of current consumption as opposed to higher savings.

In the empirical estimation, the change in the real interest rate negatively affects real consumption. In the equation below, CONSR_BiH is real private household consumption, IL_BiH denotes the nominal long-term interest rate, INFL_BiH is the annual growth rate of the consumer price index (CPI), and YDR_BiH is real disposable income. The term in square brackets contains the long-run, i.e. the cointegrating relationship. This cointegrating relation, which has been estimated in a first step and then included in the estimation of the short-run error correction model, shows that in the long run, private consumption depends on real disposable income.

$$\log(CONSR\_BiH/CONSR\_BiH_{-4}) = \underset{(2.922)}{0.367} + \underset{(4.505)}{0.395} \log(YDR\_BiH/YDR\_BiH_{-4})$$

$$- \underset{(-2.311)}{0.281} [\log(CONSR\_BiH_{-4}) - 3.036 - 0.609 \log(YDR\_BiH_{-4})]$$

$$- \underset{(-3.733)}{0.005} [(IL\_BiH - INFL\_BiH)-(IL\_BiH_{-4}-INFL\_BiH_{-4})] + \underset{(2.431)}{0.060} DUM2010q1$$

Adjusted R^2: 0.832 LM(2): 0.112

Remittances

During the war, many inhabitants left Bosnia and Herzegovina. A substantial number of these people are still living and working abroad. They send a considerable proportion of their income to their relatives in Bosnia and Herzegovina. These remittances (REMIT_BiH) increase disposable income. Due to their importance for the disposable income of private households in Bosnia and Herzegovina, remittances are explicitly modelled. They are positively related to the global economic situation, approximated by world trade (WTRADE). The notion behind this behavioural relationship is that in an economic upswing, more people find employment abroad and their income opportunities increase.

$$\log(REMIT\_BiH/REMIT\_BiH_{-4}) = \underset{(-1.362)}{-0.017} + \underset{(2.520)}{0.346} \log(REMIT\_BiH_{-1}/REMIT\_BiH_{-5})$$

$$+ \underset{(2.600)}{0.388} \log(WTRADE/WTRADE_{-4})$$

Adjusted R^2: 0.289 LM(2): 4.528

Gross fixed capital formation

Investment is undertaken to renew the capital stock and to adjust it to changes in final demand. Hence, the accelerator theory stipulates that changes in demand determine fixed capital formation. Since it takes time to purchase and install new capital goods, it is expected rather than actual demand that has to be considered. However, in the case of adaptive expectations, as is assumed here, expectations are based on past observations. Therefore, in the investment equation, actual demand is included as an approximation for expected future demand.

According to theories focussing on the profitability of investment projects, the value of the capital stock equals the discounted future income that can be generated by employing the capital stock. Therefore, the interest rate, which is used to discount future income, is crucial for the profitability of an investment project. The market interest rate is formed on the basis of the time preferences of the individual investors. According to this strand of theories, investment is a function of the real interest rate.

The relation between the present value of the discounted future revenues that can be generated by an additional unit of the capital stock and the price for this additional unit of capital is called marginal q. This theory was introduced by Keynes (1936) and further elaborated by Brainard and Tobin (1968) and by Tobin (1969, 1978). In empirical studies the problem arises that the marginal q is unobservable and has to be approximated by observable variables. A possible candidate that may be used to approximate the present value of the future revenues of a selected number of companies is the stock index. However, this is only justified under the condition that the stock market correctly reflects the economic fundamentals of the companies concerned and is not biased by speculative bubbles or over-pessimistic expectations.

The neoclassical theory of investment combines the investment determinants according to the accelerator hypothesis and profitability considerations (see, for example, Jorgensen 1963). In this case, the investment function is derived from the profit maximisation of companies, based on a neoclassical production function with the input factor capital and a positive but diminishing marginal product. The optimal capital stock equalizes the marginal revenue product of capital and the user cost of capital. The latter consist of the depreciation rate, the real interest rate and the growth rate of the price index for capital goods. If the price for capital goods rises, this diminishes the user cost of capital, since in this case it is more profitable to invest in the current period than postpone investment to the following period. In addition to these variables, the user costs of capital are influenced by taxation. Tax allowances lower the user cost of capital whereas taxation of profits reduces the profitability of investment projects. In empirical estimations, however, the inclusion of these variables is often limited by data availability.

The aforementioned investment theories can be extended by considering uncertainty. Investment decisions are affected by uncertainty as future price and demand developments are unknown ex ante. The same is true for future costs. Hence, empirical studies find a negative influence of revenue and cost uncertainties on investment (Deutsche Bundesbank 2001). In the model for Bosnia and Herzegovina, due to data availability as well as the significance and sign of the estimated coefficients, the user costs of capital are approximated by the sum of the real long-term interest rate and the depreciation rate. As can be seen from the following specification, in the sub-model for Bosnia and Herzegovina, the growth rate of real gross fixed capital formation (IFIXR_BiH) depends on the growth rate of real GDP from the expenditure side (GDPR_EXP_BiH) and the user cost of capital (UCC_BiH). In the long run, real fixed investment depends solely on real GDP.

$$\log(IFIXR\_BiH/IFIXR\_BiH_{-4}) = \underset{(6.872)}{0.596} \log(IFIXR\_BiH_{-1}/IFIXR\_BiH_{-5})$$

$$+ \underset{(5.611)}{0.817} \log(GDPR\_EXP\_BiH/GDPR\_BiH\_EXP_{-4}) - \underset{(-1.849)}{0.002}\, UCC\_BiH - \underset{(-6.699)}{0.295}\, DUM2006q1$$

$$- \underset{(-3.462)}{0.401} [\log(IFIXR\_BiH_{-4}) - 0.7222 - 0.7404 \, LOG(GDPR\_EXP\_BiH_{-4})]$$

Adjusted R^2: 0.951 LM(2): 4.217

Exports of goods and services

As elaborated above, every country model contains equations for exports to every other country in the model, as well as to the rest of the world. Hence, for Bosnia and Herzegovina, exports to Slovenia, Serbia, Croatia and the rest of the world are modelled. The relevant equations are presented in this section.

Exports from Bosnia and Herzegovina to Croatia (EXR_BiHCRO) depend on final demand in Croatia (DEMANDR_CRO), the real exchange rate between the Bosnian mark and the Croatian kuna, and some dummy variables.

Since Bosnia and Herzegovina runs a currency board with a fixed exchange rate of 1.9558 mark to the euro, the nominal exchange rate between the mark and the kuna can be approximated by the exchange rate of the euro and the kuna (HRKEUR). In the model, HRKEUR denotes the price of the euro in kunas. Hence, the inverse of this exchange rate enters the equation for exports from Bosnia and Herzegovina to Croatia to account for the fact that a nominal depreciation of the Bosnian mark (or, due to the currency board arrangement, the euro) *ceteris paribus* benefits Bosnian exports. An increase in the inverse of HRKEUR reflects a depreciation of the euro. The real exchange rate between the mark and the kuna includes the price ratio between Bosnia and Croatia (CPI_CRO/CPI_BiH) in addition to the nominal exchange rate between the Bosnian mark (or the euro) and the kuna.

$$\log(\text{EXR\_BiHCRO}/\text{EXR\_BiHCRO}_{-4}) = \underset{(4.752)}{0.376} \log(\text{EXR\_BiHCRO}_{-1}/\text{EXR\_BiHCRO}_{-5})$$

$$+ \underset{(4.836)}{0.930} \log(\text{DEMANDR\_CRO}/\text{DEMANDR\_CRO}_{-4}) + \underset{(2.938)}{0.172}\ \text{DUM2007q1}$$

$$+ \underset{(1.550)}{0.817} \log(((1/\text{HRKEUR}_{-2}) \cdot \text{CPI\_CRO}_{-2}/\text{CPI\_BiH}_{-2})/((1/\text{HRKEUR}_{-6}) \cdot \text{CPI\_CRO}_{-6}/\text{CPI\_BiH}_{-6}))$$

$$- \underset{(-6.009)}{0.351} \log(\text{EXR\_BiHCRO}_{-4}) + \underset{(5.525)}{0.565} \log(\text{DEMANDR\_CRO}_{-4})$$

$$+ \underset{(5.212)}{2.440} \log((1/\text{HRKEUR}_{-4}) \cdot \text{CPI\_CRO}_{-4}/\text{CPI\_BiH}_{-4}) + \underset{(5.286)}{0.176}\ \text{DUM2004}$$

Adjusted R^2: 0.885 LM(2): 0.023

Exports from Bosnia and Herzegovina to Slovenia (EXR_BiHSLO) are influenced by real final demand in Slovenia (DEMAND_SLO) and by the price ratio between Bosnia and Slovenia. Due to the fact that Slovenia has the euro as its legal tender and Bosnia and Herzegovina runs a currency board with the euro as the reference currency, the real exchange rate between these two countries only consists of the price ratio (CPI_SLO/CPI_BiH) while the nominal exchange rate is fixed.

$$\log(EXR\_BiHSLO/EXR\_BiHSLO_{-4}) = \underset{(-1.756)}{-4.410} + \underset{(7.102)}{0.666} \log(EXR\_BiHSLO_{-1}/EXR\_BiHSLO_{-5})$$

$$+ \underset{(2.862)}{1.017} \log(DEMAND\_SLO/DEMAND\_SLO_{-4}) - \underset{(-3.912)}{0.476} \log(EXR\_BiHSLO_{-4})$$

$$+ \underset{(2.153)}{0.665} \log(DEMAND\_SLO_{-4}) + \underset{(2.687)}{0.761} \log(CPI\_SLO_{-4}/CPI\_BiH_{-4}) + \underset{(3.311)}{0.251} DUM2010Q1$$

Adjusted R^2: 0.872 LM(2): 1.798

Exports from Bosnia and Herzegovina to Serbia (EXR_BiHSRB) are a function of real final demand in Serbia (DEMANDR_SRB) and the real exchange rate. The latter consists of the nominal exchange rate between the euro (due to the currency board and the fixed exchange rate between the euro and the Bosnian mark) and the Serbian dinar (DINEUR) and the ratio between the consumer price indices in Serbia (CPI_SRB) and Bosnia (CPI_BiH). As in the case of the kuna exchange rate, the exchange rate between the euro and the dinar is defined in such a way that its inverse enters the calculation of the real exchange rate between Bosnia and Serbia.

$$\log(EXR\_BiHSRB/EXR\_BiHSRB_{-4}) = \underset{(-1.358)}{-0.020} + \underset{(3.656)}{0.349} \log(EXR\_BiHSRB_{-1}/EXR\_BiHSRB_{-5})$$

$$+ \underset{(5.972)}{0.963} \log(DEMANDR\_SRB/DEMANDR\_SRB_{-4})$$

$$- \underset{(-5.764)}{0.294} [\log(EXR\_BiHSRB_{-4}) - 0.681 \log(DEMANDR\_SRB_{-4}) - 0.805 \log(((1/DINEUR_{-4}) \cdot CPI\_SRB_{-4}/CPI\_BiH_{-4}))]$$

Adjusted R^2: 0.719 LM(2): 2.217

Exports from Bosnia and Herzegovina to the rest of the world (EXR_BiHROW) depend on world trade (WTRADE) as a proxy for world demand and on the real effective exchange rate of the Bosnian mark (REER_BiH). The real effective exchange rate is a weighted average of the nominal exchange rates and the price ratios to Bosnia's most important trading partners, weighted with their respective shares in Bosnia's international trade.

$$\log(EXR\_BiHROW/EXR\_BiHROW_{-4}) = -2.24 + 0.15 \log(EXR\_BiHROW_{-1}/EXR\_BiHROW_{-5})$$
$$(-2.708) \quad (1.347)$$

$$+ 1.374 \log(WTRADE/WTRADE_{-4}) + 0.716 \log(REER\_BiH/REER\_BiH_{-4})$$
$$(7.110) \qquad (1.911)$$

$$- 0.193 \log(EXR\_BiHROW_{-4}) + 0.450 \log(WTRADE_{-4}) + 0.088\ DUM2005$$
$$(-2.036) \qquad (2.573) \qquad (3.207)$$

Adjusted R^2: 0.868 LM(2): 0.292

Imports of goods and services

Imports to Bosnia and Herzegovina from the other countries in the model are, by definition, identical to their exports to Bosnia (except for deviations between exports and imports due to measurement and other statistical errors). Hence, they are modelled as exports in the other country models, and only Bosnia's imports from the rest of the world (IMR_BiHROW) are modelled separately. They depend on total real demand in Bosnia and Herzegovina and on relative prices. Total demand is approximated by real GDP from the expenditure side (GDPR_EXP_BiH). Relative prices are approximated by the real effective exchange rate for Bosnia (REER_BiH).

$$\log(IMR\_BiHROW/IMR\_BiHROW_{-4}) = 1.695 + 0.254 \log(IMR\_BiHROW\text{-}1/IMR\_BiHROW_{-5})$$
$$(2.199) \quad (2.148)$$

$$+ 1.486 \log(GDPR\_EXP\_BiH/GDPR\_EXP\_BiH_{-4})$$
$$(3.540)$$

$$- 1.873 \log(REER\_BiH/REER\_BiH_{-4}) - 0.233\ DUM2007q3$$
$$(-2.305) \qquad (-2.229)$$

$$- 0.462 \log(IMR\_BiHROW_{-4}) + 0.194 \log(GDPR\_EXP\_BiH_{-4}) + 0.196\ DUM2005q4$$
$$(-4.381) \qquad (1.823) \qquad (1.962)$$

Adjusted R^2: 0.668 LM(2): 1.491

Money market

Due to the fact that Bosnia and Herzegovina operates a currency board with the euro as the reference currency, except for a risk premium the short-term interest rate in Bosnia and Herzegovina (IS_BiH) is essentially determined by its counterpart in the euro area (EUR3M).

$$IS\_BiH - IS\_BiH_{-4} = \underset{(1.778)}{0.277} + \underset{(6.014)}{1.091}(IS\_BiH_{-1} - IS\_BiH_{-5}) - \underset{(-2.071)}{0.333}(IS\_BiH_{-2} - IS\_BiH_{-6})$$

$$- \underset{(-2.317)}{0.062}(IS\_BiH_{-4} - EUR3M_{-4})$$

Adjusted R^2: 0.885 LM(2): 1.396

In a term structure equation, the long-term interest rate (IL_BiH) depends on the short-term interest rate (IS_BiH). In addition, due to the continuous European integration process of Bosnia and Herzegovina and the currency board arrangement, the long-term interest rate should gradually converge towards its euro area counterpart. Hence, the yield on 10 year government bonds in the euro area (EUR10Y) is included in the term structure equation as a second regressor besides the short-term interest rate.

$$IL\_BiH - IL\_BiH_{-4} = \underset{(1.698)}{1.029} + \underset{(1.765)}{0.419}(IS\_BiH_{-2} - IS\_BiH_{-6}) - \underset{(-1.477)}{0.249}(IL\_BiH_{-4} - EUR10Y_{-4})$$

Adjusted R^2: 0.386 LM(2): 5.842*

The implicit interest rate on government debt (IL_DEBT_BiH), i.e. the average interest rate on Bosnia and Herzegovina's outstanding public debt, is explained by the long-term market interest rate.

$$IL\_DEBT\_BiH = - \underset{(-3.661)}{0.527}(IL\_DEBT\_BiH_{-1}) + \underset{(9.157)}{0.115}\, IL\_BiH$$

Adjusted R^2: 0.151 LM(2): 8.387**

Foreign exchange market

Due to the currency board arrangement operated by the Central Bank of Bosnia and Herzegovina, the nominal effective exchange rate of the Bosnian mark (NEER_BiH) is determined by important bilateral exchange rates other than that between the Bosnian mark and the euro. Although the other countries of the former Yugoslavia still account for a substantial share of Bosnia and Herzegovina's external trade, in the empirical estimation it was only the exchange rate vis-à-vis the US dollar (EURUSD) that entered the equation statistically significantly and with the theoretically correct sign. The fact that the other exchange rates, i.e. the euro/kuna and the euro/dinar rates were either insignificant or had the wrong sign might be due to multicollinearity between the various exchange rates.

$$\log(NEER\_BiH/NEER\_BiH_{-4}) = \underset{(1.889)}{0.005} + \underset{(6.142)}{0.702} \log(NEER\_BiH_{-1}/NEER\_BiH_{-5})$$

$$- \underset{(-2.613)}{0.051} \log(EURUSD_{-1}/EURUSD_{-5})$$

Adjusted R^2: 0.585 LM(2): 3.647

The real effective exchange rate (REER_BiH) is influenced by the nominal effective exchange rate (NEER_BiH) and by price developments. The latter have been approximated by the inflation rate in Bosnia and Herzegovina, i.e. the annual change in the consumer price index (CPI_BiH). In reality, it is the inflation differential rather than inflation alone in Bosnia and Herzegovina that matters. However, it would have been difficult to construct an international inflation rate consistent with the regional pattern of Bosnia's external trade as reflected in the effective exchange rate. Therefore, in the real effective exchange rate equation only inflation in Bosnia and Herzegovina was included in addition to the nominal effective exchange rate.

$$\log(REER\_BiH/REER\_BiH_{-4}) - \underset{(-8.261)}{0.0280} + \underset{(5.925)}{0.440} \log(REER\_BiH_{-1}/REER\_BiH_{-5})$$

$$+ \underset{(6.616)}{0.802} \log(NEER\_BiH/NEER\_BiH_{-4}) + \underset{(8.773)}{0.624} \log(CPI\_BiH/CPI\_BiH_{-4})$$

Adjusted R^2: 0.862 LM(2): 3.136

Labour market

Labour demand by companies (i.e. actual employment, EMP_BiH) is influenced by production and labour costs. In the model, production is approximated by GDP (GDPR_EXP_BiH), while labour costs consist of the average gross wage per employee (GWAGER_BiH).

$$
\begin{aligned}
\log(EMP\_BiH/EMP\_BiH_{-4}) = {} & \underset{(0.932)}{0.004} + \underset{(7.657)}{0.486} \log(EMP\_BiH_{-1}/EMP\_BiH_{-5}) \\
& + \underset{(2.420)}{0.111} \log(GDPR\_EXP\_BiH/GDPR\_EXP\_BiH_{-4}) \\
& - \underset{(-2.260)}{0.120} \log(GWAGER\_BiH_{-3}/GWAGER\_BiH_{-7}) - \underset{(-2.775)}{0.015}\, DUM2001 \\
& + \underset{(12.771)}{0.129}\, DUM2008q1 + \underset{(3.894)}{0.051}\, DUM2008q2 - \underset{(-5.086)}{0.055}\, DUM2009q1
\end{aligned}
$$

Adjusted R^2: 0.928 LM(2): 1.591

Labour supply by private households is determined by multiplying the population by the labour force participation rate (PARTRATE_BiH). Ideally, only the population of working age (generally, persons aged 15 to 64) should be taken, but at the time of developing the model for Bosnia and Herzegovina, only total population data were available for a sufficient time span. Hence, the labour force participation rate is smaller than it would be had only the working age population been taken into account. In a behavioural equation, the participation rate is positively influenced by the real net wage (NWAGER_BiH). This implies that the substitution effect of an increasing wage dominates the income effect, since the former would imply a positive influence of higher wages on labour supply, while the income effect results, *ceteris paribus*, in a negative reaction of labour force participation to rising wages.

$$
\begin{aligned}
PARTRATE\_BiH = {} & - \underset{(-2.157)}{0.045} + \underset{(14.637)}{0.828}\, PARTRATE\_BiH_{-1} + \underset{(2.833)}{0.013} \log(NWAGER\_BiH) \\
& + \underset{(7.226)}{0.020}\, DUM2008q1 - \underset{(-4.359)}{0.012}\, DUM2008q3
\end{aligned}
$$

Adjusted R^2: 0.971 LM(2): 0.913

Due to institutional arrangements and a large informal sector, registered (un)employment in Bosnia and Herzegovina deviates substantially from employment and unemployment, respectively, as measured by the labour force survey. Since registering as unemployed is a prerequisite for being entitled to unemployment benefits, many people register with the employment agency, even if they are employed at the same time, at least part-time. Therefore, employment and underemployment as measured on the basis of the labour force survey may provide a more accurate picture of the labour market situation in Bosnia and Herzegovina. Adjusted employment, i.e. employment according to the labour force survey, exceeds registered employment. Over time, the discrepancy between employment according to the labour force survey and according to business registries has declined from 25 percent in 2006 to 17 percent in 2011. In the model, employment as determined by the behavioural equation is multiplied by a factor which declines from 1.25 at the beginning of the time series to 1.17 at the end (i.e. 2011) so as to calculate adjusted employment. Since the first labour force survey was conducted in 2006, the adjustment factor had to be extrapolated backwards to the beginning of the time series, i.e. 1999. This was done by assuming the same factor of 1.25 as observed in 2006 for the period 1999 to 2005.

In a behavioural equation, the adjusted labour force (LFORCE_ADJ) is explained by the unadjusted labour force (LFORCE_BiH).

$$\log(LFORCE\_ADJ\_BiH/LFORCE\_ADJ\_BiH_{-4}) = \underset{(-7.120)}{-0.006} + \underset{(4.455)}{0.009}\, DUM2006$$

$$+ \underset{(33.050)}{1.004} \log(LFORCE\_BiH/LFORCE\_BiH_{-4}) - \underset{(-21.977)}{0.046}\, DUM2008 + \underset{(13.353)}{0.003}\, DUM2010$$

Adjusted R^2: 0.973 LM(2): 13.121**

Adjusted (unadjusted) unemployment is defined as the difference between the adjusted (unadjusted) labour force and adjusted (unadjusted) employment.

Prices and wages

In this part of the model, consumer prices, the GDP deflator and the wage rate are determined. The wage-price system is based on a bargaining model between employers and trade unions (Layard, Nickell and Jackman 1991). In this labour market model, prices are set as a mark-up over marginal costs. The wage-setting rule is based on a Nash bargaining process which produces an expected real wage that varies inversely with the unemployment rate. As unemployment falls, insiders know that, should they be laid off, they could quickly find work elsewhere. This raises the value of their fall-back point.

In the central equation of this model block, the consumer price index (CPI_BiH) is related to internal and external determinants. The most important internal cost-push factor is the wage rate (GWAGE_BiH). In addition, rising capacity utilisation (UTIL_BiH) exerts upward pressure on prices. When current production exceeds its potential or long-run level, output may only be further increased by employees working overtime, requesting extra payments.

In addition, machines might break down more quickly and thus require more maintenance if they run longer. As an important external cost factor, the oil price in Bosnian convertible marks KM (OILKM) enters the consumer price equation.

$$\log(CPI\_BiH/CPI\_BiH_{-4}) + \underset{(11.558)}{0.754} \log(CPI\_BiH_{-1}/CPI\_BiH_{-5})$$

$$+ \underset{(1.840)}{0.046} \log(GWAGE\_BiH_{-1}/GWAGE\_BiH_{-5}) + \underset{(8.636)}{0.044} \log(OILKM/OILKM_{-4})$$

$$+ \underset{(2.081)}{0.099} \log(UTIL\_BiH_{-2}/UTIL\_BiH_{-6}) - \underset{(-3.272)}{0.031} DUM2007q1$$

Adjusted R^2: 0.887 LM(2): 0.206

The deflator of GDP from the expenditure side (PGDP_EXP_BiH) is linked to the consumer price index (CPI_BiH). The GDP deflator is then used to derive nominal GDP once real GDP has been determined by adding up the expenditure components.

$$\log(PGDP\_EXP\_BiH/PGDP\_EXP\_BiH_{-4}) = \underset{(-2.776)}{-0.579} - \underset{(-3.404)}{0.044} DUM2009q1$$

$$+ \underset{(8.519)}{0.714} \log(PGDP\_EXP\_BiH_{-1}/PGDP\_EXP\_BiH_{-5}) + \underset{(3.197)}{0.262} \log(CPI\_BiH/CPI\_BiH_{4})$$

$$- \underset{(-3.348)}{0.258} \log(PGDP\_EXP\_BiH_{-4}) + \underset{(3.236)}{0.386} \log(CPI\_BiH_{-4}) - \underset{(-4.622)}{0.0650} DUM200q1$$

Adjusted R^2: 0.918 LM(2): 0.013

In an extended Phillips curve equation, the average gross wage rate (GWAGE_BiH) is negatively influenced by the difference between the actual unemployment rate (UR_BiH) and the structural unemployment rate (the NAIRU). The notion behind this relationship is that the negotiation power of trade unions increases if actual unemployment falls below its structural level, resulting in rising wage pressure. In addition, wages are positively influenced by consumer prices (CPI_BiH) and by labour productivity (PROD_BiH). The former explanatory variable accounts for the fact that employees are interested in keeping the purchasing power of nominal wages at least constant in the event of rising prices. The inclusion of labour productivity rests on the notion that employees will demand to participate in productivity advancements. In the long run, the real wage is constant. This is captured by entering the lagged real wage (GWAGE_BiH/CPI_BiH) as the cointegrating relationship.

$$\log(GWAGE\_BiH/GWAGE\_BiH_{-4}) = \underset{(2.949)}{0.169} + \underset{(4.742)}{0.549}\log(GWAGE\_BiH_{-1}/GWAGE\_BiH_{-5})$$

$$+ \underset{(3.107)}{0.403}\log(CPI\_BiH_{-1}/CPI\_BiH_{-5}) - \underset{(-2.608)}{0.064}\log(GWAGE\_BiH_{-4}/CPI\_BiH_{-4})$$

$$+ \underset{(1.332)}{0.031}\log(PROD\_BiH_{-4}) - \underset{(-1.758)}{0.007}(UR\_BiH - NAIRU\_BiH)$$

Adjusted R^2: 0.752 LM(2): 3.957

Public sector

This model block contains equations for the most important government revenue and expenditure items. Notwithstanding the rather complicated and fragmented political structure of Bosnia and Herzegovina, where many competences in the field of fiscal policy-making are assigned to the Entities, i.e. the Federation of Bosnia and Herzegovina, the Republika Srpska and Brčko District, in the aggregated macroeconometric model for Bosnia and Herzegovina the focus lies on the consolidated general government. Hence, aggregated revenues and expenditures at all levels of public administration are related to the relevant explanatory variables such as policy instruments or the economic situation.

Expenditures

In a fiscal rule, public expenditures on goods and services, i.e. public consumption according to fiscal statistics (GCONS_BiH) is inversely related to the past change in the debt level (DEBT_BiH). This rule prevents public debt from increasing permanently since a rise in the debt level is counteracted by spending restraint in the next period.

In order to account for differences between national accounts and public finance data, the model includes a behavioural equation relating government consumption according to national accounts (G_BiH) to government consumption according to public finance accounting (GCONS_BiH).

$$\log(GCONS\_BiH/GCONS\_BiH_{-4}) = \underset{(4.082)}{0.065} + \underset{(3.896)}{0.446} \log(GCONS\_BiH_{-1}/GCONS\_BiH_{-5})$$

$$- \underset{(-2.997)}{0.326} \log(DEBT\_BiH_{-2}/DEBT\_BiH_{-6}) - \underset{(-3.345)}{0.108}\, DUM2004 + \underset{(4.607)}{0.247}\, DUM2006q3$$

$$- \underset{(-3.078)}{0.167}\, DUM2007q3 + \underset{(1.939)}{0.109}\, DUM2007q4 - \underset{(-4.194)}{0.237}\, DUM2008q4$$

Adjusted R^2: 0.699 LM(2): 1.813

$$\log(G\_BiH/G\_BiH_{-4}) = \underset{(4.322)}{0.040} + \underset{(11.842)}{0.776} \log(GCONS\_BiH/GCONS\_BiH_{-4})$$

$$- \underset{(-4.172)}{0.565} \log(G\_BiH_{-4})-\log(GCONS\_BiH_{-4})$$

Adjusted R^2: 0.789 LM(2): 18.461^{***}

Transfer payments (TRANSFERS_BiH) to private households consist, to a large extent, of pensions and unemployment benefits. In the model for Bosnia and Herzegovina, the number of pensioners is not explicitly taken into account. Hence, in the behavioural equation for transfer payments, only unemployment benefits are considered. They are related to the number of unemployed people and to the unemployment benefit per person. The latter is related to the compensation per employee. Hence, transfers are explained by the number of unemployed persons (UN_BiH) and by compensation per employee (COMP_EMP_BiH).

$$\log(TRANSFERS\_BiH/TRANSFERS\_BiH_{-4}) = \underset{(-2.700)}{- 0.046}$$

$$+ \underset{(4.423)}{0.588} \log(TRANSFERS\_BiH_{-1}/TRANSFERS\_BiH_{-5}) + \underset{(2.861)}{0.645} \log(UN\_BiH/UN\_BiH_{-4})$$

$$+ \underset{(3.633)}{0.713} \log(COMP\_EMP\_BiH/COMP\_EMP\_BiH_{-4}) + \underset{(3.155)}{0.137}\, DUM2006q2$$

$$- \underset{(-3.759)}{0.161}\, DUM2006q4 + \underset{(2.959)}{0.122}\, DUM2007q3 + \underset{(3.371)}{0.145}\, DUM2007q4$$

Adjusted R^2: 0.840 LM(2): 3.469

Subsidies (SUBSIDIES_BiH) to private enterprises are positively related to the general economic situation, which is approximated by GDP at current prices (GDP_EXP_BiH). This equation is based on the notion that an increasing GDP brings about rising government revenues, which enable the government to spend more, among others, on subsidies.

$$\log(SUBSIDIES\_BiH/SUBSIDIES\_BiH_{-4}) = \underset{(1.203)}{0.040} - \underset{(-3.511)}{0.447}\,DUM2007q3.$$

$$+ \underset{(1.981)}{0.306}\log(SUBSIDIES\_BiH_{-1}/SUBSIDIES\_BiH_{-5}) + \underset{(4.020)}{0.626}\,DUM2007q4$$

$$+ \underset{(1.266)}{0.580}\log(GDP\_EXP\_BiH/GDP\_EXP\_BiH_{-4}) + \underset{(3.346)}{0.432}\,DUM2008q3 - \underset{(-3.255)}{0.457}\,DUM2008q4$$

Adjusted R^2: 0.661 LM(2): 4.349

Other government expenditures (EXPOTHER_BiH) are explained by other revenues (REVOTHER_BiH), since higher revenues enable the government to spend more.

$$\log(EXPOTHER\_BiH/EXPOTHER\_BiH_{-4}) = \underset{(1.904)}{0.065} - \underset{(-4.649)}{0.986}\,DUM2007q1$$

$$+ \underset{(1.915)}{0.268}\log(EXPOTHER\_BiH_{-1}/EXPOTHER\_BiH_{-5}) + \underset{(2.540)}{0.513}\,DUM2007q4$$

$$+ \underset{(1.854)}{0.248}\log(REVOTHER\_BiH/REVOTHER\_BiH_{-4})$$

Adjusted R^2: 0.452 LM(2): 6.701^{**}

Revenues

In a definitional equation, social security contributions are derived by multiplying the average social security contribution rate by the wage rate and by the number of employees.

Since income tax revenues (TAXINCOME_BiH) behave pro-cyclically, in the model they are linked to GDP at current prices (GDP_EXP_BiH) as the most comprehensive measure of economic activity.

$$\log(TAXINCOME\_BiH/TAXINCOME\_BiH_{-4}) + \underset{(0.157)}{0.007}$$

$$+ \underset{(9.965)}{0.855} \log(TAXINCOME\_BiH_{-1}/TAXINCOME\_BiH_{-5})$$

$$+ \underset{(1.302)}{0.481} \log(GDP\_EXP\_BiH_{-1}/GDP\_EXP\_BiH_{-5})$$

$$- \underset{(-2.492)}{0.312} DUM2005q1 - \underset{(-4.832)}{0.639} DUM2008q1 + \underset{(5.255)}{0.667} DUM2009q1$$

Adjusted R^2: 0.762 LM(2): 5.896*

Value added tax (VAT) revenues (TAXVAT_BiH) are determined by private consumption expenditures (CONS_BiH), multiplied by the value added tax rate (VATRATE_BiH). Some goods and services are taxed at lower rates than the general VAT rate, and some goods and services are VAT-exempt. Hence, there is no definitional relation between VAT revenues and private consumption multiplied by the VAT rate. Any deviations are reflected in the residuals of the behavioural equation. A dummy variable accounts for the fact that it was not until 2006 that VAT replaced the sales tax that had been in place before. Other dummies account for special developments of value added tax revenues in single quarters.

$$\log(TAXVAT\_BiH/TAXVAT\_BiH_{-4}) = \underset{(17.480)}{0.773} \log(TAXVAT\_BiH_{-1}/TAXVAT\_BiH_{-5})$$

$$+ \underset{(3.793)}{0.290} \log((CONS\_BiH * VATRATE\_BiH)/(CONS\_BiH_{-4} \cdot VATRATE\_BiH_{-4}))$$

$$- \underset{(-3.353)}{0.184} \log(TAXVAT\_BiH_{-4}) + 2.2067 - 1.3631 \cdot (\log(CONS\_BiH_{-4} \cdot VATRATE\_BiH_{-4}))$$

$$- \underset{(-4.606)}{0.074} DUM2004q1 + \underset{(6.123)}{0.110} DUM2005q1 + \underset{(6.711)}{0.110} DUM2006q1$$

$$- \underset{(-4.143)}{0.070} DUM2008q1 - \underset{(-8.002)}{0.129} DUM2009q1 + \underset{(7.313)}{0.129} DUM2010q1$$

+Adjusted R^2: 0.970 LM(2): 0.000

Other government revenues (REVOTHER_BiH) are positively related to the economic situation as measured by nominal GDP (GDP_EXP_BiH). In general, an increase in total income causes rising government revenues.

$$\log(REVOTHER\_BiH/REVOTHER\_BiH_{-4}) = -\underset{(-1.761)}{0.087} + \underset{(3.390)}{0.623}\ DUM2003q4$$

$$+ \underset{(3.685)}{1.912}\ \log(GDP\_EXP\_BiH/GDP\_EXP\_BiH_{-4}) - \underset{(-3.118)}{0.563}\ DUM2006q2$$

$$+ \underset{(2.345)}{0.436}\ DUM2006q4 - \underset{(-3.291)}{0.598}\ DUM2008q4$$

Adjusted R^2: 0.522 LM(2): 9.348^{***}

The wedge on labour income, i.e. the difference between gross and net wages (WEDGE_BiH), is determined by an average social security contribution rate (SOCCONTRATE_BiH) which is multiplied by the average gross wage (GWAGE_BiH). Besides social security contributions, the wedge between gross and net wages is determined by income taxes. However, only data for total income taxes, but no separate data for personal and corporate income tax payments were available for Bosnia and Herzegovina at the time of setting up the model. This is taken into account by specifying a behavioural rather than a deterministic equation for the tax wedge. The fact that the wedge consists of income taxes in addition to social security contributions is captured by a coefficient smaller than 1 for social security contributions.

$$\log(WEDGE\_BiH) = \underset{(1.351)}{0.229} + \underset{(9.701)}{0.795}\ \log(WEDGE\_BiH_{-4})$$

$$+ \underset{(2.362)}{0.179}\ \log(GWAGE\_BiH*SOCCONTRATE\_BiH/100)$$

Adjusted R^2: 0.971 LM(2): 15.785^{***}

Theoretically, the change in the debt level should be identical to the fiscal balance, i.e. a budget surplus (deficit) should result in an equivalent reduction (increase) in the level of public debt. In the reality of economic accounting, however, certain operations only affect either the budget balance or the debt level. Therefore, the model includes a behavioural equation for the change in the debt level (DELTADEBT_BiH). As the only explanatory variables, the budget balance (BALANCE_BiH) and two dummy variables are considered.

$$\underset{}{DELTADEBT\_BiH} = \underset{(-2.837)}{-\,0.206}\ BALANCE\_BiH + \underset{(2.979)}{423.688}\ DUM2009q3 + \underset{(3.002)}{426.839}\ DUM2010q1$$

Adjusted R^2: 0.296 LM(2): 0.882

Identities

$$trendemp\_bih = lforce\_bih * (1 - nairu\_bih / 100)$$

$$capr\_bih = capr\_bih_{-1} * (1 - deprate\_bih / 100) + ifixr\_bih$$

$$\log(ypot\_bih) = 0.65 * \log(trendemp\_bih) + 0.35 * \log(capr\_bih) + \log(trendtfp\_bih)$$

$$util\_bih = gdpr\_exp\_bih / ypot\_bih * 100$$

$$util\_sa\_bih = util\_sa\_bih_{-4} * [1 + ((util\_bih/util\_bih_{-4})*100) / 100]$$

$$yd\_bih = gdp\_exp\_bih - taxincome\_bih - soccontr\_bih + transfers\_bih + remit\_bih$$

$$ydr\_bih = yd\_bih / cpi\_bih * 100$$

$$demandr\_bih = consr\_bih + gr\_bih + ifixr\_bih + inventr\_bih + exr\_bih$$

$$oilkm = oil * kmusd$$

$$nwage\_bih = gwage\_bih - wedge\_bih$$

$$\text{gwager\_bih} = \text{gwage\_bih} / \text{cpi\_bih} * 100$$

$$\text{nwager\_bih} = \text{nwage\_bih} / \text{cpi\_bih} * 100$$

$$\text{infl\_bih} = (\text{cpi\_bih} / \text{cpi\_bih}_{-4} - 1) * 100$$

$$\text{ilreal\_bih} = \text{il\_bih} - \text{infl\_bih}$$

$$\text{ucc\_bih} = \text{ilreal\_bih} + \text{deprate\_bih}$$

$$\text{inventr\_bih} = \text{moving avarage (inventr\_bih, 8)}$$

$$\text{investr\_bih} = \text{ifixr\_bih} + \text{inventr\_bih}$$

$$\text{gr\_bih} = \text{g\_bih} / \text{pgdp\_exp\_bih} * 100$$

$$\begin{aligned}\text{gdpr\_exp\_bih} = {} & \text{consr\_bih} + \text{gr\_bih} + \text{ifixr\_bih} + \text{inventr\_bih} \\ & + \text{exr\_bih} - \text{imr\_bih}\end{aligned}$$

$$\text{cons\_bih} = \text{consr\_bih} * \text{pgdp\_exp\_bih} / 100$$

$$\text{gdp\_exp\_bih} = \text{gdpr\_exp\_bih} * \text{pgdp\_exp\_bih} / 100$$

$$\text{lforce\_bih} = \text{partrate\_bih} * \text{pop\_bih}$$

$$\text{emp\_adj\_bih} = \text{empfactor\_bih} * \text{emp\_bih}$$

$$\text{un\_bih} = \text{lforce\_bih} - \text{emp\_bih}$$

$$\text{ur\_bih} = \text{un\_bih} / \text{lforce\_bih} * 100$$

$$\text{un\_adj\_bih} = \text{lforce\_adj\_bih} - \text{emp\_adj\_bih}$$

$$\text{ur\_adj\_bih} = \text{un\_adj\_bih} / \text{lforce\_adj\_bih} * 100$$

$$\text{prod\_bih} = \text{gdpr\_exp\_bih} / \text{emp\_bih} * 1000$$

$$\begin{aligned}\text{soccontr\_bih} = {} & (\text{gwage\_bih} * \text{soccontrate\_bih} * \text{emp\_bih}) \\ & / 100000000\end{aligned}$$

$$\text{soccontremp\_bih} = \text{soccontr\_bih} * 1000000 / \text{emp\_bih}$$

$$\text{comp\_emp\_bih} = \text{gwage\_bih} * \text{emp\_bih} / 1000000 + \text{soccontr\_bih}$$

$$\text{interest\_bih} = \text{il\_debt\_bih} * \text{debt\_bih}_{-1} / 100$$

$$revtotal\_bih = taxincome\_bih + taxvat\_bih + soccontr\_bih + revother\_bih$$

$$exptotal\_bih = gcons\_bih + interest\_bih + subsidies\_bih + transfers\_bih + expother\_bih$$

$$balance\_curr\_bih = revtotal\_bih - exptotal\_bih$$

$$balance\_bih = balance\_curr\_bih - pubinvest\_bih$$

$$balanceratio\_bih = balance\_bih / gdp\_exp\_bih * 100$$

$$balance\_curr\_ratio\_bih = balance\_curr\_bih / gdp\_exp\_bih * 100$$

$$debt\_bih = debt\_bih_{-1} + deltadebt\_bih$$

$$debtratio\_bih = debt\_bih / (gdp\_exp\_bih + gdp\_exp\_bih_{-1} + gdp\_exp\_bih_{-2} + gdp\_exp\_bih_{-3}) * 100$$

$$exr\_bih = exr\_bihcro + exr\_bihsrb + exr\_bihslo + exr\_bihrow$$

$$imr\_bih = exr\_crobih / hrkeur * 1.95583 + exr\_srbbih / dineur * 1.95583 + exr\_slobih * 1.95583 + imr\_bihrow$$

THE MODEL FOR SLOVENIA

Introduction and data issues

The Slovenia sub-model already has a long tradition as a stand-alone model. Its development started in 1998 as part of an international collaboration between the Slovenian Ministry of Economic Affairs, a Klagenfurt based energy consulting company, the University of Klagenfurt, and the Institute of Macroeconomic Analysis and Development (IMAD) in Ljubljana. The model developed within this project combined a macroeconomic model and an energy-system model for carrying out energy-sector related analyses. Based upon this blueprint, a structural macroeconometric model of the Slovenian economy was built, called SLOPOLi (SLOvenian economic POLicy model, version no. i, with i denoting the version i = 1, 2, …,8). The different model versions have been described in several publications (see, e.g., Weyerstrass and Neck 2001, 2007 and Weyerstrass 2011).

The behavioural equations were estimated using quarterly data for the period 1995:1 to 2011:4. The data were taken from databases and publications by the Slovenian Statistical Office, the Bank of Slovenia, and the Eurostat database. Macroeconomic data for Slovenia are of much better quality than data for the other successor states of the former Yugoslavia included in the multi-country model. This has several reasons. Slovenia was one of the first countries to become independent, its declaration of independence was not followed by a war with major destruction, and Slovenia was the first country from the former Yugoslavia to become a member state of the EU and the euro area. Hence, it had to meet the strict EU standards regarding the quality of macroeconomic statistics much earlier than the other former Yugoslav republics. Furthermore, Slovenia was the most advanced state within the former Yugoslavia; hence its transformation process towards a modern Western economy – which also has impacts on macroeconomic statistics – was less severe than the transformation of the other former Yugoslav republics. Due to the better data quality, no data transformations were necessary, unlike the other three sub-models in the multi-country model.

Model equations

Like the other country models, the model for Slovenia contains behavioural equations and identities for several markets and sectors: the goods market, the labour market, the foreign exchange market, the money market, and the government sector. Rigidities of wages and prices are taken into account. The model combines Keynesian and neoclassical elements. The former determine the short and medium-run solutions in the sense that the model is demand-driven, and persistent disequilibria in the goods and labour markets are possible. The supply side incorporates neoclassical features. In this section, the behavioural equations of these model blocks are described in detail. Since all four country sub-models have similar theoretical foundations, the model equations for Slovenia in this section and for Serbia and Croatia in the following sections are described in less detail than the model equations for Bosnia and Herzegovina above. As in the previous section on the model for Bosnia, t-statistics are provided in parentheses below the estimated coefficients. In addition, the adjusted R^2 and the Breusch-Godfrey test for serial correlation are provided. The suffix _SLO in the variable names indicates the sub-model for Slovenia.

Supply side

Similar to the other sub-models, in the supply block potential GDP is determined on the basis of a Cobb-Douglas production function with constant returns to scale. In addition to the production factors labour and capital, autonomous technical progress is considered. The production function has the following form:

$$\log(YPOT\_SLO) = 0.65 \log(TRENDEMP\_SLO) + 0.35 \log(CAPR\_SLO) + TRENDTFP\_SLO.$$

YPOT_SLO is potential GDP, TRENDEMP_SLO is the trend labour force, i.e. the labour force minus structural unemployment, CAPR_SLO is the real capital stock, and TRENDTFP_SLO is the long-run trend of total factor productivity (TFP). The production elasticities of employment (0.65) and capital (0.35) are based on international empirical evidence. In addition, in line with economic theory these production elasticities are close to the shares of wages and capital income in national income.[11] Furthermore, these production elasticities are also used by the European Commission in its potential output estimations for the EU Member States, hence also for Slovenia (D'Auria et al. 2010).

Before calculating potential GDP according to the above equation, trend employment and trend total factor productivity are determined in the same way

[11] 0.6 and 0.4 respectively.

as in the sub-model for Bosnia and Herzegovina. Trend employment is calculated by subtracting natural or structural unemployment from the labour force. The non-accelerating inflation rate of unemployment (or the NAIRU) is again estimated by applying the Hodrick-Prescott (HP) filter to the actual unemployment rate in order to extract the trend. The NAIRU is then endogenised by an 8 quarter moving average process.

Applying growth accounting, total factor productivity (TFP) is calculated as that part of real GDP that is not due to labour and capital input, where both production factors are weighted with their production elasticities:

$$\log(TFP\_SLO) = \log(GDPR\_SLO) - 0.65 \log(EMP\_SLO) - 0.35 \log(CAPR\_SLO)$$

In this equation, TFP_SLO denotes actual (i.e. not trend) total factor productivity, GDPR_SLO is real GDP, EMP_SLO stands for actual employment, and CAPR_SLO is, as before, the real capital stock. For the production possibilities, the long-run trend rather than the current level of total factor productivity is relevant. Therefore, the actual TFP series is smoothed by applying the Hodrick-Prescott filter so as to remove short-run fluctuations which are caused by the business cycle or by any short-run shocks. In order to endogenise trend TFP, the following equation has been estimated and implemented in the model.

$$
\begin{aligned}
\log(TRENDTFP\_SLO/TRENDTFP\_SLO_{-4}) = {} & \underset{(1.500)}{0.00004} \\
& + \underset{(66.026)}{3.872} \log(TRENDTFP\_SLO_{-1}/TRENDTFP\_SLO_{-5}) \\
& - \underset{(-32.759)}{5.680} \log(TRENDTFP\_SLO_{-2}/TRENDTFP\_SLO_{-6}) \\
& + \underset{(21.537)}{3.739} \log(TRENDTFP\_SLO_{-3}/TRENDTFP\_SLO_{-7}) \\
& - \underset{(-15.821)}{0.932} \log(TRENDTFP\_SLO_{-4}/TRENDTFP\_SLO_{-8}) \\
& - \underset{(-3.224)}{0.00004} DUM2009q3 - \underset{(-3.627)}{0.00004} DUM2009q4
\end{aligned}
$$

Adjusted R^2: 0.999 LM(2): 10.409***

Demand side

Consumption of private households

Real consumption of private households (CR_SLO) is explained by a combination of a Keynesian consumption function and a function in accordance with the permanent income hypothesis and the life cycle hypothesis. Thus, private consumption depends on current real disposable income (INCOMER_SLO). In addition, the long-term real interest rate (GOV10YR_SLO) enters the consumption equation with a negative sign. The growth rate of current disposable income is retained in the short-run equation for theoretical reasons although it is not significant.

$$\log(CR\_SLO/CR\_SLO_{-4})=\underset{(9.709)}{0.036}+\underset{(0.665)}{0.015}\log(INCOMER\_SLO/INCOMER\_SLO_{-4})$$

$$-\underset{(-3.129)}{0.040}[\log(CR\_SLO_{-4})-0.974\log(INCOMER\_SLO_{-4})]-\underset{(-4.444)}{0.007}GOV10YR\_SLO$$

$$+\underset{(3.804)}{0.069}DUM1999q2-\underset{(-2.621)}{0.049}DUM2000q2+\underset{(3.437)}{0.060}DUM2007q3$$

Adjusted R^2: 0.505 LM(2): 9.996^{***}

Disposable income is defined as the sum of wage income and capital income. The former is calculated by multiplying the average gross wage per employee by the number of employees, subtracting direct taxes and social security contributions, and adding transfer payments. Capital income or income from financial wealth is determined by multiplying the average long-term interest rate by the stock of financial wealth.

The stock of financial wealth (FINWEALTH_SLO) is related to the nominal capital stock, i.e. the real capital stock (CAPR_SLO) multiplied by the GDP deflator (GDPDEF_SLO).

$$\log(FINWEALTH\_SLO/FINWEALTH\_SLO_{-4})=\underset{(2.292)}{0.024}+\underset{(7.889)}{0.132}DUM2007$$

$$+\underset{(4.319)}{0.422}\log[(CAPR\_SLO*GDPDEF\_SLO)/(CAPR\_SLO_{-4}*GDPDEF\_SLO_{-4})]$$

Adjusted R^2: 0.561 LM(2): 41.032^{***}

Gross fixed capital formation

Real private (i.e. non-government) investment in machinery, equipment and buildings (PRINVR_SLO) is influenced by the change in total domestic demand (in accordance with the accelerator hypothesis) and by the user costs of capital (UCC_SLO), where the latter are defined as the real interest rate plus the depreciation rate of the capital stock. Total demand is approximated by real GDP (GDPR_SLO). Changes in inventories (INVENTR_SLO) are modelled as an eight quarter moving average process.

$$\log(PRINVR\_SLO/CONSR\_SLO_{-4}) = \underset{(-2.359)}{-2.612} + \underset{(10.360)}{2.724} \log(GDPR\_SLO/GDPR\_SLO_{-4})$$

$$- \underset{(-1.802)}{0.0008} (UCC\_SLO - UCC\_SLO_{-4}) + \underset{(2.305)}{0.554} \log(UTIL\_SLO_{-4})$$

$$- \underset{(-2.306)}{0.178} [\log(PRINVR\_SLO_{-4}) - 0.850 \log(GDPR\_SLO_{-4}) + 0.056\, UCC\_SLO_{-4}]$$

Adjusted R^2: 0.782 LM(2): 4.553

Exports of goods and services

As elaborated above, every country sub-model contains equations for exports to every other country in the model, as well as to the rest of the world. Hence, for Slovenia, exports to Bosnia and Herzegovina, Serbia, Croatia and the rest of the world are modelled separately.

Exports from Slovenia to Bosnia and Herzegovina (EXR_SLOBiH) are influenced by real final demand in Bosnia and Herzegovina (DEMANDR_BiH) and by the price ratio between Slovenia and Bosnia. Due to the fact that Slovenia has the euro as its legal tender and Bosnia and Herzegovina operates a currency board with the euro as the reference currency, the real exchange rate between these two countries only consists of the price ratio (CPI_BiH/CPI_SLO) while the nominal exchange rate between the Bosnian mark and the euro is fixed.

$$\log(EXR\_SLOBiH/EXR\_SLOBiH_{-4}) = \underset{(1.908)}{1.212} + \underset{(2.947)}{0.314}\log(EXR\_SLOBiH_{-1}/EXR\_SLOSLO_{-5})$$

$$+ \underset{(3.530)}{0.599}\log(DEMANDR\_BiH/DEMANDR\_BiH_{-4})$$

$$+ \underset{(2.235)}{0.432}\log(CPI\_BiH/CPI\_SLO) - \underset{(-3.966)}{0.506}\log(EXR\_SLOBIH_{-4}) + \underset{(2.793)}{0.142}\log(DEMANDR\_BiH_{-4})$$

Adjusted R^2: 0.775 LM(2): 10.648^{***}

Exports from Slovenia to Serbia (EXR_SLOSRB) are a function of real final demand in Serbia (DEMANDR_SRB) and the real exchange rate. The real exchange rate consists of the nominal exchange rate between the euro and the Serbian dinar (DINEUR) and the ratio between the consumer price indices in Serbia (CPI_SRB) and Slovenia (CPI_SLO). The exchange rate between the euro and the dinar is defined in such a way that its inverse enters the calculation of the real exchange rate between Slovenia and Serbia.

$$\log(EXR\_SLOSRB/EXR\_SLOSRB_{-4}) = \underset{(-4.639)}{-7.710} + \underset{(5.277)}{0.474}\log(EXR\_SLOSRB_{-1}/EXR\_SLOSRB_{-5})$$

$$+ \underset{(2.398)}{0.488}\log(DEMANDR\_SRB/DEMANDR\_SRB_{-4})$$

$$- \underset{(-5.797)}{0.593}\log(EXR\_SLOSRB_{-4}) + \underset{(5.093)}{0.839}\log(DEMANDR\_SRB_{-4})$$

$$+ \underset{(1.354)}{0.080}\log(((1/DINEUR_{-4})*CPI\_SRB_{-4}/CPI\_SLO_{-4}))] + \underset{(4.176)}{0.366}\,DUM2007q1$$

Adjusted R^2: 0.773 LM(2): 2.005

Exports from Slovenia to Croatia (EXR_SLOCRO) depend on final demand in Croatia (DEMANDR_CRO) and the real exchange rate between the euro and the Croatian kuna. The real exchange rate between the euro and the kuna includes the price ratio between Slovenia and Croatia (CPI_CRO/CPI_SLO) in addition to the nominal exchange rate between the euro and the kuna (HRKEUR). The nominal exchange rate has been defined in such a way that the inverse, i.e. 1/HRKEUR enters the definition of the real exchange rate. In this equation, the long-run, cointegrating relation was estimated in a first step. It then enters the error correction model with a lag.

$$\log(EXR\_SLOCRO/EXR\_SLOCRO_{-4}) = \underset{(9.819)}{0.605} \log(EXR\_SLOCRO_{-1}/EXR\_SLOCRO_{-5})$$

$$+ \underset{(5.632)}{0.969} \log(DEMANDR\_CRO/DEMANDR\_CRO_{-4})$$

$$+ \underset{(2.809)}{0.651} \log(((1/HRKEUR)*CPI\_CRO/CPI\_SLO)/((1/HRKEUR_{-4})\cdot CPI\_CRO_{-4}/CPI\_SLO_{-4}))$$

$$- \underset{(-5.889)}{0.480} [\log(EXR\_SLOCRO_{-4}) + 13.767 - 1.871 \log(DEMANDR\_CRO_{-4}) - 0.825 \log((1/HRKEUR_{-4})*CPI\_CRO_{-4}/CPI\_SLO_{-4}) - 0.090\, Q1 + 0.062\, Q3]$$

$$- \underset{(-7.048)}{0.310}\, DUM2009q1 + \underset{(2.262)}{0.093}\, DUM2009q4$$

Adjusted R^2: 0.947 LM(2): 3.943

Exports from Slovenia to the rest of the world (EXR_SLOROW) depend on world trade (WTRADE) as a proxy for world demand, and on the real effective exchange rate for Slovenia (REER41_SLO). The real effective exchange rate is a weighted average of the nominal exchange rates and the price ratios to Slovenia's 41 most important trading partners. Due to Slovenia's euro area membership, the nominal exchange rate between Slovenia and the other euro area countries does not exist. However, the real exchange rate is also defined within the euro area, due to inflation and, hence, price level differentials.

$$\log(EXR\_SLOROW/EXR\_SLOROW_{-4}) = \underset{(5.114)}{4.939} + \underset{(20.866)}{1.181} \log(WTRADE/WTRADE_{-4})$$

$$- \underset{(-2.216)}{0.492} \log(REER41\_SLO/REER41\_SLO_{-4})$$

$$- \underset{(-3.055)}{0.368} \log(EXR\_SLOROW_{-4}) + \underset{(3.549)}{0.504} \log(WTRADE_{-4}) - \underset{(-6.081)}{1.296} \log(REER41\_SLO_{-4})$$

Adjusted R^2: 0.938 LM(2): 6.547^{**}

Imports of goods and services

Imports to Slovenia from the other countries in the model are, by definition, identical to their exports to Slovenia (except for deviations between exports and imports due to measurement and other statistical errors). Hence, they are modelled as exports in the other country models, and only Slovenia's imports from the rest of the world (IMR_SLOROW) are modelled separately. They depend on total real demand in Slovenia (DEMAND_SLO) and on relative prices. Similar to the equation for Slovenia's exports to the rest of the world, relative prices are approximated by the real effective exchange rate for Slovenia with respect to its 41 most important trading partners (REER41_SLO).

$$\log(IMR\_SLOROW/IMR\_SLOROW_{-4}) = \underset{(-2.057)}{-0.009} + \underset{(2.090)}{0.333} \log(REER41\_SLO_{-2}/REER41\_SLO_{-6})$$

$$+ \underset{(26.050)}{1.737} \log(DEMAND\_SLO/DEMAND\_SLO_{-4}) - \underset{(-3.839)}{0.094} DUM2005q2$$

Adjusted R^2: 0.941 LM(2): 6.680^{**}

Money market

In the money market section of the model, the short-term interest rate, the long-term interest rate and the implicit interest rate on outstanding public debt are determined.

The short-term interest rate, i.e. the three-month money market rate (SLO3M) is linked to its euro area counterpart (EUR3M). Within the euro area, short-term money market interest rates are identical for all Member States. However, the data used for estimating the model equations include data for the period before Slovenia's euro area accession in 2007. From January 1, 2007 onwards, SLO3M is replaced by EUR3M.

$$SLO3M - SLO3M_{-4} = \underset{(9.785)}{0.937} (EUR3M - EUR3M_{-4}) - \underset{(-6.003)}{0.693} (SLO3M_{-4} - EUR3M_{-4})$$

Adjusted R^2: 0.631 LM(2): 46.470^{***}

The long-term euro area interest rate (EUR10Y) is included in the equation determining the long-term interest rate in Slovenia so as to capture Slovenia's euro area membership since 2007. In the model, the long-term interest rate is defined as the yield on government bonds with a maturity of ten years (GOV10Y_SLO). Contrary to money market rates, government bond yields can and do differ between the Member States of a currency union, reflecting, in particular, differences in the perceived default risks. However, for countries with a similar default risk, there is a tendency towards convergence for government bond yields. This convergence tendency is the foundation for including the euro area long-term rate in the equation determining the bond yield in Slovenia. In addition to the euro area average bond yield, the Slovenian long-term interest rate is linked to the short-term rate, representing the term structure of interest rates.

$$GOV10Y\_SLO - GOV10Y\_SLO_{-4} = \underset{(1.106)}{0.146}\,(SLO3M_{-1} - SLO3M_{-5}) \underset{(-2.143)}{- 0.183}\,(GOV10Y\_SLO_{-4} - EUR10Y_{-4})$$

Adjusted R^2: 0.107 LM(2): 31.123***

The implicit interest rate on public debt (IGOVDEBT_SLO) is influenced by the maturity structure of debt that the government has incurred in the past. This implicit interest rate adjusts gradually to the current long-term market rate, where the speed of adjustment is influenced by the roll-over of maturing liabilities.

$$IGOVDEBT\_SLO - IGOVDEBT\_SLO_{-1} = \underset{(0.615)}{0.041}\,(GOV10Y\_SLO - GOV10Y\_SLO_{-1}) + \underset{(6.165)}{1.167}\,Q1 - \underset{(-5.957)}{1.092}\,Q2$$

Adjusted R^2: 0.524 LM(2): 28.406***

Foreign exchange market

The foreign exchange market is modelled by the real effective exchange rate against a group of 41 countries (REER41_SLO). As the time series on which the estimation of the behavioural equations are based include the period before Slovenia's euro area accession in 2007, the bilateral exchange rate between the Slovenian tolar and the euro (SITEUR) is included as one of the explanatory variables in the real effective exchange rate equation. In addition, the exchange rate between the euro and the US dollar (EURUSD) is considered. As the real exchange rate takes the nominal exchange rate and price developments into account, the inflation rate in Slovenia is included as a further explanatory variable. From a theoretical point of view, the ratio between the price level in Slovenia and the weighted average price level in the 41 trading partners that enter the calculation of the real effective exchange rate should be taken as explanatory variables. However, a calculation of such a weighted average price level would involve many exogenous variables which would have to be extrapolated in forecasts and *ex ante* simulations. Hence, in the estimation, only price developments in Slovenia are taken into account. This is justified as a long-run cointegrating relationship was not supported by the data. Hence, only the annual change in the exchange rates and inflation in Slovenia (i.e. the annual change in the consumer price index, CPI_SLO) were included in the equation. Thus, the consideration of average inflation in Slovenia's 41 most important trading partners would have implied including the difference between inflation in Slovenia and an exogenous variable. The omission of this exogenous inflation only influences the constant in the estimation.

$$\log(REER41\_SLO/REER41\_SLO_{-4}) = \underset{(-4.271)}{-0.021} + \underset{(8.587)}{0.544} \log(REER41\_SLO_{-1}/REER41\_SLO_{-5})$$

$$+ \underset{(2.159)}{0.319} \log(SITEUR/SITEUR_{-4}) + \underset{(4.830)}{0.098} \log(EURUSD/EURUSD_{-4})$$

$$+ \underset{(3.904)}{0.559} \log(CPI\_SLO/CPI\_SLO_{-4})$$

$$+ \underset{(5.102)}{0.040}\, DUM2009 + \underset{(4.256)}{0.058}\, DUM1998q4 - \underset{(-3.012)}{0.039}\, DUM2010q1$$

Adjusted R^2: 0.837 LM(2): 9.186^{***}

Labour market

Turning to the labour market, labour demand by companies (actual employment, EMP_SLO) is influenced by the final demand for goods and services (which is approximated by real GDP) and by the real gross wage (GWAGER_SLO). In accordance with the Cobb-Douglas production function with constant returns to scale which is used to determine potential GDP, the long-run elasticity of real production with respect to employment was restricted to 1.

$$\log(EMP\_SLO/EMP\_SLO_{-4}) = \underset{(6.623)}{0.223} \log(GDPR\_SLO)$$

$$- \underset{(-5.441)}{0.233} \log(GWAGER\_SLO) - \underset{(-3.228)}{0.042} \log(EMP\_SLO_{-4}/GDPR\_SLO_{-4})$$

Adjusted R^2: 0.775 LM(2): 30.912^{***}

Labour supply by private households is modelled via the participation rate (PARTRATE_SLO), i.e. the labour force (employed plus unemployed persons) divided by the working-age population (the population aged 15 to 64 years). The participation rate depends positively on the real net wage (NWAGER_SLO). For this equation, only the short-run part, but no long-run, cointegrating relation, was supported by the data. Wage growth enters the equation with a considerable lag, implying that it takes time to adjust labour supply to changes in wages. Wages enter labour supply with a positive sign. Hence, the substitution effect of higher wages dominates the income effect.

$$(PARTRATE\_SLO - PARTRATE\_SLO_{-4}) = \underset{(-1.038)}{-0.00005} + \underset{(9.119)}{0.786}\,(PARTRATE\_SLO_{-1} - PARTRATE\_SLO_{-5}) + \underset{(2.450)}{0.030}\,\log(NWAGER\_SLO_{-4}/NWAGER\_SLO_{-8})$$

Adjusted R^2: 0.600 LM(2): 0.419

Prices and wages

In the wage-price system, gross wages, the consumer price index (CPI) and various deflators are determined. The average gross wage rate (GWAGE_SLO) depends on the price level (CPI_SLO), labour productivity (PROD_SLO) and the difference between the actual and the natural rate of unemployment (or the NAIRU) (UR_SLO-NAIRU_SLO). The latter relationship ensures that in the long run the output gap is closed, i.e. actual output converges towards potential GDP. If actual production exceeds its long-run, sustainable level, actual unemployment will be lower than structural unemployment. In such a situation, trade unions have a stronger position in wage negotiations and enforce higher wage increases. These higher wages imply higher costs for companies, which either reduce their investment activity or pass the increased wage costs onto their customers. In either case, real effective demand is reduced, thus pushing actual towards potential production. In the case of a negative output gap, i.e. if actual output falls behind its long-run level, the unemployment rate exceeds the NAIRU, and the adjustment process goes in the opposite direction via lower prices and costs and ultimately higher real demand. Furthermore, trade unions claim compensations for higher inflation, and employees try to participate in productivity advances. In order to avoid multicollinearity problems, inflation enters the wage equation with a one quarter lag.

$$\log(GWAGE\_SLO/GWAGE\_SLO_{-4}) = \underset{(2.169)}{0.007} + \underset{(6.770)}{0.639} \log(GWAGE\_SLO_{-1}/GWAGE\_SLO_{-5})$$

$$+ \underset{(3.146)}{0.331} \log(CPI\_SLO_{-1}/CPI\_SLO_{-5}) + \underset{(0.442)}{0.021} \log(PROD\_SLO/PROD\_SLO_{-4})$$

$$- \underset{(-1.500)}{0.002} (UR\_SLO-NAIRU\_SLO) - \underset{(-2.317)}{0.020} DUM2000q1 - \underset{(-7.825)}{0.074} DUM2008q4$$

$$+ \underset{(3.514)}{0.039} DUM2009q1$$

Adjusted R^2: 0.917 LM(2): 8.694^{**}

Consumer prices (CPI_SLO) depend on domestic and international factors. The most important internal cost factors are wages (GWAGE_SLO). In addition, for Slovenia as a small open economy, international prices are important determinants of domestic prices. Imported inflation is modelled via the import deflator (IMPDEF_SLO).

$$\log(CPI\_SLO/CPI\_SLO_{-4}) = \underset{(-1.566)}{-0.125} + \underset{(7.623)}{0.554} \log(CPI\_SLO_{-1}/CPI\_SLO_{-5})$$

$$+ \underset{(3.412)}{0.099} \log(IMPDEF\_SLO/IMPDEF\_SLO_{-4}) + \underset{(4.332)}{0.280} \log(GWAGE\_SLO/GWAGE\_SLO_{-4})$$

$$- \underset{(-2.424)}{0.122} \log(CPI\_SLO_{-4}) + \underset{(1.449)}{0.051} \log(GWAGE\_SLO_{-4}) + \underset{(1.446)}{0.059} \log(IMPDEF_{-4})$$

Adjusted R^2: 0.940 LM(2): 2.976

The GDP deflator (GDPDEF_SLO) and the deflators for private (CDEF_SLO) and public consumption (GDEF_SLO) are directly linked to consumer prices. The export deflator (EXPDEF_SLO) depends on unit labour costs in Slovenia (ULC_SLO) and on import prices (IMPDEF_SLO). The former assumes that Slovenian companies can partly pass on increases in domestic costs to output prices, provided that international competition allows this. The inclusion of import prices accounts for the import content of export goods. As many exported goods contain either raw materials or intermediate goods, of which large parts are imported, the prices of these primary and intermediate products significantly influence the prices of export goods. The import deflator (IMPDEF_SLO) is influenced by the oil price in euro

(OILEUR) as a proxy for international raw material prices, which constitute an important determinant of the price level in a small open economy like Slovenia.

$$\log(GDPDEF\_SLO/GDP\_SLO_{-4}) = \underset{(6.987)}{0.511} + \underset{(6.468)}{0.642} \log(CPI\_SLO/CPI\_SLO_{-4})$$

$$\underset{(-6.233)}{-\,0.904} \log(GDPDEF\_SLO_{-4}) + \underset{(5.887)}{0.796} \log(CPI\_SLO_{-4}) \underset{(-3.748)}{-\,0.016} Q1$$

Adjusted R^2: 0.836 LM(2): 18.369^{***}

$$\log(CDEF\_SLO/CDEF\_SLO_{-4}) = \underset{(2.821)}{0.154} + \underset{(2.814)}{0.260} \log(CDEF\_SLO_{-1}/CDEF\_SLO_{-5})$$

$$+ \underset{(6.747)}{0.689} \log(CPI\_SLO/CPI\_SLO_{-4}) \underset{(-2.263)}{-\,0.006} Q1$$

$$\underset{(-3.345)}{-\,0.343} \log(CDEF\_SLO_{-4}) + \underset{(3.285)}{0.310} \log(CPI\_SLO_{-4})$$

Adjusted R^2: 0.917 LM(2): 4.957^{*}

$$\log(GDEF\_SLO/GDEF\_SLO_{-4}) = \underset{(-2.638)}{-0.153} + \underset{(9.057)}{0.612} \log(GDEF\_SLO_{-1}/GDEF\_SLO_{-5})$$

$$+ \underset{(5.269)}{0.530} \log(CPI\_SLO/CPI\_SLO_{-4}) \underset{(-2.881)}{-\,0.030} DUM2007q4$$

$$\underset{(-3.837)}{-\,0.254} \log(GDEF\_SLO_{-4}) + \underset{(3.942)}{0.285} \log(CPI\_SLO_{-4})$$

Adjusted R^2: 0.902 LM(2): 4.161

$$\log(EXPDEF\_SLO/EXPDEF\_SLO_{-4}) = \underset{(3.032)}{0.114} + \underset{(5.569)}{0.356} \log(EXPDEF\_SLO_{-1}/EXPDEF\_SLO_{-5})$$

$$+ \underset{(1.822)}{0.067} \log(ULC\_SLO/ULC\_SLO_{-4}) \underset{(-3.487)}{-\,0.033} DUM1997q1$$

$$+ \underset{(10.119)}{0.447} \log(IMPDEF\_SLO/IMPDEF\_SLO_{-4})$$

$$\underset{(-3.065)}{-\,0.241} \log(EXPDEF\_SLO_{-4}) + \underset{(2.825)}{0.216} \log(IMPDEF\_SLO_{-4})$$

Adjusted R^2: 0.929 LM(2): 0.836

$$\log(IMPDEF\_SLO/IMPDEF\_SLO_{-4}) = \underset{(2.685)}{0.452} + \underset{(7.473)}{0.545} \log(IMPDEF\_SLO_{-1}/IMPDEF\_SLO_{-5})$$

$$+ \underset{(6.940)}{0.067} \log(OILEUR/OILEUR_{-4}) - \underset{(-2.509)}{0.122} \log(IMPDEF\_SLO_{-4}) + \underset{(1.945)}{0.031} \log(OILEUR_{-4})$$

Adjusted R^2: 0.829 LM(2): 1.432

The GDP deflator is needed to deflate real GDP, which is determined by adding up the expenditure components. The private consumption deflator is used to transpose real consumption, which is derived from the consumption function, into nominal consumption, which enters the equation for the determination of value added tax revenues. The export and import deflators are used to calculate nominal net exports, and the import deflator also enters the CPI equation.

Public sector

In the government sector of the model, the most important expenditure and revenue items of the general Slovenian budget are determined. Turning first to government revenues, in a definitional equation social security contributions by employees are calculated by multiplying the average social security contribution rate by the gross wage rate and the number of employees. In the same vein, income tax payments by employees are determined by multiplying the average income tax rate by the gross wage rate and the number of employees.

In a behavioural equation, social security payments by companies (SOCCOMP_SLO) are linked to social security contributions by employees (SOCEMP_SLO). Profit tax payments by companies (INCTAXCORP_SLO) are explained by nominal GDP (GDPN_SLO) as an indicator for the economic situation, taking account of the fact that profits and hence profit tax payments display a strongly pro-cyclical behaviour. In this equation, several dummies account for outliers in profit tax revenues. Such outliers are often caused by changes in the legal framework. Value added tax revenues (VAT_SLO) depend on the value added tax rate (VATAXRATE_SLO) and on private consumption (CN_SLO). Value added tax revenues cannot be simply determined in a definitional equation by multiplying the VAT rate by total private consumption because some items like food are taxed at a lower than the normal rate, and some consumption items are totally exempt from value added tax. Finally, the remaining government revenues (REVREST_SLO) are explained by nominal GDP, considering their pro-cyclical behaviour.

$$\log(SOCCOMP\_SLO/SOCCOMP\_SLO_{-4}) = \underset{(-15.790)}{-0.387} - \underset{(-11.094)}{0.448}\, DUM1997$$
$$+ \underset{(32.953)}{0.987} \log(SOCEMP\_SLO/SOCEMP\_SLO_{-4}) - \underset{(-3.983)}{0.034}\, DUM2000q4 + \underset{(2.754)}{0.021}\, DUM2003q2$$
$$- \underset{(-46.386)}{0.605} \log(SOCCOMP\_SLO_{-4}) + \underset{(52.059)}{0.637} \log(SOCEMP\_SLO_{-4})$$

Adjusted R^2: 0.987 LM(2): 33.861***

$$(INCTAXCORP\_SLO - INCTAXCORP\_SLO_{-4}) = \underset{(-4.368)}{-16.274} + \underset{(15.459)}{238.408}\, DUM2011q2$$
$$+ \underset{(3.633)}{0.115} (INCTAXCORP\_SLO_{-1} - INCTAXCORP\_SLO_{-5})$$
$$+ \underset{(8.007)}{0.064} (GDPN\_SLO - GDPN\_SLO_{-4}) + \underset{(14.698)}{224.489}\, DUM2006q2$$
$$- \underset{(-4.280)}{66.773}\, DUM2007q2 - \underset{(-18.494)}{321.155}\, DUM2009q2 - \underset{(-7.363)}{113.465}\, DUM2010q2$$

Adjusted R^2: 0.956 LM(2): 2.710

$$\log(VAT\_SLO/VAT\_SLO_{-4}) = \underset{(-3.169)}{-1.550} - \underset{(-5.107)}{0.557}\, DUM2001q1 - \underset{(-5.772)}{0.676}\, DUM2002q1$$
$$+ \underset{(4.823)}{1.342} \log((VATAXRATE\_SLO_{-1}*CN\_SLO_{-1})/(VATAXRATE\_SLO_{-5}*CN\_SLO_{-5}))$$
$$- \underset{(-8.142)}{0.606} \log(VAT\_SLO_{-4}) + \underset{(7.166)}{0.481} \log(VATAXRATE\_SLO_{-4}*CN\_SLO_{-4})$$

Adjusted R^2: 0.648 LM(2): 6.407**

$$\log(REVREST\_SLO/REVREST\_SLO_{-4}) = \underset{(1.305)}{0.032} + \underset{(4.107)}{0.545} \log(GDPN\_SLO/GDPN\_SLO_{-4})$$

Adjusted R^2: 0.201 LM(2): 0.526

On the expenditure side of the budget, interest payments are calculated by multiplying the stock of public debt by the implicit interest rate on public debt. Public consumption according to national accounts (GN_SLOI) is determined in a fiscal rule, where the annual change in public consumption is negatively related to the year-over-year change in the debt level (DEBT_SLO) lagged by one quarter. In a behavioural equation, public consumption according to fiscal statistics (GNFIN_SLO) is linked to public consumption according to national accounts (GN_SLO); the two are very closely related but not identical due to some differences in statistical definitions. The remaining government expenditures (RESTEXP_SLO) are linked to remaining government revenues (REVREST_SLO) so as to make sure that revenues and expenditures do not permanently deviate over time, which would create an ever rising public deficit and debt level.

$$\log(GN\_SLO/GN\_SLO_{-4}) = \underset{(-0.265)}{-0.001} + \underset{(23.658)}{1.033} \log(GN\_SLO_{-1}/GN\_SLO_{-5}) - \underset{(-3.829)}{0.054}\, DUM2009q1$$

$$- \underset{(-1.462)}{0.025} \log(DEBT\_SLO_{-1}/DEBT\_SLO_{-5}) - \underset{(-3.402)}{0.047}\, DUM2007q1 + \underset{(5.626)}{0.080}\, DUM2008q1$$

Adjusted R^2: 0.904 LM(2): 1.141

$$\log(GNFIN\_SLO/GNFIN\_SLO_{-4}) = \underset{(-3.346)}{-0.043} + \underset{(3.492)}{0.303} \log(GNFIN\_SLO_{-1}/GNFIN\_SLO_{-5})$$

$$+ \underset{(3.633)}{0.972} \log(GN\_SLO/GNSLO\_SLO_{-4}) - \underset{(-2.159)}{0.109} \log(GNFIN\_SLO_{-4}/GNSLO_{-4})$$

$$- \underset{(-4.485)}{0.142}\, DUM2000q4$$

Adjusted R^2: 0.778 LM(2): 2.013

$$\log(RESTEXP\_SLO/RESTEXP\_SLO_{-4}) = \underset{(1.305}{-0.043} - \underset{(-4.697)}{0.447}\, DUM2000q1 + \underset{(4.018)}{0.206}\, DUM2004$$

$$+ \underset{(2.654)}{0.262} \log(REVREST\_SLO/REVREST\_SLO_{-4})$$

$$- \underset{(-3.379)}{0.194} \log(EXPREST\_SLO_{-4}/REVREST\_SLO_{-4})$$

Adjusted R^2: 0.505 LM(2): 1.593

The budget balance is given by the difference between total government revenues and expenditures. Public debt level is extrapolated on the basis of the budget balance plus debt adjustment operations which occur as some fiscal activities affect only either the deficit or the debt level. Such debt adjustments occur irregularly. Hence they are exogenous in the model.

Identities

oileur = oil / eurusd

gr_slo = gn_slo / gdef_slo * 100

gwager_slo = gwage_slo / cpi_slo * 100

can_slo = exr_slo * expdef_slo / 100 - impr_slo * impdef_slo / 100

cagdp_slo = can_slo / gdpn_slo * 100

grgdpr_slo = gdpr_slo / gdpr_slo$_{-4}$ * 100 - 100

grypot_slo = (ypot_slo / ypot_slo$_{-4}$ - 1) * 100

prod_slo = gdpr_slo / emp_slo * 100

ulc_slo = gwage_slo / prod_slo

demand_slo = invr_slo + cr_slo + gr_slo + exr_slo

income_slo = nwage_slo * emp_slo / 1000000 + resttransfers_slo
+ pensions_slo + unbenefit_slo - inctaxcorp_slo
+ finwealth_slo * gov10y_slo

incomer_slo = income_slo / cpi_slo * 100

infl_slo = (cpi_slo / cpi_slo$_{-4}$ - 1) * 100

ucc_slo = gov10yr_slo + deprate_slo

gov10yr_slo = gov10y_slo - infl_slo

inctaxpers_slo=inctaxrate_slo*gwage_slo * emp_slo/1000000)/100

socemp_slo = socemprate_slo*(socemprate_slo*
(gwage_slo*emp_slo/1000000)/100

wedge_slo=gwage_slo*(inctaxrate_slo/100+socemprate_slo / 100)

nwage_slo=gwage_slo*(1-inctaxrate_slo/100-socemprate_slo/ 100)

nwager_slo = nwage_slo / cpi_slo * 100

soctotal_slo = soccomp_slo + socemp_slo

inctax_slo = inctaxpers_slo + inctaxcorp_slo

capr_slo = (1 - deprate_slo / 100) * capr_slo$_{-1}$ + invr_slo

gdpr_slo = cr_slo+gr_slo+invr_slo+inventr_slo+exr_slo-impr_slo

gdpn_slo = gdpr_slo * gdpdef_slo / 100

cn_slo = cr_slo * cdef_slo / 100

trendemp_slo = lforce_slo * (1 - nairu_slo / 100)

util_slo = gdpr_slo / ypot_slo * 100

interest_slo = igovdebt_slo * debt_slo-1 / 100

balancen_slo = vat_slo + soctotal_slo + inctax_slo
+ revrest_slo - gnfin_slo - ginvn_slo - pensions_slo
- unbenefit_slo - resttransfers_slo - interest_slo exprest_slo

balancegdp_slo = balancen_slo / gdpn_slo * 100

debt_slo = debt_slo$_{-1}$ - balancen_slo + debtadj_slo

debtgdp_slo = debt_slo
/ (gdpn_slo+gdpn_slo$_{-1}$+gdpn_slo$_{-2}$+gdpn_slo$_{-3}$)*100

ginvr_slo = ginvn_slo / gdpdef_slo * 100

invr_slo = prinvr_slo + ginvr_slo

exr_slo = exr_slobih + exr_slocro + exr_slosrb + exr_slorow

impr_slo = exr_croslo/hrkeur + exr_bihslo / 1.95583
+exr_srbslo/dineur + imr_slorow

inventr_slo = moving average (inventr_slo, 8)+0.07 * inventr_slo$_{-4}$

pensioners_slo = Pensioners1549_slo + Pensioners50_slo
+ Pensioners51_slo + Pensioners52_slo
+ Pensioners53_slo + Pensioners54_slo
+ Pensioners55_slo + Pensioners56_slo

$$+ \text{Pensioners57\_slo} + \text{Pensioners58\_slo} + \text{Pensioners59\_slo} + \text{Pensioners60\_sl} + \text{Pensioners61\_slo} + \text{Pensioners62\_slo} + \text{Pensioners63\_slo} + \text{Pensioners64\_slo} + \text{Pensioners65\_slo} + \text{Pensioners66\_slo} + \text{Pensioners67\_slo} + \text{Pensioners68\_slo} + \text{Pensioners69\_slo} + \text{Pensioners70plus\_slo}$$

$$\text{pop1564\_slo} = \text{POP1549\_slo} + \text{POP50\_slo} + \text{POP51\_slo} + \text{POP52\_slo} + \text{POP53\_slo} + \text{POP54\_slo} + \text{POP55\_slo} + \text{POP56\_slo} + \text{POP57\_slo} + \text{POP58\_slo} + \text{POP59\_slo} + \text{POP60\_slo} + \text{POP61\_slo} + \text{POP62\_slo} + \text{POP63\_slo} + \text{POP64\_slo}$$

$$\text{avpension\_slo} = \text{reprate\_slo} * \text{gwage\_slo}$$

$$\text{pensions\_slo} = \text{avpension\_slo} * \text{pensioners\_slo} / 1000000$$

$$\text{avunbenefit\_slo} = \text{unbenefitrate\_slo} * \text{gwage\_slo}$$

$$\text{unbenefit\_slo} = \text{avunbenefit\_slo} * \text{un\_slo} / 1000000$$

$$\text{lforce\_slo} = \text{partrate\_slo} * \text{pop1564\_slo}$$

$$\text{un\_slo} = \text{lforce\_slo} - \text{emp\_slo}$$

$$\text{ur\_slo} = \text{un\_slo} / \text{lforce\_slo} * 100$$

$$\text{nairu\_slo} = \text{moving average}(\text{ur\_slo}, 8)$$

$$\log(\text{ypot\_slo}) = 0.65 * \log(\text{trendemp\_slo}) + 0.35 * \log(\text{capr\_slo}) + \log(\text{trendtfp\_slo})$$

THE MODEL FOR SERBIA

Introduction and data issues

In this section, the Serbian sub-model is described, including necessary data transformations and the model equations. Similarly to the other country models, the model for Serbia contains equations for the goods market, the labour market, the foreign exchange market, the money market, and the government sector. Rigidities of wages and prices are taken into account. The model combines Keynesian and neoclassical elements. The former determine the short and medium-run solutions in the sense that the model is demand-driven and persistent disequilibria in the goods and labour markets are possible. The supply side incorporates neoclassical features. A detailed description of the most recent version of the model, but excluding the links to the other countries in the multi-country model for the former Yugoslavia, can be found in Weyerstrass and Grozea-Helmenstein (2013a).

Data availability

As in the cases of Bosnia and Herzegovina and Croatia, some data transformations were also necessary for the Serbian sub-model. At the time of creating the model version described in this book, the available reliable macroeconomic data for Serbia covered at best the period 1997 to 2010. Although preliminary data for 2011 would have also been available, macroeconomic data are often revised significantly over time as more precise information from underlying data sources becomes available. Such frequent data revisions are also present in more advanced economies with a longer record of reliable statistical data collection and processing like the USA or the EU Member States, but in the case of transformation economies which still have to establish reliable data collection, this issue is by far more problematic as, for example, the revisions are larger. Therefore, it was decided to use data until 2010 and no later. For many aggregates, the time series start later after 1997; in some cases data are only available from 1999 or even 2000 onwards. Hence, as for the other sub-models, econometric estimation of the behavioural equations for Serbia was based on a higher than annual frequency. For some aggregates such as wages, prices, labour market indicators and interest rates, monthly data are available. However, for GDP only annual and quarterly data are available. Overall, it seemed most appropriate to use quarterly data.

Detailed data on GDP and public finances are scarce for Serbia. For the expenditure components of GDP, only annual data at current prices are available. Quarterly data are published for total real GDP but not for the expenditure components. Hence, these data had to be constructed by reverting to related time series that are available at least at quarterly frequency. In addition, data on the capital stock are not available for Serbia at all. Hence, a time series of the capital stock had to be constructed by generating an initial value in a base year and then applying the Perpetual Inventory Method (PIM). The initial capital stock in 1997 was determined by resorting to a capital-output ratio found for Macedonia. This initial value of the capital stock was then extrapolated by adding gross investment and subtracting depreciation, in accordance with the PIM. In the following, the derivation of quarterly GDP by expenditure, the capital stock, and public sector aggregates is addressed in detail.

Data transformations

In Serbia, at the time of setting up the model, reliable data on quarterly GDP as published by the Statistical Office covered total GDP at constant prices for the period 1997q1 to 2010q4. As explained above, preliminary data for 2011 would have also been available, but these data were not used for estimating the equations of the model version described here. Due to the ongoing adaptation of Serbian macroeconomic statistics to EU standards, data revisions for Serbia are usually larger than revisions for countries with more advanced economic statistics. Hence, only those data that are relatively final were used for the model estimation. Data on the GDP expenditure components at current prices are available on an annual frequency for the period 1997 to 2010 as well. No data have been published on the expenditure aggregates at constant prices. In order to derive a quarterly series for total GDP at current prices, it was assumed that GDP at current prices follows the same quarterly pattern as GDP at constant prices.

Quarterly GDP by expenditure

For quarterly data on the GDP expenditure components at current prices, the following computations were performed:

- Exports and imports of goods and services: the National Bank of Serbia (NBS) publishes quarterly balance of payments data in euros and US dollars. The quarterly profile of these data on the export and import of goods and services from the balance of payments statistics were assigned to exports and imports in Serbian dinars (RSD) according to the national accounts statistics.

- Public consumption: for the quarterly division of public consumption according to national accounts, public finance data were used. The Serbian Ministry of Finance publishes monthly figures on a detailed breakdown of revenues and expenditures. The sum of the items "expenditures for employees" and "purchases of goods and services" was used as an approximation for government consumption. The quarterly profile of the sum of these public expenditures was used to derive government consumption according to national accounts.

- Consumption of private households: as an indicator for the expenditure of private households, revenues from value added tax (VAT) were used. These figures were taken from the "Bulletin Public Finances" of the Serbian Ministry of Finance. Using annual data on VAT revenues and private household consumption, a behavioural equation of the following form was estimated, with private consumption as the dependent variable and VAT revenues as the explanatory variable:

$$\text{Consumption}_t = c + \beta\ \text{VAT}_t + €_t,$$

The constant c and the coefficient β are estimated with annual data on consumption and VAT revenues in period t. € denotes the residuals. By dividing the constant c by four, adding quarterly value added tax revenues multiplied by the coefficient β, and adding a quarter of the annual residuals of the estimation, a quarterly series for private consumption, adding up to the actual annual figures, was calculated.

- Gross fixed capital formation: as an indicator for the sub-annual development of fixed investment is missing, the same quarterly profile as for total GDP was taken.

- Changes in inventories: for the period 1997 to 2003, quarterly changes in inventories were determined as the residual between total GDP and the final demand components. For the years since 2004, changes in inventories and a series for statistical discrepancy have been published; before 2004, the statistical discrepancy was included in the changes in inventories. Hence, for the period since 2004 the annual changes in inventories were divided by quarters by resorting to the same quarterly shares as in the cases of total GDP and fixed investment, and the residual was assigned to the statistical discrepancy.

Annual data on total nominal and real GDP are published officially. No data are available for the expenditure components at constant prices, nor for quarterly GDP at current prices. In order to derive real GDP by expenditure, some assumptions and calculations had to be made. A series of the total GDP deflator could be calculated. For the annual GDP deflator, actually published data could be used, while the calculation of the quarterly deflator was based on official data for real GDP and the calculated series of quarterly GDP at current prices. It was assumed that the same deflator as for total GDP also pertains to each expenditure component. This assumption is problematic, since consumer prices, export prices and prices for investment goods are known to develop quite differently. However, since no further information on the various deflators was available, this approximation can be justified. These calculations resulted in quarterly series for the GDP expenditure components at constant prices.

Capital stock

For Serbia, no official data on the capital stock are available. Hence, as in the cases of Croatia and of Bosnia and Herzegovina, a capital stock series was constructed based on the Perpetual Inventory Method (PIM). As elaborated in detail above, according to the PIM the net capital stock at the end of the current year (K_t) is equal to the capital stock at the end of the previous year (K_{t-1}) plus gross fixed capital formation in the current year (I_t) minus depreciation in the current year (DEP_t):

$$K_t = K_{t-1} + {}_{I}t + DEP_t$$

Application of the Perpetual Inventory Method requires the determination of an initial value of the capital stock in the starting year t_0. One option would be to assume that at the beginning of the economic transformation process at the end of the 1990s, the capital stock in Serbia was totally outdated, implying an initial value of zero in 1997. However, it seems reasonable to assume that not the entire capital stock was obsolete. Therefore, similarly to the model for Bosnia and Herzegovina, it was decided to base the starting value of the capital stock on the capital-output ratio found by Roberts (2002) for Macedonia. The first year for which GDP data for Serbia is available is 1997; hence the starting value of the capital stock was determined by multiplying the annual GDP figure for 1997 by the assumed capital-output ratio of 1.6. This figure was then taken as the initial value of the capital stock at the end of 1996 or the beginning of 1997. From the first quarter of 1997 onwards, the capital stock was then extrapolated by applying the Perpetual Inventory Method, i.e. by adding quarterly gross fixed capital formation and subtracting depreciation.

The above equation for the calculation of the capital stock can be rewritten in the following form, where δ denotes the depreciation rate:

$$K_t = (1-\delta)\cdot K_{t-1} + I_t$$

For Serbia, no full income account of GDP has been published yet. Hence, no official data on depreciation are available. Even if they were available, depreciation according to national accounts statistics deviates from the consumption of fixed capital. The physical depletion of the capital stock is not necessarily identical to the economic depreciation as accounted for in the national accounts statistics. Were capital stock data available, depreciation could be calculated accordingly by re-arranging the above equation for the PIM. As already mentioned, capital stock data are not available for Serbia. Hence, the depreciation rate could not be derived in this way.

Since no information on the depreciation of the capital stock in Serbia is available, the depreciation rate for the calculation of the capital stock according to the Perpetual Inventory Method was based on data for other countries. Again, as in the case of the model for Bosnia and Herzegovina, the depreciation rate for Serbia was based on the values found by the OECD (1997). There, the unweighted average of the depreciation rate amounts to 5 percent. Hence, for industrialised countries a depreciation rate of about 5 to 6 percent per year seems a reasonable assumption.

Applying the Perpetual Inventory Method to Serbia with an annual depreciation rate of 6 percent (1.47 percent per quarter), the capital-output ratio rises from 1.6 in 1997 to 1.8 in 2010. Due to the legacy of the former Yugoslav era, physical capital in Serbia needs to be considerably rebuilt and modernised. Hence, a rising capital-output ratio should also be expected in the future. In the OECD countries, this value lies in the range of about 2.5 to 3.

Model equations

In this section, the estimation results for the Serbian sub-model are documented together with a description of their theoretical underpinnings. As in the previous sections on the other country models, t-statistics are provided in parentheses below the estimated coefficients. In addition, the adjusted R^2 and the Breusch-Godfrey test for serial correlation are provided. The suffix _SRB in the variable names indicates the sub-model for Serbia.

Supply side

In the supply block, the determination of potential GDP follows the same principles as in the other sub-models. Hence, the calculation of potential output is based on a Cobb-Douglas production function with constant returns to scale and with the production factors labour and capital. In addition, autonomous technical progress influences potential output. Since potential GDP is a measure of the long-run production possibilities of an economy, it is the long-run trends rather than the actual realisations of the production factors that enter the production function. An exception is the capital stock where it is assumed that it is normally fully utilised. Autonomous technical progress is defined as total factor productivity (TFP). Under these assumptions, trend employment, the capital stock and trend total factor productivity determine potential output. The production function has the following form:

$$\log(YPOT\_SRB) = 0.65 \log(TRENDEMP\_SRB) + 0.35 \log(CAPR\_SRB) + TRENDTFP\_SRB$$

In this equation, YPOT_SRB is potential GDP, TRENDEMP_SRB is the labour force adjusted for structural unemployment, CAPR_SRB is the real capital stock, and TRENDTFP_SRB is the long-run trend of total factor productivity (TFP). Since for the time being no income data of the national account exist for Serbia, the production elasticities of the production factors employment (0.65) and capital (0.35) were based on international empirical evidence.

Before calculating potential GDP according to the above equation, trend employment and trend total factor productivity have to be determined. Trend employment is calculated by subtracting natural or structural unemployment from the labour force. Structural unemployment is defined as the inflation-stable unemployment rate, i.e. the NAIRU. Since structural unemployment is non-observable, this variable has to be approximated. In the model for Serbia, this is done by applying a Hodrick-Prescott (HP) filter to the actual unemployment rate in order to extract the trend. Structural unemployment is then defined as the long-run trend in actual unemployment. In order to endogenise the NAIRU, it is modelled as a moving average (MA) process.

In a growth accounting exercise, total factor productivity (*TFP*) is calculated as that part of (the change in) real GDP that is not due to (increased) labour and capital input, where both production factors are weighted with their production elasticities, i.e. 0.35 for the capital stock and 0.65 for labour respectively. For the production possibilities, the long-run trend rather than the current level of total factor productivity is relevant. Therefore, the actual *TFP* series is smoothed by applying the Hodrick-Prescott filter so as to remove short-run fluctuations that are caused by the business cycle or by any short-run shocks.

Demand side

Consumption of private households

For modelling consumption of private households, the Keynesian consumption theory and the permanent income hypothesis are combined. As already explained, according to the Keynesian view, private consumption depends solely on current disposable income while the permanent income hypothesis stipulates that it is the present value of expected future income rather than current disposable income which is relevant for consumption decisions. Taking both consumption theories together, real private consumption (CONSR_SRB) depends on real current disposable income (YDR_SRB) and on the real long-term interest rate, i.e. the nominal interest rate (ILEND_SRB) minus inflation (INFL_SRB). In addition to being used for discounting future labour income, the real interest rate as a determinant of consumption also accounts for the fact that some households finance part of their consumption via bank loans. Furthermore, the real interest rate is relevant for the intertemporal decision on the allocation of income to consumption in the present period and in the future. The higher the real interest rate, the higher the opportunity costs are of spending income for current consumption. Although the real interest rate is not significant in the short-run part of the equation, it has been retained because it is in line with more modern consumption theories and it allows for a transmission channel of monetary policy in addition to its impacts on investment. As can be seen, the long-run, cointegrating relationship was estimated in a first step and then included in the error correction model in a second step.

$$\log(CONSR\_SRB/CONSR\_SRB_{-4}) = \underset{(1.431)}{0.020} + \underset{(2.146)}{0.268} \log(CONSR\_SRB_{-1}/CONSR\_SRB_{-5})$$

$$+ \underset{(2.194)}{0.337} \log(YDR\_SRB/YDR\_SRB_{-4}) - \underset{(-0.856)}{0.002} (ILEND\_SRB - INFL\_SRB)$$

$$- \underset{(-6.589)}{1.070} [\log(CONSR\_SRB_{-4}) - 2.468 - 0.761 \log(YDR\_SRB_{-4})]$$

Adjusted R^2: 0.662 LM(2): 0.794

Gross fixed capital formation

As elaborated in the section on the sub-model for Bosnia and Herzegovina, gross fixed capital formation is undertaken to renew the capital stock and to adjust it to changes in final demand. The accelerator theory stipulates that changes in demand determine fixed capital formation. Since it takes time to purchase and install new capital goods, it is expected rather than actual demand that has to be considered. However, with adaptive expectations, as is assumed here, expectations are based on past observations. Therefore, in the investment equation, actual demand is included as an approximation of expected future demand. According to theories focussing on the profitability of investment projects, the value of the capital stock equals the discounted future income that can be generated by employing the capital stock. Therefore, the interest rate, which is used to discount future revenues, is crucial for the profitability of an investment project. The Neoclassical theory of investment combines the investment determinants according to the accelerator hypothesis and profitability considerations. In this case, the investment function is derived from companies' profit maximisation, based on a neoclassical production function with the input factor capital and a positive but diminishing marginal product. The optimal capital stock equalises the marginal revenue product of capital and the user cost of capital.

Based on these theoretical considerations, real gross fixed capital formation, i.e. investment in machinery, equipment and buildings (GFCFR_SRB), is influenced by the change in total domestic demand (DEMANDR_SRB), in accordance with the accelerator hypothesis, and by the user cost of capital (UCC_SRB). Due to data limitations, in the sub-model for Serbia, the user costs of capital are defined as the real interest rate plus the depreciation rate of the capital stock. For theoretical reasons, the user cost of capital was retained in the investment equation although the coefficient is not significant. Changes in inventories (INVENTR_SRB) are modelled as an eight quarter moving average process.

$$\log(GFCFR\_SRB/GFCFR\_SRB_{-4}) = \underset{(7.461)}{0.665} \log(GFCFR\_SRB_{-1}/GFCFR\_SRB_{-5})$$

$$+ \underset{(2.005)}{0.244} \log(DEMANDR\_SRB/DEMANDR\_SRB_{-4}) - \underset{(-0.634)}{0.0005} UCC\_SRB_{-3}$$

$$- \underset{(-2.889)}{0.153} [\log(GFCFR\_SRB_{-4}) + 2.950 - 1.073 \log(DEMANDR\_SRB_{-4})]$$

Adjusted R^2: 0.674 LM(2): 6.284^{**}

Exports of goods and services

As mentioned earlier, every country model contains equations for exports to every other country in the model and to the rest of the world. Hence, for Serbia, exports to Bosnia and Herzegovina, Slovenia, Croatia and the rest of the world are modelled. The relevant equations are presented in this section. In general, exports to a certain country depend on demand in the recipient country and on the real exchange rate. A real depreciation of the currency makes domestic goods and services more competitive on the world market. Hence, export demand would increase. In the models, the real exchange rate is included in the export and import equations in such a way that an increase represents a depreciation of the home currency. Hence, the real exchange rate is expected to influence exports positively and imports negatively, as domestically produced goods and services become less competitive when the currency depreciates in nominal terms or if prices at home increase more than abroad.

Exports from Serbia to Croatia (EXR_SRBCRO) depend on final demand in Croatia (DEMANDR_CRO) and the real exchange rate between the Serbian dinar and the Croatian kuna. The real exchange rate between the dinar and the kuna includes the price ratio between Croatia and Serbia (CPI_CRO/CPI_SRB) in addition to the nominal exchange rate between the dinar and the kuna (HRKDIN).

$$\log(EXR\_SRBCRO/EXR\_SRBCRO_{-4})' = \underset{(-4.737)}{-19.016} + \underset{(2.610)}{0.368}\ DUM2004q4 + \underset{(2.639)}{0.380}\ DUM2005q1$$

$$+ \underset{(4.585)}{2.114} \log(DEMANDR\_CRO/DEMANDR\_CRO_{-4})$$

$$+ \underset{(1.611)}{0.117} \log(((1/HRKDIN_{-1})*CPI\_CRO_{-1}/CPI\_SRB_{-1})/((1/HRKDIN_{-5})*CPI\_CRO_{-5}/CPI\_SRB_{-5}))$$

$$- \underset{(-4.815)}{0.419} \log(EXR\_SRBCRO_{-4}) + \underset{(4.492)}{1.795} \log(DEMANDR\_CRO_{-4})$$

$$+ \underset{(6.815)}{0.825} \log((1/HRKDIN_{-4})*CPI\_CRO{-4}/CPI\_SRB_{-4})$$

Adjusted R^2: 0.795 LM(2): 3.458

Exports from Serbia to Bosnia and Herzegovina (EXR_SRBBiH) are influenced by real final demand in Bosnia and Herzegovina (DEMANDR_BiH) and by the real exchange rate between the Serbian dinar and the Bosnian convertible mark (KM). Due to the fact that Bosnia and Herzegovina runs a currency board with the euro as the reference currency and a fixed conversion rate of 1.9558 between the KM and the euro, the nominal exchange rate between the dinar and the euro was used as an approximation of the exchange rate between the dinar and the convertible mark. The real exchange rate between Serbia and Bosnia and Herzegovina thus consists of the nominal exchange rate between the dinar and the euro (DINEUR) and the price ratio (CPI_BiH/CPI_SRB).

$$\log(EXR\_SRBBiH/EXR\_SRBBiH_{-4}) = \underset{(-2.900)}{-2.897} + \underset{(2.754)}{0.823} \log(DEMANDR\_BiH/DEMANDR\_BiH_{-4})$$

$$- \underset{(-6.464)}{0\ 354} \log(EXR\_SRBBiH_{-4}) + \underset{(2.589)}{0.344} \log(DEMANDR\_BiH_{-4})$$

$$+ \underset{(10.769)}{0.707} \log((DINEUR_{-4}*CPIBiH_{-4})/CPI\_SRB_{-4})) - \underset{(-2.971)}{0.370}\ DUM2002q1 - \underset{(-3.431)}{0.213}\ DUM2006$$

Adjusted R^2: 0.852 LM(2): 11.830^{***}

Exports from Serbia to Slovenia (EXR_SRBSLO) are a function of real final demand in Slovenia (DEMAND_SLO) and the real exchange rate. In this case, the real exchange rate consists of the nominal exchange rate between the Serbian dinar and the euro (DINEUR) and the ratio between the consumer price indices in Slovenia (CPI_SLO) and Serbia (CPI_SRB).

$$\log(EXR\_SRBSLO/EXR\_SRBSLO_{-4}) = \underset{(-4.376)}{-12.021} + \underset{(5.365)}{0.474} \log(DEMAND\_SLO/DEMAND\_SLO_{-4})$$

$$- \underset{(-4.686)}{0.361} \log(EXR\_SRBSLO_{-4}) + \underset{(3.596)}{1.271} \log(DEMAND\_SLO_{-4})$$

$$+ \underset{(9.254)}{0.691} \log((DINEUR_{-4})*CPI\_SLO_{-4}/CPI\_SRB_{-4}))$$

Adjusted R^2: 0.802 LM(2): 10.588***

Exports from Serbia to the rest of the world (EXR_SRBROW) depend on world trade (WTRADE) as a proxy for world demand, and on the real effective exchange rate of the Serbian dinar (REER_SRB). The real effective exchange rate is a weighted average of the nominal exchange rates and the price ratios with respect to Serbia's most important trading partners.

$$\log(EXR\_SRBROW/EXR\_SRBROW_{-4}) = \underset{(-2.678)}{-6.184} + \underset{(2.005)}{1.102} \log(WTRADE/WTRADE_{-4})$$

$$- \underset{(-4.869)}{0.742} \log(EXR\_SRBROW_{-4}) + \underset{(4.757)}{1.873} \log(WTRADE_{-4}) - \underset{(-1.793)}{0.110} \log(REER\_SRB_{-4})$$

Adjusted R^2: 0.469 LM(2): 11.566***

Imports of goods and services

Except for deviations between exports and imports due to measurement and other statistical errors, imports to Serbia from the other countries in the model are, by definition, identical to their exports to Serbia. Hence, similarly to the foreign trade sectors of the other sub-models, Serbian imports from Slovenia, Bosnia and Herzegovina and Croatia are modelled as exports in the other country models, and only Serbia's imports from the rest of the world (IMR_SRBROW) are modelled separately. They depend on real final demand in Serbia (DEMANDR_SRB) and on relative prices. Similarly to the equation for Serbia's exports to the rest of the world, relative prices are approximated by the real effective exchange rate with respect to Serbia's most important trading partners (REER_SRB). Although it is not significant, for theoretical consistency the real effective exchange rate was retained in the equation.

$$\log(IMR\_SRBROW/IMR\_SRBROW_{-4}) = \underset{(-2.057)}{-9.243}$$

$$+ \underset{(7.360)}{2.571} \log(DEMANDR\_SRB/DEMANDR\_SRB_{-4}) + \underset{(3.769)}{0.245} \log(REER\_SRB/REER\_SRB_{-4})$$

$$- \underset{(-5.395)}{0.835} \log(IMR\_SRBROW_{-4}) + \underset{(5.104)}{1.416} \log(DEMANDR\_SRB_{-4}) + \underset{(1.023)}{0.077} \log(REER\_SRB_{-4})$$

Adjusted R^2: 0.832 LM(2): 21.551^{***}

Money market

In the money market section of the model, the short-term interest rate, the long-term interest rate and the implicit interest rate on outstanding public debt are determined.

Since the National Bank of Serbia (NBS) runs an independent monetary policy, the short-run interest rate, i.e. the NBS interest rate for open market operations, has been included in the model as the relevant monetary policy instrument. The NBS interest rate for open market operations (NBSRATE_SRB) is determined in a Taylor rule (Taylor 1993). In this equation, the monetary policy interest rate depends positively on the inflation rate (INFL_SRB) and the capacity utilisation rate (UTIL_SRB) in Serbia. This approach implies that the National Bank of Serbia follows both an inflation and an output target. Monetary policy becomes more restrictive, i.e. the interest rate is raised, when inflation rises and/or actual output exceeds potential output. In the latter case, i.e. when resources are fully or even over-employed, inflationary pressure arises since trade unions have more power to claim higher wage increases, and as machines run at full capacity, costs for maintenance and repairs rise. The short-term interest rate of the previous quarter was included as an additional explanatory variable, accounting for interest rate smoothing, i.e. the fact that erratic changes in the policy instruments are not possible in practical monetary policy-making.

$$NBSRATE\_SRB = \underset{(5.833)}{0.562} NBSRATE\_SRB_{-1} + \underset{(1.798)}{0.045} INFL\_SRB + \underset{(4.102)}{0.045} UTIL\_SRB$$

Adjusted R^2: 0.813 LM(2): 14.127^{***}

In a term structure equation, the long-term interest rate in Serbia is explained mainly by the NBS rate for open market operations. This implies that by changing the short-term interest rate, the National Bank of Serbia is able to influence interest rates at the long end of the term structure as well. Due to its increasing integration in the EU capital market, the long-term interest rate in Serbia is also influenced by the long-term interest rate in the EU. The latter was approximated by the yield on government bonds with a maturity of 10 years in the euro area (EUR10Y). The long-term interest rate (ILEND_SRB) is defined as the average interest rate on loans to households and non-financial corporations.

$$\begin{aligned} ILEND\_SRB - ILEND\_SRB_{-4} = {} & \underset{(5.202)}{0.392} (ILEND\_SRB_{-1} - ILEND\_SRB_{-5}) \\ & + \underset{(5.846)}{0.521} (NBSRATE\_SRB - NBSRATE\_SRB_{-4}) - \underset{(-3.482)}{0.150} (ILEND\_SRB_{-4} - EUR10Y_{-4}) \end{aligned}$$

Adjusted R^2: 0.927 LM(2): 5.589^*

The implicit interest rate on public debt (IL_DEBT_SRB) is influenced by the maturity structure of debt that the government incurred in the past. This implicit interest rate adjusts gradually to the current long-term market rate (ILEND_SRB), whereby the speed of adjustment is influenced by the annual roll-over of maturing liabilities. Data on the implicit interest rate on public debt are not published officially. This time series could be constructed by dividing the annual interest payments by the public debt level at the end of the previous year.

$$\begin{aligned} IL\_DEBT\_SRB-IL\_DEBT\_SRB_{-4} = {} & \underset{(3.185)}{0.524} (IL\_DEBT\_SRB_{-1} - IL\_DEBT\_SRB_{-5}) \\ & + \underset{(1.370)}{0.016} (ILEND\_SRB - ILEND\_SRB_{-4}) \end{aligned}$$

Adjusted R^2: 0.279 LM(2): 0.000

Foreign exchange market

The foreign exchange market is modelled with respect to the nominal and the real effective exchange rates against Serbia's most important trading partners. In the model, the nominal effective exchange rate (NEER_SRB) depends exclusively on the exchange rate between the Serbian dinar and the euro (DINEUR). When trying to include the US dollar in the equation as well, this bilateral exchange rate had the wrong sign, and the dinar/euro exchange rate became insignificant. This probably has two reasons. Firstly, the countries of the euro area are Serbia's most important trading partners. Hence, the euro is the most relevant foreign currency for Serbian companies. Secondly, the exchange rates between the dinar on the one hand and the euro or the US dollar on the other hand are highly correlated, causing multicollinearity when both exchange rates are included together in the equation.

$$\log(NERR\_SRB/NEER\_SRB_{-4}) = \underset{(-2.294)}{-0.113} + \underset{(5.648)}{0.487} \log(NEER\_SRB_{-1}/NEER\_SRB_{-5})$$

$$- \underset{(-6.002)}{0.598} \log(DINEUR/DINEUR_{-4})$$

Adjusted R^2: 0.736 LM(2): 25.206***

As the real effective exchange rate (REER_SRB) takes the nominal effective exchange rate (NEER_SRB) and price developments into account, in the equation for the real effective exchange rate, the inflation rate in Serbia is included in addition to the nominal effective exchange rate. From a theoretical point of view, the ratio between the price level in Serbia and the weighted average price level in those trading partners that are included in the calculation of the real effective exchange rate should be taken as explanatory variables. However, calculating such a weighted average price level would involve many exogenous variables which would have to be extrapolated in forecasts and ex ante simulations. Hence, in the estimations only price developments in Serbia are taken into account, as was the case in the sub-models for the other countries. As a long-run, cointegrating relationship was not supported by the data, only the annual change in the exchange rates and inflation in Serbia (i.e. the annual change in the consumer price index, CPI_SRB) were included in the equation.

$$\log(REER\_SRB/REER\_SRB_{-4}) = \underset{(0.166)}{0.008} + \underset{(16.083)}{0.845} \log(REER\_SRB_{-1}/REER\_SRB_{-5})$$

$$+ \underset{(10.679)}{0.656} \log(NEER\_SRB/NEER\_SRB_{-4}) - \underset{(-6.735)}{0.490} \log(NEER\_SRB_{-1}/NEER\_SRB_{-5})$$

$$+ \underset{(3.371)}{0.374} \log(CPI\_SRB/CPI\_SRB_{-4}) + \underset{(5.368)}{0.801}\, DUM2001q4$$

Adjusted R^2: 0.951 LM(2): 8.025**

Labour market

Labour demand by Serbian companies (i.e. actual employment, EMP_SRB) is influenced by production and by labour costs. In the model, production is approximated by real GDP (GDPR_SRB) while the average gross wage rate per employee (GWAGER_SRB) is taken as the labour cost indicator. In order to make labour demand compatible with the Cobb-Douglas production function which is used to estimate potential GDP, the long-run elasticity of employment with respect to GDP was restricted to 1.

$$\log(EMP\_SRB/EMP\_SRB_{-4}) = \underset{(1.632)}{0.043} + \underset{(2.445)}{0.113} \log(GDPR\_SRB/GDPR\_SRB_{-4})$$

$$- \underset{(-4.619)}{0.092} \log(GWAGER\_SRB/GWAGER\_SRB_{-4}) - \underset{(-8.222)}{0.060} DUM2001 + \underset{(11.366)}{0.087} DUM2002$$

$$- \underset{(-1.813)}{0.024} [\log(EMP\_SRB_{-4}) - \log(GDPR\_SRB_{-4})] - \underset{(-6.690)}{0.057} DUM2009 - \underset{(-6.950)}{0.054} DUM2010$$

Adjusted R^2: 0.881 LM(2): 2.354

Labour supply by private households is modelled via the participation rate (PARTRATE_SRB), i.e. the labour force divided by the working-age population (those aged 15 to 64). The participation rate depends positively on the real net wage (NWAGER_SRB). The positive influence implies that the substitution effect of a higher wage rate dominates the income effect. Since a higher wage rate means that the same income level can be maintained with reduced labour effort, the income effect implies a negative impact of higher wages on labour supply. On the other hand, rising wages are associated with higher opportunity costs of leisure. Hence, the substitution effect calls for a positive relationship between rising wages and labour supply. Such a positive relation is supported by the aggregate data for Serbia, as in the other country sub-models.

$$PARTRATE\_SRB - PARTRATE\_SRB_{-4} = \underset{(-1.922)}{-0.004} + \underset{(9.213)}{0.736} (PARTRATE\_SRB_{-1} - PARTRATE\_SRB_{-5})$$

$$+ \underset{(3.115)}{0.022} \log(NWAGER\_SRB/NWAGER\_SRB_{-4})$$

Adjusted R^2: 0.708 LM(2): 3.589

Prices and wages

In the wage-price system, gross wages, the consumer price index (CPI) and various deflators are determined. Like the other country models, the wage-price system is based on a bargaining model between employers and trade unions (Layard, Nickell, Jackman 1991). In this labour market model, prices are set as a mark-up over marginal costs, and wages are determined in an extended Phillips curve relationship. Based on the theoretical underpinning, the average gross wage rate in Serbia (GWAGE_SRB) depends on the price level (CPI_SRB), labour productivity (PROD_SRB) and the difference between the actual and the structural rate of unemployment (or the NAIRU) (UR_SRB-NAIRU_SRB). Unfortunately, only the change in the difference between structural and natural unemployment comes anywhere near being significant at the 10 percent level, and only with a lag of three quarters. However, for theoretical reasons this explanatory variable was retained in the wage equation. This relationship ensures that in the long run the output gap is closed, i.e. actual employment converges to its long-run level. In this situation, all remaining unemployment is structural, and actual output equals potential GDP. In order to avoid multicollinearity problems, inflation enters the wage equation with a one quarter lag. For the cointegrating relationship it was assumed that in the long run, real wages remain constant and real wages develop in line with productivity.

$$\log(GWAGE\_SRB/GWAGE\_SRB_{-4}) = \underset{(2.309)}{0.648} + \underset{(12.440)}{0.523} \log(GWAGE\_SRB_{-1}/GWAGE\_SRB_{-5})$$

$$+ \underset{(9.025)}{0.438} \log(CPI\_SRB_{-1}/CPI\_SRB_{-5}) + \underset{(4.363)}{0.341} \log(PROD\_SRB/PROD\_RBO_{-4})$$

$$- \underset{(-2.244)}{0.082} \log[(GWAGE\_SRB_{-4}/CPI\_SRB_{-4})/PROD\_SRB_{-4}]$$

$$- \underset{(-1.258)}{0.184} D(UR\_SRB_{-3} - NAIRU\_SRB_{-3})$$

$$- \underset{(-6.019)}{0.176} DUM2001q1 + \underset{(3.724)}{0.117} DUM2001q2 - \underset{(-4.874)}{0.121} DUM2002q2 - \underset{(-7.462)}{0.103} DUM2009$$

Adjusted R^2: 0.992 LM(2): 4.304

Consumer prices (CPI_SRB) depend on domestic and international factors. The most important internal cost factor is wage costs (GWAGE_SRB). Furthermore, rising capacity utilisation (UTIL_SRB) exerts price pressures as machines require more maintenance when they are used more intensively, and workers probably get wage supplements as they work overtime. In addition to internal factors, for Serbia as a small open economy, international prices are important determinants of domestic prices. The oil price in Serbian dinar (OILDIN) is included as a proxy for the prices of imported raw materials in general.

$$\log(CPI\_SRB/CPI\_SRB_{-4}) = \underset{(2.576)}{0.051} + \underset{(7.801)}{0.144} \log(OILDIN/OILDIN_{-4}) + \underset{(9.966)}{0.528}\, DUM2001$$

$$+ \underset{(2.771)}{0.182} \log(GWAGE\_SRB_{-1}/GWAGE\_SRB_{-5}) + \underset{(2.603)}{0.589} \log(UTIL\_SRB_{-2}/UTIL\_SRB_{-6})$$

Adjusted R^2: 0.874 LM(2): 1.468

Due to the lack of quarterly data on the nominal and real expenditure components, in the Serbian sub-model the GDP deflator and the deflators for the expenditure components are identical. Hence, the model contains a behavioural equation only for the GDP deflator (PGDP_SRB), which is simply linked to the consumer price index (CPI_SRB).

$$\log(PGDP\_SRB/PGDP\_SRB_{-4}) = \underset{(0.629)}{0.009} + \underset{(5.675)}{0.546} \log(PGDP\_SRB_{-1}/PGDP\_SRB_{-5})$$

$$+ \underset{(4.494)}{0.401} \log(CPI\_SRB/CPI\_SRB_{-4})$$

Adjusted R^2: 0.882 LM(2): 0.682

Public sector

In the public sector block, the model contains behavioural equations for the most important revenue and expenditure items of the consolidated general government of Serbia, i.e. the Republic of Serbia (central government), the Autonomous Province of Vojvodina, the municipalities and cities, and the Social Security Organisations (i.e. the Pension Fund, the Health Fund, and the National Employment Agency). Turning first to the *expenditure* side, in a fiscal rule public consumption according to national accounts (G_SRB) is related to the past change in the debt level (DEBT_SRB). This rule prevents public debt from increasing continuously since a rise in the debt level is counteracted by spending restraint in the next period. In order to account for differences between national accounts and public finance data, the model includes a behavioural equation relating government consumption according to public finance statistics (GOVCONS_SRB) to government consumption according to national accounts (G_CONS).

$$\log(G\_SRB/G\_SRB_{-4}) = \underset{(5.589)}{0.097} + \underset{(6.097)}{0.450} \log(G\_SRB_{-1}/G\_SRB_{-5}) - \underset{(-2.624)}{0.163}\, DUM2008q4$$

$$- \underset{(-3.209)}{0.280} \log(DEBT\_SRB_{-1}/DEBT\_SRB_{-5}) - \underset{(-2.702)}{0.171}\, DUM2003q1 - \underset{(-3.405)}{0.209}\, DUM2004q3$$

Adjusted R^2: 0.692 LM(2): 0.341

$$\log(GOVCONS\_SRB/GOVCONS\_SRB_{-4}) = \underset{(-1.911)}{-0.065} + \underset{(4.254)}{0.832} \log(G\_SRB/G\_SRB_{-4})$$

$$+ \underset{(2.439)}{0.311} \log(GOVCONS\_SRB_{-1}/GOVCONS\_SRB_{-5}) - \underset{(-4.084)}{0.419} \log(GOVCONS\_SRB_{-4}/G\_SRB_{-4})$$

Adjusted R^2: 0.722 LM(2): 6.701^{**}

Subsidies (SUBSIDIES_SRB) to the corporate sector are positively related to the general economic situation, which is approximated by GDP at current prices (GDP_SRB). The notion behind this specification is that higher public revenues usually initiate pressure from interest groups to increase spending as well.

$$\log(SUBSIDIES\_SRB/SUBSIDIES\_SRB_{-4}) = \underset{(-1.624)}{-4.419} + \underset{(2.367)}{2.333} \log(GDP\_SRB/GDP\_SRB_{-4})$$

$$- \underset{(-3.447)}{0.675} \log(SUBSIDIES\_SRB_{-4}) + \underset{(2.973)}{0.811} \log(GDP\_SRB_{-4})$$

Adjusted R^2: 0.377 LM(2): 3.521

The remaining government expenditures (EXPREST_SRB) are related to the remaining government revenues (REVREST_SRB). This ensures that, at least with regard to those expenditures which are not modelled separately, public spending is limited by the revenues of the general government.

$$\log(EXPREST\_SRB/EXPREST\_SRB_{-4}) = \underset{(-5.396)}{-0.848} - \underset{(-3.913)}{1.113}\, DUM2005q4$$

$$+ \underset{(3.589)}{1.248} \log(REVREST\_SRB/REVREST\_SRB_{-4}) - \underset{(-5.859)}{0.862} \log(EXPREST\_SRB_{-4}/REVREST\_SRB_{-4})$$

Adjusted R^2: 0.700 LM(2): 6.627^{**}

On the *revenues* side of the general government budget, social security contributions (SOCCONTR_SRB) are determined by the average gross wage per employee (GWAGE_SRB), multiplied by the average social security contribution rate (SOCCONTRATE_SRB) and the employment level (EMP_SRB). Since, in addition to employees, employers also have to pay social contributions, total social security contributions are not determined in a definition equation but in a behavioural equation. Following similar reasoning, personal income tax revenues (TACINC_SRB) are related to the average wage rate per employee, the employment level and the average personal income tax rate (PINCTAXRATE_SRB). Corporate tax payments (TAXCORP_SRB) are explained by the average corporate tax rate (CORPTRATE_SRB) in Serbia, multiplied by nominal GDP (GDP_SRB) as an indicator for corporate profits which behave pro-cyclically.

$$\log(SOCCONTR\_SRB/SOCCONTR\_SRB_{-4}) = \underset{(-2.309)}{-4.268} - \underset{(-2.720)}{0.531} \log(SOCCONTR\_SRB_{-4})$$

$$+ \underset{(2.718)}{0.406} \log(SOCCONTR\_SRB_{-1}/SOCCONTR\_SRB_{-5})$$

$$+ \underset{(1.709)}{0.296} \log[(EMP\_SRB*GWAGE\_SRB*SOCCONTRATE\_SRB/100) /(EMP\_SRB_{-4}*GWAGE\_SRB_{-4}*SOCCONTRATE\_SRB_{-4}/100)]$$

$$+ \underset{(2.757)}{0.437} \log(EMP\_SRB_{-4}*GWAGE\_SRB_{-4}*SOCCONTRATE\_SRB_{-4}/100)$$

Adjusted R^2: 0.679 LM(2): 1.153

$$\log(TAXINC\_SRB/TAXINC\_SRB_{-4}) = \underset{(-3.650)}{-5.75}$$

$$+ \underset{(3.243)}{0.624} \log((EMP\_SRB*GWAGE\_SRB*PINCTRATE\_SRB/100) /(EMP\_SRB_{-4}*GWAGE\_SRB_{-4}*PINCTRATE\_SRB_{-4}/100))$$

$$- \underset{(-4.574)}{0.866} \log(TAXINC\_SRB_{-4}) + \underset{(4.836)}{0.642} \log(EMP\_SRB_{-4}*GWAGE\_SRB_{-4}*PINCTRATE\_SRB_{-4}/100))$$

Adjusted R^2: 0.567 LM(2): 1.974

$$\log(TAXCORP\_SRB/TAXCORP\_SRB_{-4}) = \underset{(-0.876)}{-0.088} + \underset{(1.650)}{0\ 356}\ DUM2007q2$$

$$+ \underset{(1.993)}{0.395} \log(TAXCORP\_SRB_{-2}/TAXCORP\_SRB_{-6})$$

$$+ \underset{(1.919)}{1.617} \log[(GDP\_SRB_{-2}*CORPTRATE\_SRB_{-2})/(GDP\_SRB_{-6}*CORPTRATE\_SRB_{-6}))]$$

Adjusted R^2: 0.512 LM(2): 8.038^{**}

Value added tax (VAT) revenues (VAT_SRB) are determined by nominal private consumption expenditures (CONS_SRB), multiplied by the value added tax rate (VATRATE_SRB). Since some goods and services are taxed at a lower rate than standard VAT and some goods and services are exempt from VAT, value added tax revenues cannot be calculated in an identity but are determined in a behavioural equation.

$$\log(VAT\_SRB/VAT\_SRB_{-4}) = \underset{(-2.190)}{-2.033} + \underset{(2.694)}{0\ 273} \log(VAT\_SRB_{-1}/VAT\_SRB_{-5})$$

$$+ \underset{(6.411)}{1.629} \log[(CONS\_SRB*VATRATE\_SRB/100)/(CONS\_SRB_{-4}*VATRATE\_SRB_{-4}/100)$$

$$- \underset{(-6.155)}{0.896} \log(VAT\_SRB_{-4}) + \underset{(5.464)}{1.052} \log(CONS\_SRB_{-4}*VATRATE\_SRB_{-4}/100)$$

Adjusted R^2: 0.844 LM(2): 8.038^{**}

The remaining government revenues (REVREST_SRB) are explained by the economic situation as measured by nominal GDP.

$$\log(REVREST\_SRB/REVREST\_SRB_{-4}) = \underset{(-2.966)}{-4.322} + \underset{(4.428)}{1\ 547} \log(GDP\_SRB/GDP\_SRB_{-4})$$

$$- \underset{(5.920)}{0.765} \log(REVREST\_SRB_{-4}) + \underset{(4.664)}{0.971} \log(GDP\_SRB_{-4}) + \underset{(3.079)}{0.218}\ DUM2006q1$$

Adjusted R^2: 0.804 LM(2): 2.684

Identities

$oildin = oil * dinusd$

$nwage\_srb = gwage\_srb * (1 - av\_tax\_rate\_srb / 100)$

$nwager\_srb = nwage\_srb / cpi\_srb * 100$

$gwager\_srb = gwage\_srb / cpi\_srb * 100$

$infl\_srb = (cpi\_srb / cpi\_srb_{-4} - 1) * 100$

$ucc\_srb = ilend\_srb-[(pgdp\_srb / pgdp\_srb_{-4} -1)*100] + deprate\_srb$

$prod\_srb = gdpr\_srb / emp\_srb$

$ulc\_srb = gwage\_srb / prod\_srb$

$un\_srb = lforce\_srb - emp\_srb$

$ur\_srb = un\_srb / lforce\_srb * 100$

$$gdpr\_srb = consr\_srb + gr\_srb + gfcfr\_srb + inventr\_srb + exr\_srb - imr\_srb$$

$grgdpr\_srb = (gdpr\_srb / gdpr\_srb_{-4} - 1) * 100$

$gdp\_srb = gdpr\_srb * pgdp\_srb / 100$

$yd\_srb = gdp\_srb-taxinc\_srb-vat\_srb-soccontr\_srb+socbenefit\_srb$

$ydr\_srb = yd\_srb / cpi\_srb * 100$

$cons\_srb = consr\_srb * pgdp\_srb / 100$

$gr\_srb = g\_srb / pgdp\_srb * 100$

$demandr\_srb = consr\_srb+gr\_srb+gfcfr\_srb+inventr\_srb+exr\_srb$

$exr\_srb = exr\_srbbih + exr\_srbcro + exr\_srbslo + exr\_srbrow$

$$imr\_srb = exr\_bihsrb / 1.95583 * dineur + exr\_slosrb * dineur + exr\_crosrb / hrkdin + imr\_srbrow$$

$$lforce\_srb = partrate\_srb * pop\_srb$$

$$inventr\_srb = (inventr\_srb + inventr\_srb_{-1} + inventr\_srb_{-} + inventr\_srb_{-3} + inventr\_srb_{-4} + inventr\_srb_{-5} + inventr\_srb_{-6} + inventr\_srb_{-7}) / 8$$

$$interest\_srb = il\_debt\_srb * debt\_srb_{-1} / 100$$

$$balance\_srb = taxinc\_srb + taxcorp\_srb + vat\_srb + soccontr\_srb + revrest\_sr - socbenefit\_srb - subsidies\_srb - govcons\_srb - interest\_srb - exprest\_srb$$

$$balanceratio\_srb = (balance\_srb + balance\_srb_{-1} + balance\_srb_{-2} + balance\_srb_{-3}))/(gdpr\_srb + gdpr\_srb_{-1} + gdpr\_srb_{-2} + gdpr\_srb_{-3}) * 100$$

$$debt\_srb = debt\_srb_{-1} - balance\_srb + deltadebt\_srb$$

$$debtratio\_srb = debt\_srb / (gdpr\_srb + gdpr\_srb_{-1} + gdpr\_srb_{-2} + gdpr\_srb_{-3}) * 100$$

$$capr\_srb = capr\_srb_{-1} * (1 - deprate\_srb / 100) + gfcfr\_srb$$

$$trendemp\_srb = lforce\_srb * (1 - nairu\_srb / 100)$$

$$\log(ypot\_srb) = 0.7 * \log(trendemp\_srb) + 0.3 * \log(capr\_srb) + \log(trendtfp\_srb)$$

$$util\_srb = gdpr\_srb / ypot\_srb * 100$$

THE MODEL FOR CROATIA[12]

Introduction and data issues

Croatia's economic development was characterised by the transition from a socialist-type economy to a market economy, as well as the Croatian War of Independence (1991-1995) and the associated loss of markets. It took about a decade until Croatia's production re-attained its 1990 level. Between 2000 and 2007 real GDP growth was quite moderate compared to the other countries from Central, Eastern and South-Eastern Europe (CESEE). After this period of moderate growth and slow income convergence towards the EU, Croatia was hit hard by the global economic and financial crisis. Since the onset of the crisis and until 2013, real GDP in Croatia did not reach positive growth rates. It declined by 6.9 percent in 2009 and by 2.3 percent in 2010, remained stable in 2011, but declined again afterwards. According to the latest available data, real GDP decreased by 2.0 percent in 2012, and in its Autumn 2013 forecast the European Commission (European Commission 2013a) expected a further decline by 0.7 percent in 2013, followed by a meagre recovery (+0.5 percent) in 2014. Especially due to the war-related destruction and the transformation of the economy, empirical data for Croatia before the Dayton-Paris Agreement of November 1995 are not of appropriate quality for an econometric model. In order to base the equations on stable economic relations, data from the "Tuđman era" (1990-1999) are also mostly ignored as in this period major privatisation took place. As a result of the brevity of the time period for which the data are of sufficient quality with respect to consistency, reliability and the capability to reflect a relatively stable economic framework, it was necessary to use data with a higher than annual frequency. For most macroeconomic aggregates, data are available either on a monthly basis (like price indices, wages, exchange rates, monetary aggregates, interest rates) or quarterly (like national accounts data). As a result, the macroeconometric model of the small open economy of Croatia was constructed on the basis of quarterly data for the period 1999q1 until 2011q1/2011q2. The data were taken from the websites of the Croatian Bureau of Statistics (DZS), the Croatian Central Bank (CCB) and the Croatian Ministry of Finance. As for the other sub-models here, seasonally unadjusted data were used since the limited time frame makes a reliable detection and removal of regular seasonal patterns nearly impossible.

---

[12] The model for Croatia was described for the first time in Behrens, Haber and Weyerstrass (2011).

At the end of March 2011 the *revised national income accounting data* for the time period 2000q1 – 2010q4 were published by the Croatian Bureau of Statistics (DZS), where GDP estimates had been adjusted to meet the requirements of the European System of Accounts (ESA95).[13] These estimates are reported on a quarterly basis and include gross domestic product (GDP) and its expenditure components. GDP data for 1999 had also been published on a quarterly basis with 1997 as the reference year instead of 2000 and was transformed accordingly. Data for 2011 were taken directly from the most recent DZS reports.

Model equations

The equations of the sub-model for Croatia embody all relevant aspects to represent the essential features of the Croatian economy, combining Keynesian with neoclassical features. As in the sub-models for the other countries in the multi-country model, the Keynesian elements determine the short-run behaviour of the model, assuming that the economy is demand-driven, and persistent disequilibria in the market for goods and services and especially in the labour market are possible. The supply side is built on neoclassical foundations. In the following, the estimation results for the Croatian sub-model are documented in connection with a description of the underlying theoretical considerations of the different equations. As in the previous sections on the other country models, t-statistics, the adjusted R^2 and the Breusch-Godfrey test for serial correlation are provided. The suffix _CRO in the variable names indicates the sub-model for Croatia.

Supply side

In the supply block, the determination of potential GDP follows the same principles as in the other sub-models. Hence, the calculation of potential output is based on a Cobb-Douglas production function with constant returns to scale and with the production factors labour and capital. In addition, autonomous technical progress influences potential output. Since potential GDP is a measure of the long-run production possibilities of an economy, it is the long-run trends rather than the actual realisations of the production factors that enter the production function. An exception is the capital stock for which the actual level is taken. Autonomous technical progress is defined as total

[13] For the entire data set see First Release of the Croatian Bureau of Statistics ("Quarterly gross domestic product estimate 2000q1-2010q4"), No 12.1.1/4., published 31 March 2011.

factor productivity (TFP). Under these assumptions, trend employment, the capital stock and trend total factor productivity determine potential output. The production function has the following form:

log(YPOT_CRO) = 0.67 log(TRENDEMP_CRO)
+ 0.33 log(CAPR_CRO) + TENDTFP_CRO

In this equation, YPOT_CRO is potential GDP, TRENDEMP_CRO is the labour force adjusted for structural unemployment, CAPR_CRO is the real capital stock, and TRENDTFP_CRO is the long-run trend of total factor productivity (TFP). Since, for the time being, no income data of the national account exist for Croatia, the production elasticities of the production factors employment (2/3) and capital (1/3) were based on international empirical evidence.

Trend employment is determined by adjusting the actual labour force by the number of those unemployed for structural reasons. Since the natural (or structural) unemployment rate cannot be observed, it needs to be estimated. Defining the natural rate of unemployment as the long-run trend of the actual unemployment rate (yielding the NAIRU, the rate of unemployment that leaves the rate of inflation constant), a Hodrick-Prescott (HP) filter was used to extract this trend from observed unemployment data. Trend employment is then determined as follows:

$$TRENDEMP\_CRO_t = LFORCE\_CRO_t \cdot \left(1 - \frac{NAIRU\_CRO_t}{100}\right).$$

The NAIRU is endogenised by the following equation:

log(NAIRU_CRO/NAIRU_CRO$_{-4}$) = -0.00005 + 3.996 log(NAIRU_CRO$_{-1}$/NAIRU_CRO$_{-5}$)
(-2.672) (66.773)

- 6.120 log(NAIRU_CRO$_{-2}$/NAIRU_CRO$_{-6}$) + 4.253 log(NAIRU_CRO$_{-3}$/NAIRU_CRO$_{-7}$)
(-34.462) (23.756)

- 1.131 log(NAIRU_CRO$_{-4}$/NAIRU_CRO$_{-8}$)
(-18.449)

Adjusted R^2: 0.999 LM(2): 2.913

The calculation of the capital stock is based on the Perpetual Inventory Method (PIM). According to this method the capital stock at the end of the current period is identical to the capital stock at the end of the previous period plus gross fixed capital formation minus depreciation. Hence, an estimation of Croatia's aggregated capital stock in the starting period, i.e. in the first quarter of 1999 is needed first. This initial capital stock was constructed as the present value of a persistent stream of average quarterly gross investments (at constant prices) for an infinite period. For the time period spanning the first quarter of 1999 to the fourth quarter of 2010, real average quarterly gross investment was equal to 13.31 billion Croatian kuna (HRK). Using the average long-run interest rate on loans to companies (which is equal to 7.21 percent p.a. according to data from the Croatian National Bank), the present value of persistent quarterly gross investment measured in billion HRK for an infinite time horizon is equal to

$$CAPR\_CRO_0 = 13.31 \cdot \sum_{t=0}^{\infty} \frac{1}{(1+0.018)^t} \cong \frac{13.31}{1-(1-0.018))} \cong 738.417$$

In accordance with Weyerstrass et al. (2009), a quarterly depreciation rate of 1.47 percent (corresponding to an annual depreciation rate of 6 percent) is applied. This provides the information needed to compute a time series for Croatia's stock of aggregated capital (where $IFIXR\_CRO_t$ denotes real gross investment):

$$CAPR\_CRO = (1-0.0147) \cdot CAPR\_CRO_{t-1} + IFIXR\_CRO_t,$$

The variable TRENDTFP_CRO is determined as the trend of total factor productivity (TFP), where total factor productivity is calculated as that part of the annual change in real GDP that is caused neither by rising labour nor by higher capital input. Weighing labour and capital by their respective production elasticities, 2/3 and 1/3, the production function is used to calculate the time series for *TFP* by applying growth accounting, where GDPR_CRO represents real gross domestic product, EMP_CRO denotes the actual number of persons in employment and CAPR_CRO is Croatia's aggregate capital stock:

$$\log(TFP\_CRO_t) = \log(GDPR\_CRO_t) - 0.67 \log(EMP\_CRO_t) - 0.33 \log(CAPR\_CRO_t)$$

The long-run trend of total factor productivity is determined by applying the HP filter to the actual TFP series. To endogenise trend total factor productivity, the following estimation is included in the model:

$$\log(TRENDTFP\_CRO/TRENDTFP\_CRO_{-4}) = \underset{(2.245)}{0.0003} - \underset{(-2.512)}{0.000005}\ TREND$$

$$+ \underset{(25.215)}{3.938} \log(TRENDTFP\_CRO_{-1}/TRENDTFP\_CRO_{-5})$$

$$- \underset{(-11.024)}{6.396} \log(TRENDTFP\_CRO_{-2}/TRENDTFP\_CRO_{-6})$$

$$+ \underset{(6.174)}{5.397} \log(TRENDTFP\_CRO_{-3}/TRENDTFP\_CRO_{-7})$$

$$- \underset{(-3.731)}{2.377} \log(TRENDTFP\_CRO_{-4}/TRENDTFP\_CRO_{-8})$$

$$+ \underset{(2.310)}{0.435} \log(TRENDTFP\_CRO_{-5}/TRENDTFP\_CRO_{-9})$$

Adjusted R^2: 0.999 LM(2): 4.027

Demand side

Consumption of private households

Consumption of private households (CONSUMR_CRO) is influenced by current disposable income (YDR_CRO), as the Keynesian consumption theory stipulates, and on the real long-term interest rate (IR_LR_CRO), in line with both the permanent income hypothesis and the life cycle hypothesis. The real interest rate, which is approximated by the nominal interest rate minus consumer price inflation, as a determinant of consumption accounts both for the fact that some households finance part of their consumption via bank loans and for the intertemporal decision on the allocation of income to consumption in the present period and in the future. The higher the real interest rate, the higher the opportunity costs are of spending income for current consumption.

$$\log(CONSUMR\_CRO/CONSUMR\_CRO_{-4}) = \underset{(9.180)}{0.668} \log(YDR\_CRO_{-1}/YDR\_CRO_{-5})$$

$$- \underset{(-0.856)}{0.005} (IR\_LR\_CRO - IR\_LR\_CRO_{-4}) + \underset{(6.104)}{0.067} DUM2002 - \underset{(-2.750)}{0.061} DUM2009q1$$

$$- \underset{(-1.233)}{0.051} [\log(CONSUMR\_CRO_{-4} - 3.849 - 0.599 \log(YDR\_CRO_{-4})]$$

Adjusted R^2: 0.791 LM(2): 11.482^{***}

Gross fixed capital formation

As elaborated in the sections on the other sub-models above, gross fixed capital formation is undertaken to renew the capital stock and to adjust it to changes in final demand. Hence, the accelerator theory stipulates that changes in demand determine fixed capital formation. Since it takes time to purchase and install new capital goods, it is expected rather than actual demand that has to be considered. However, in the case of adaptive expectations, as is assumed here, expectations are based on past observations. Therefore, in the investment equation, actual demand is included as an approximation for expected future demand. According to theories focussing on the profitability of investment projects, the value of the capital stock equals the discounted future income that can be generated by employing the capital stock. Therefore, the interest rate, which is used to discount future income, is crucial for the profitability of an investment project. Based on these theoretical considerations, real gross fixed capital formation (IFIXR_CRO) is influenced by the change in total domestic demand (DEMANDR_CRO), in accordance with the accelerator hypothesis, and by the real long-term interest rate (IR_LR_CRO), the latter approximating the user cost of capital.

Changes in inventories (INVENTR_CRO) are modelled as an eight quarter moving average process.

$$\log(IFIXR\_CRO/IFIXR\_CRO_{-4}) = \underset{(-4.323)}{-5.340} + \underset{(2.385)}{0.195} \log(IFIXR\_CRO_{-1}/IFIXR\_CRO_{-5})$$

$$+ \underset{(6.274)}{0.971} \log(DEMANDR\_CRO/DEMANDR\_CRO_{-4}) - \underset{(-2.003)}{0.009} IR\_LR\_CRO_{-1}$$

$$- \underset{(-6.421)}{0.578} \log(IFIXR\_CRO_{-4}) + \underset{(5.470)}{0.959} \log(DEMANDR\_CRO_{-4}) + \underset{(4.296)}{0.102} DUM2003$$

Adjusted R^2: 0.906 LM(2): 10.082^{***}

Exports of goods and services

As elaborated above, every country model contains equations for exports to every other country in the model and to the rest of the world. Hence, for Croatia, exports are modelled to Bosnia and Herzegovina, Slovenia, Serbia, and the rest of the world, the relevant equations being presented in this section. In general, exports to a certain country depend on demand in the recipient country and on the real exchange rate between the exporting and the importing country. A real depreciation of the currency makes domestic goods and services more competitive on the world market. Hence, export demand increases. In the model, the exchange rate is included in the export and import equations in such a way that an increase represents a depreciation of the home currency. Hence, the exchange rate is expected to influence exports positively and imports negatively, as domestically produced goods and services become less competitive when the currency depreciates in nominal terms or prices at home increase more than abroad.

Exports from Croatia to Serbia (EXR_CROSRB) depend on final demand in Serbia (DEMANDR_SRB) and the real exchange rate between the Croatian kuna and the Serbian dinar. The real exchange rate between the kuna and the dinar includes the price ratio between Serbia and Croatia (CPI_SRB/CPI_CRO) in addition to the nominal exchange rate between the dinar and the kuna (DINHRK).

$$\log(EXR\_CROSRB/EXR\_CROSRB_{-4}) = \underset{(4.530)}{0.528} \log(EXR\_SRBCRO_{-1}/EXR\_SRBCRO_{-5})$$

$$+ \underset{(2.889)}{0.655} \log(DEMANDR\_SRB/DEMANDR\_SRB_{-4})$$

$$+ \underset{(0.483)}{0.0003} \log((HRKDIN*CPI\_SRB/CPI\_CRO)/(HRKDIN_{-4}*CPI\_SRB_{-4}/CPI\_CRO_{-4}))$$

$$- 0.112 [\log(EXR\_CROSRB_{-4}) - 0.726 \log(DEMANDR\_SRB_{-4}) - 1.086 \log((HRKDIN_{-4}*CPI\_SRB_{-4})/CPI\_CRO_{-4}) - 0.489\ Q3]$$

Adjusted R^2: 0.551 LM(2): 4.483

Exports from Croatia to Bosnia and Herzegovina (EXR_CROBiH) are influenced by real final demand in Bosnia and Herzegovina (DEMANDR_BiH) and by the real exchange rate between the Croatian kuna and the Bosnian convertible mark (KM). Due to Bosnia and Herzegovina's currency board with the euro as the reference currency, the nominal exchange rate between the kuna and the euro was taken as an approximation of the exchange rate between the kuna and the convertible mark. The real exchange rate between Croatia and Bosnia and Herzegovina thus consists of the nominal exchange rate between the kuna and the euro (HRKEUR) and the price ratio (CPI_BIH/CPI_CRO).

$$\log(EXR\_CROBiH/EXR\_CROBiH_{-4}) = \underset{(6.992)}{0.598} \log(EXR\_CROBIH_{-1}/EXR\_CROBIH_{-5})$$

$$+ \underset{(3.168)}{0.678} \log(DEMANDR\_BiH/DEMANDR\_BiH_{-4}) - \underset{(-2.880)}{0.219} DUM2009q1$$

$$- \underset{(-2.443)}{0\ 188} \log(EXR\_CROBiH_{-4}) + \underset{(1.456)}{0.135} \log(DEMANDR\_BiH_{-4})$$

$$+ \underset{(0.749)}{0.146} \log(HRKEUR_{-4}*CPIBIH_{-4}/CPI\_CRO_{-4})) + \underset{(1.942)}{0.078} Q3$$

Adjusted R^2: 0.823 LM(2): 2.983

Exports from Croatia to Slovenia (EXR_CROSLO) are a function of real final demand in Slovenia (DEMAND_SLO) and the real exchange rate. In this case, the real exchange rate consists of the nominal exchange rate between the Croatian kuna and the euro (HRKEUR) and the ratio between the consumer price indices in Slovenia (CPI_SLO) and Croatia (CPI_CRO).

$$\log(EXR\_CROSLO/EXR\_CROSLO_{-4}) = \underset{(-1.623)}{-1.508} + \underset{(3.298)}{0.313} \log(EXR\_CROSLO_{-1}/EXR\_CROSLO_{-5})$$

$$+ \underset{(6.679)}{2.049} \log(DEMAND\_SLO/DEMAND\_SLO_{-4})$$

$$- \underset{(-3.701)}{0.313} \log(EXR\_CROSLO_{-4}) + \underset{(2.152)}{0.384} \log(DEMAND\_SLO_{-4})$$

$$+ \underset{(0.421)}{0.121} \log((HRKEUR_{-4})*CPI\_SLO_{-4}/CPI\_CRO_{-4})) - \underset{(-2.383)}{0.167} DUM2008q1 + \underset{(3.047)}{0.156} Q3$$

Adjusted R^2: 0.852 LM(2): 0.383

Exports from Croatia to the rest of the world (EXR_CROROW) depend on world trade (WTRADE) as a proxy for world demand and on the real effective exchange rate of the Croatian kuna (REER_CRO). The real effective exchange rate is a weighted average of the nominal exchange rates and the price ratios with respect to Croatia's most important trading partners.

$$\log(EXR\_CROROW/EXR\_CROROW_{-4}) = \underset{(8.403)}{0.600} \log(WTRADE/WTRADE_{-4})$$

$$+ \underset{(2.179)}{0.403} \log(REER\_CRO_{-3}/REER\_CRO_{-7}) + \underset{(3.454)}{0.068}\, DUM2003 - \underset{(-6.385)}{0.240}\, DUM2011$$

$$- \underset{(-3.885)}{0.497} [\log(EXR\_CROROW_{-4} - 0.794 \log(WTRADE_{-4}) - 0.718 \log(REER\_CRO_{-4}) + 0.209\, Q1 - 0.495\, Q3]$$

Adjusted R^2: 0.780 LM(2): 0.912

Imports of goods and services

Except from deviations between exports and imports due to statistical errors, imports to Croatia from the other countries in the model are, by definition, identical to their exports to Croatia. Hence, like in the foreign trade sectors of the other sub-models, they are modelled as exports in the country models themselves, and only Croatia's imports from the rest of the world (IMR_CROROW) are modelled separately. They depend on total real demand in Croatia (DEMANDR_CRO) and on relative prices. Similar to the equation for Croatia's exports to the rest of the world, relative prices are approximated by the real effective exchange rate with respect to Croatia's most important trading partners (REER_CRO).

$$\log(IMR\_CROROW/IMR\_CROROW_{-4}) = \underset{(-1.384)}{-0.008} + \underset{(2.082)}{0.033}\, DUM2003 - \underset{(-4.396)}{0.076}\, DUM2004$$

$$+ \underset{(18.427)}{1.612} \log(DEMANDR\_CRO/DEMANDR\_CRO_{-4}) - \underset{(-0.334)}{0.067} \log(REER\_CRO/REER\_CRO_{-4})$$

$$- \underset{(-2.441)}{0.259} [\log(IMR\_CROROW_{-4}) - 1.011 \log(DEMANDR\_CRO_{-4} + 0.278 \log(REER\_CRO_{-4})]$$

Adjusted R^2: 0.929 LM(2): 3.488

Labour market

According to the Croatian Employment Service, the registered unemployment rate in Croatia is currently about 18 percent. Thus, increasing the number of employed persons is a major concern of the Croatian government, and understanding the development of (un)employment is an important requirement for public policy making. In this context it is important to note that the unemployment figures that allow for international comparison (and that are used for estimating the macroeconomic model of the Croatian economy presented here) are collected in a different manner from the registered ones, namely according to the standards of the International Labour Organization (ILO). According to the ILO, persons regarded as employed are defined as follows: "Persons in employment are those who did any work for payment in cash or kind during the reference week. Those are employees, self-employed persons and family members who help in some kind of family business (family enterprise, firm, craft, free-lance, farm) or some other kind of gainful activity, as well as persons who worked on a contract basis, for direct payment in cash or kind. Therefore, the [Labour Force] Survey covers all persons who worked in the reference period, no matter what their formal status or means of payment was. In this way, a retired person, a student or a housewife can also be classified as an employed person. Persons in employment are also those who were temporarily not working but had a job to return to with the same employer after the reason for absence no longer existed." [Croatian Bureau of Statistics, The Labour Force Survey 2010]. The ILO unemployment rate is usually far below its "national" registered alternative. For example, according to the Croatian Employment Service the ILO unemployment rate for the first quarter of 2011 amounted to "only" 11.2 percent.

Similarly to the other sub-models, labour demand in the Croatia sub-model is influenced by labour costs and by Croatia's aggregate production level. Hence, the number of persons employed (EMP_CRO) depends positively on real GDP (GDPR_CRO) and negatively on the real gross wage (GROSS_WAGER_CRO).

$$\log(EMP\_CRO/EMP\_CRO_{-4}) = \underset{(5.714)}{4.614} + \underset{(2.404)}{0.213} \log(EMP\_CRO_{-1}/EMP\_CRO_{-5})$$

$$+ \underset{(2.794)}{0.183} \log(GDPR\_CRO/GDPR\_CRO_{-4}) - \underset{(-3.602)}{0.045} DUM2001 - \underset{(-3.536)}{0.030} DUM2010$$

$$- \underset{(-1.504)}{0.278} \log(GROSS\_WAGER\_CRO/GROSS\_WAGER\_CRO_{-4})$$

$$- \underset{(-4.342)}{0.757} \log(EMP\_CRO_{-4}) + \underset{(3.658)}{0.224} \log(GDPR\_CRO_{-4}) - \underset{(-2.291)}{0.173} \log(GROSS\_WAGER\_CRO_{-4})$$

Adjusted R^2: 0.817 LM(2): 6.886^{**}

Labour supply by private households is modelled via the participation rate (PARTRATE_CRO), i.e. the labour force divided by the working-age population (those aged 15 to 64). The participation rate depends positively on the real net wage (NTE_WAGER_CRO). The positive influence implies that the substitution effect of a higher wage rate (increasing opportunity costs of leisure) dominates the income effect (maintenance of the income level with reduced labour effort as the wage rises).

$$PARTRATE\_CRO = \underset{(5.287)}{-0.0002} + \underset{(4.157)}{0.439}\ PARTRATE\_CRO_{-1} - \underset{(-4.274)}{0.00003}\ DUM2001q1$$

$$+ \underset{(2.484)}{0.0001} \log(NET\_WAGER\_CRO/NET\_WAGER\_CRO_{-4}) + \underset{(4.275)}{0.00002}\ DUM2000q3$$

Adjusted R^2: 0.560 LM(2): 9.510^{***}

Prices and wages

In the wage-price system, gross wages, the consumer price index (CPI) and various deflators are determined. For the period 2000 to 2010 the average nominal earnings have been reported by the Croatian Central Bureau of Statistics.[14] Based on data for 2000[15], the average wages for 1999 were constructed by breaking down thc rcported biannual numbers according to the quarterly pattern observed in 2000.

Real average gross wages in Croatia are determined by deflating real gross wages with the consumer price index. Nominal average net wages in Croatia are determined following

$$NET\_WAGE\_CRO_t = (1 - AV\_TAXRATE\_CRO/100) \cdot GROSS\_WAGE\_CRO_t$$

where AV_TAXRATE_CRO denotes the average tax rate on wages and is given exogenously. Real average net wages are then computed according to the following rule:

$$NET\_WAGER\_CRO_t = 100 \cdot \frac{NET\_WAGE\_CRO_t}{CPI\_CRO_t}.$$

[14] For example, net wages are derived from the First Release of the Croatian Bureau of Statistics ("Average monthly paid off net earnings of persons in paid employment, 2000-2008"), No. 9.1.8., published on 30 June 2009. Data for 2009q1-2011q1 are taken from the monthly publications provided by the Central Bureau of Statistics. See http://www.dzs.hr/eng/publication/2009/9-1-8_1e2009.htm.

[15] http://www.dzs.hr/Eng/Publication/2001/9-1-2_12e2001.htm.

Similarly to the other sub-models, in an extended Phillips curve relationship the average gross wage rate in Croatia (GROSS_WAGE_CRO) depends positively on the price level (CPI_CRO) and on labour productivity (PROD_CRO) and negatively on the difference between the actual and the natural rate of unemployment (or the NAIRU) (UR_CRO-NAIRU_CRO). In order to avoid multicollinearity problems, inflation enters the wage equation with a one quarter lag. The notion behind this bargaining model is that employees or their representatives, i.e. trade unions, strive at least to maintain the purchasing power of wages (hence the positive influence of the price level), and to participate in productivity gains. The relative position of employees in wage negotiations improves as the labour market improves, reflected in actual unemployment eventually being lower than the structural unemployment rate (the NAIRU).

$$\log(GROSS\_WAGE\_CRO/GWAGE\_CRO_{-4}) = \underset{(-2.857)}{-0.551} \underset{(-2.525)}{- 0.028} DUM2001q1 \underset{(-2.861)}{- 0.014} Q1$$

$$\underset{(4.693)}{+ 0.515} \log(GROSS\_WAGE\_CRO_{-1}/GROSS\_WAGE\_CRO_{-5})$$

$$\underset{(1.997)}{+ 0.240} \log(CPI\_CRO_{-1}/CPI\_CRO_{-5}) \underset{(3.686)}{+ 0.159} \log(PROD\_CRO/PROD\_CRO_{-4})$$

$$\underset{(-3.446)}{- 0.297} \log(GROSS\_WAGE\_CRO_{-4}) \underset{(1.848)}{+ 0.244} \log(CPI\_CRO\text{-}4) \underset{(4.681)}{+ 0.244} \log(PROD\_CRO_{-4})$$

$$\underset{(-2.460)}{- 0.004} (UR\_CRO_{-1} - NAIRU\_CRO_{-1})$$

Adjusted R^2: 0.845 LM(2): 0.012

In the central price equation, the consumer price index (CPI_CRO) depends on domestic and international factors. The most important internal cost factors are wage costs (GROSS_WAGE_CRO). In addition, rising capacity utilisation (UTIL_CRO) exerts price pressure as machines require more maintenance when they are used longer hours and workers are paid compensation for working overtime. In addition to internal factors, for Croatia as a small open economy, international prices are important determinants of domestic prices. The oil price in Croatian kuna (OILHRK) is included as a proxy for the prices of imported raw materials in general.

$$\log(CPI\_CRO/CPI\_CRO_{-4}) = \underset{(-1.103)}{-0.057} + \underset{(11.923)}{0.837} \log(CPI\_CRO_{-1}/CPI\_CRO_{-5})$$

$$+ \underset{(1.808)}{0.105} \log(GROSS\_WAGE\_CRO_{-2}/GROSS\_WAGE\_CRO_{-6})$$

$$+ \underset{(4.157)}{0.014} \log(OILHRK/OILHRK_{-4}) + \underset{(2.180)}{0.047} \log(UTIL\_CRO_{-1}/UTIL\_CRO_{-5})$$

$$- \underset{(-1.584)}{0.125} \log(CPI\_CRO_{-4}) + \underset{(1.798)}{0.075} \log(GROSS\_WAGE\_CRO_{-4})$$

$$- \underset{(-2.456)}{0.014} \, DUM200q3 - \underset{(-2.154)}{0.012} \, DUM2006q4 - \underset{(-3.151)}{0.020} \, DUM2008q4$$

Adjusted R^2: 0.884 LM(2): 1.162

The GDP deflator (P_GDP_CRO), the deflator of private consumption (P_CONSUM_CRO) and the deflator of public consumption (P_G_CRO) essentially depend on the consumer price index (CPI_CRO). The GDP deflator is, in addition, influenced by unit labour costs (ULC_CRO). In the model, real GDP is derived by adding up the real expenditure components which were determined in behavioural equations. Nominal GDP is then calculated by deflating real GDP with the GDP deflator. The deflator for public consumption is needed to determine real public consumption, since this variable is first determined in nominal terms, in contrast to the other expenditure items of GDP. Finally, the private consumption deflator is used to determine nominal consumption, which is needed to derive value added tax revenues.

$$\log(P\_GDP\_CRO/P\_GDP\_CRO_{-4}) = \underset{(0.966)}{0.004} + \underset{(6.483)}{0.449} \log(P\_GDP\_CRO_{-1}/P\_GDP\_CRO_{-5})$$

$$+ \underset{(3.162)}{0.440} \log(CPI\_CRO/CPI\_CROB_{-4}) + \underset{(1.370)}{0.068} \log(ULC\_CRO/ULC\_CRO_{-4})$$

$$+ \underset{(6.679)}{0.088} \, DUM200q3 - \underset{(6.317)}{0.087} \, DUM2004q1 + \underset{(-6.484)}{0.085} \, DUM2005q1$$

Adjusted R^2: 0.836 LM(2): 4.204

$$\log(P\_CONSUM\_CRO/P\_CONSUM\_CRO_{-4}) = \underset{(-1.357)}{-0.099} + \underset{(14.660)}{0.980} \log(CPI\_CRO/CPI\_CRO_{-4})$$

$$- \underset{(-5.944)}{0.544} \log(P\_CONSUM\_CRO_{-4}) + \underset{(5.475)}{0.562} \log(CPI\_CRO_{-4})$$

Adjusted R^2: 0.890 LM(2): 8.925^{**}

$$\log(P\_G\_CRO/P\_G\_CRO_{-4}) = -0.821 + 0.544 \log(P\_G\_CRO_{-1}/P\_G\_CRO_{-5})$$
$$\qquad (-2.610) \quad (5.164)$$

$$- 0.401 \log(P\_G\_CRO_{-4}) + 0.574 \log(CPI\_CRO_{-4})$$
$$(-3.891) \qquad\qquad (3.799)$$

Adjusted R^2: 0.608 LM(2): 2.048

Money market

As Croatia is not yet a member of the euro area, the Croatian National Bank (HNB) is able to conduct, essentially, an independent monetary policy. Hence, it is assumed that the HNB sets its short-term interest rate according to a Taylor rule, where the market-determined short-term interest rate is taken as an approximation of the monetary policy instrument, since the market-determined short-term interest rate is normally very close to the monetary policy rate. The short-term interest rate I_SR_CRO therefore depends positively on the output gap, i.e. the ratio between actual and potential GDP (GDPR_CRO/YPOT_CRO). A rising capacity utilisation signals increasing inflationary pressure and triggers an increase in the interest rate. The second term which is normally included in a Taylor rule policy rule, i.e. the inflation rate, was not supported by the Croatian data.

$$I\_SR\_CRO_{-1} - I\_SR\_CRO_{-5} = 0.895 (I\_SR\_CRO_{-1}-I\_SR\_CRO_{-5})$$
$$(14.711)$$

$$+ 2.237 \log(GDPR\_CRO/YPOT\_CRO)$$
$$(1.438)$$

Adjusted R^2: 0.795 LM(2): 6.781^{**}

In a term structure equation, the long-term interest rate (I_LR_CRO) depends on the short-term rate of interest (I_SR_CRO). In addition, the Croatian long-term interest rate is influenced by its counterpart in the euro area (EUR10Y). It is sensible to assume that the financial market of the small open economy of Croatia is strongly influenced by world financial markets, whereby the European financial market is of particular importance for an EU Member State.

$$I\_LR\_CRO - I\_LR\_CRO_{-4} = \underset{(4.158)}{0.492} + \underset{(6.312)}{0.547} (I\_LR\_CRO_{-1} - I\_LR\_CRO_{-5})$$
$$+ \underset{(2.101)}{0.1476} [(I\_SR\_CRO_{-4} - I\_SR\_CRO_{-8}) - 0.224 (I\_LR\_CRO_{-4} - EUR10Y_{-4})]$$

Adjusted R^2: 0.892 LM(2): 2.078

The implicit – or average – interest rate on public debt (I_DEBT_CRO) is largely determined by the long-term market interest rate I_LR_CRO. However, the implicit interest rate converges only gradually to the market rate since a large part of public debt has a long maturity, and therefore in every year only a fraction of public debt becomes due and has to be resolved. The implicit interest rate on public debt was first calculated by dividing annual interest payments by the stock of public debt at the end of the previous year or, equivalently, at the beginning of the current year.

$$I\_DEBT\_CRO - I\_DEBT\_CRO_{-1} = \underset{(1.748)}{0.318} (I\_LR\_CRO_{-1} - I\_LR\_CRO_{-2})$$
$$+ \underset{(9.542)}{1.089} Q1 - \underset{(-8.837)}{1.110} Q2$$

Adjusted R^2: 0.814 LM(2): 14.812^{***}

Foreign exchange market

The foreign exchange market is modelled by the nominal and the real effective exchange rate against Croatia's most important trading partners. In the model, the nominal effective exchange rate (NEER_CRO) depends on the bilateral exchange rates between the Croatian kuna and the most important currencies, i.e. the euro (HRKEUR) and the US dollar (HRKUSD).

$$\log(NERR\_CRO/NEER\_CRO_{-4}) = \underset{(-1.953)}{-0.002} + \underset{(4.456)}{0.274} \log(NEER\_CRO_{-1}/NEER\_CRO_{-5})$$
$$+ \underset{(7.907)}{0.079} \log(HRKUSD/HRKUSD_{-4}) + \underset{(7.993)}{0.522} \log(HRKEUR/HRKEUR_{-4})$$
$$\underset{(-2.546)}{-0.013} DUM200q2 + \underset{(4.618)}{0.012} DUM2010$$

Adjusted R^2: 0.914 LM(2): 9.230^{***}

Theoretically, the real effective exchange rate (REER_CRO) depends on the nominal effective exchange rate (NEER_CRO) as well as on relative prices between Croatia and its trading partners. However, the model does not include foreign price levels or inflation rates, except for those of the other countries from the former Yugoslavia that are included in the multi-country model. Hence, instead of the inflation differential, only domestic inflation in Croatia was included as a determinant of the real exchange rate. The same approximation was also made in the sub-models for the other countries.

$$\log(REER\_CRO/REER\_CRO_{-4}) = \underset{(12.300)}{0.811} \log(REER\_CRO_{-1}/REER\_CRO_{-5})$$

$$+ \underset{(5.636)}{1.019} \log(NEER\_CRO/NEER\_CRO_{-4}) - \underset{(-2.906)}{0.617} \log(NEER\_CRO_{-1}/NEER\_CRO_{-5})$$

$$- \underset{(-2.325)}{0.002} (INFL\_CRO - INFL\_CRO_{-4})$$

Adjusted R^2: 0.878 LM(2): 1.983

Public sector

This model block contains behavioural equations and identities for Croatia's most important governmental revenue and expenditure items, quite a difficult task given that even over the last ten years public sector aggregates as published by the Croatian Ministry of Finance have been subject to several changes, redefinitions and reclassifications. The main structural break in reporting Croatian public finance data occurred about between the first and the second half of 2004.[16] Since then monthly time series for most, albeit not all, relevant items of the Croatian general budget are of relatively good quality and are quite easily accessible from the Croatian Ministry of Finance.

---

16 For 1999q1-2004q2 public finance accounting data can found in the Ministry of Finance Statistical Review being published in a monthly pattern, while for 2004q3-today public finance accounting data are provided at http://www.mfin.hr/en/time-series-data.

Expenditures

General government expenditures consist primarily of public consumption according to public finance data, all kinds of transfer payments and interest payments. Thus, total expenditures (TOTALEXP_CRO) can be set up as

$$TOTALEXP\_CRO_t = G\_CONS\_CRO_t + G\_SUBSIDIES\_CRO_t + G\_TRANSFER\_CRO_t + INTEREST\_CRO_t + G\_OTHEREXP\_CRO_t,$$

where the endogenous variable G_CONS_CRO measures public consumption and includes all public expenses on goods and services plus wages and salaries and employers' social security contributions for persons employed in the public sector. The variable G_SUBSIDIES_CRO stands for the endogenously determined transfer payments to companies. The variable G_TRANSFER_CRO is the only item on the expenditure side that is not determined endogenously and contains all sorts of social benefit payments to private households. The endogenous variable INTEREST_CRO represents interest payments on public debt, and the endogenously determined variable G_OTHEREXP_CRO includes all remaining government expenditures.

In a fiscal rule, public expenditures on goods and services (G_CRO) are inversely related to the past change in the debt level (DEBT_CRO). This rule prevents public debt from increasing permanently, since a rise in the debt level is counteracted by a spending restraint in the next period.

$$\log(G\_CRO/G\_CRO_{-4}) = \underset{(2.966)}{0.029} + \underset{(6.923)}{0.676} \log(G\_CRO_{-1}/G\_CRO_{-5})$$

$$\underset{(-2.711)}{- 0.161} \log(DEBT\_CRO_{-1}/DEBT\_CRO_{-5})$$

Adjusted R^2: 0.746 LM(2): 0.733

In spite of the lacking identity of public consumption according to national income accounting (G_CRO) and public consumption according to public finance accounting (G_CONS_CRO), these two items are strongly correlated. This pertains to a long-run as well as to a short-run relationship. The influence of the lagged dependent variable accounts for inertia inherent in public consumption, since, mainly due to contractual relations and legally defined spending rules, public consumption cannot fluctuate erratically from one year to the next.

$$\log(G\_CONS\_CRO/G\_CONS\_CRO_{-4}) = \underset{(2.684)}{1.748} + \underset{(3.407)}{0.814} \log(G\_CRO/G\_CRO_{-4})$$

$$+ \underset{(4.552)}{0.445} \log(G\_CONS\_CRO_{-1}/G\_CONS\_CRO_{-5})$$

$$- \underset{(-5.220)}{0.621} \log(G\_CONS\_CRO_{-4}) + \underset{(3.685)}{0.399} \log(G\_CRO_{-4})$$

Adjusted R^2: 0.672 LM(2): 9.379***

Subsidies to private companies (SUBSIDIES_CRO) correlate strongly with the state of the economy, which is approximated by the nominal gross domestic product (GDP_CRO). This specification accounts for the empirical observation that an improvement in the public budgetary situation inspires interest groups to demand higher spending.

$$\log(G\_SUBSIDIES\_CRO/G\_SUBSIDIES\_CRO_{-4}) = \underset{(-3.086)}{-6.016} + \underset{(3.416)}{0.353} Q1$$

$$+ \underset{(2.355)}{0.223} \log(G\_SUBSIDIES\_CRO_{-1}/G\_SUBSIDIES\_CRO_{-5}) + \underset{(2.324)}{0.237} Q4$$

$$- \underset{(-8.094)}{1.063} \log(G\_SUBSIDIES\_CRO_{-4}) + \underset{(5.322)}{1.214} \log(GDP\_CRO_{-4})$$

Adjusted R^2: 0.632 LM(2): 2.215

Interest payments on outstanding government debt are calculated by multiplying the debt level at the end of the previous year (DEBT_CRO) by the implicit interest rate on public debt (I_DEBT_CRO). Hence, interest payments are determined in a definitional rather than a behavioural equation.

The remaining public expenditures (G_OTHEREXP_CRO) are mainly determined by other public revenues (REV_OTHER_CRO) to ensure that public expenditures are, by and large, covered by revenues so as to avoid an ever increasing gap between expenditures and revenues.

$$\log(G\_OTHEREXP\_CRO/G\_OTHEREXP\_CRO_{-4}) = \underset{(2.893)}{0.275}$$
$$+ \underset{(3.087)}{0.387} \log(G\_OTHEREXP\_CRO_{-1}/G\_OTHEREXP\_CRO_{-5})$$
$$+ \underset{(4.316)}{0.334} \log(REV\_OTHER\_CRO/REV\_OTHER\_CRO_{-4})$$
$$- \underset{(-3.254)}{0.357} \log(G\_OTHEREXP\_CRO_{-4}/REV\_OTHER\_CRO_{-4})$$

Adjusted R^2: 0.331 LM(2): 3.391

Revenues

The main two sources of general governmental revenues are taxes and social security contributions Most of the tax revenues consist of general taxes on goods and services (mainly value added taxes, VAT). Thus, total government revenues (TOTALREV_CRO) can be set up as

$$TOTALREV\_CRO_t = TOTALTAX\_CRO_t + SOCIALCONT\_CRO_t + REVOTHER\_CRO_t,$$

where the variable REV_OTHER_CRO includes all general government revenues other than taxes or social contributions.

Social security contributions (SOCIALCONT_CRO) are determined by multiplying the average gross wage per employee (GROSS_WAGE_CRO) by the number of employees (EMP_CRO), yielding the total wage bill, which is then multiplied by the average social security contribution rate (SOCIALCONTRATE_CRO):

$$SOCIALCONT\_CRO_t = (SOCIALCONTRATE\_CRO_t \cdot GROSS\_WAGE\_CRO_t \cdot EMP\_CRO_t)/100\ 000$$

The average social security contribution rate is exogenous and available as a policy instrument in model simulations.

Total tax revenues (TOTALTAX_CRO) consist of income taxes paid by persons (INCTAXPERS_CRO) and by companies (INCTAXCORP_CRO), taxes on goods and services, of which value added taxes (TAX_VAT_CRO) are the most important ones, and other tax revenues (TAX_OTHER_CRO):

$$TOTALTAX\_CRO_t = INCTAXPERS\_CRO_t + INCTAXCORP\_CRO_t + TAX\_VAT\_CRO_t + TAXOTHER\_CRO_t.$$

Personal income tax revenues are computed as

$$INCTAXPERS\_CRO_t = (INCTAXRATE\_CRO_t \cdot GROSS\_WAGE\_CRO_t \cdot EMP\_CRO_t)/100000$$

i.e. the average personal income tax rate (INCTAXRATE_CRO) is multiplied by the total wage bill. The personal income tax rate is treated as a policy instrument.

Corporate income taxes (INCTAXCORP_CRO) are determined by multiplying an average corporate income tax rate (INCTAXRATE_CRO), which is defined as corporate income taxes as a percentage of nominal GDP and treated as another fiscal policy instrument, by GDP:

$$INCTAXCORP\_CRO_t = NCTAXRATECORP\_CRO_t \cdot GDPN\_CRO_t/100$$

Revenues from general taxes on goods and services, represented by the variable TAX_VAT_CRO, consist essentially of value added tax revenue and excises, whereby 66 to 75 percent of the revenues are generated by value added taxes. Croatia applies a standard VAT rate of 23 percent, albeit with a number of exceptions. A zero percent VAT rate is applied to some goods and services such as bread, milk, books, educational material and medical products. Moreover, in July 2005, a uniform VAT rate of 10 percent was introduced for the tourism sector. Furthermore, although the variable is called TAX_VAT_CRO, it comprises excises in addition to value added taxes. Hence, the average "VAT rate" in the model, which is determined by dividing the revenues from taxes on goods and services by nominal private consumption, is higher than the official VAT rate. In the model, taxes on goods and services are then calculated by multiplying the average "VAT rate" (VATRATE_CRO) by nominal private consumption (CONSUM_CRO):

$$TAX\_VAT\_CRO_t = (VATRATE\_CRO_t \cdot CONSUM\_CRO_t)/100$$

The remaining tax revenues (TAX_OTHER_CRO) as well as all other government revenues (REV_OTHER_CRO) are determined in behavioural equations with nominal GDP as the explanatory variable, accounting for the fact that tax and non-tax revenues behave pro-cyclically.

$$TAX\_OTHEREXP\_CRO - TAX\_OTHEREXP\_CRO_{-4} = \underset{(-2.984)}{-132.644} + \underset{(2.494)}{344.979}\, DUM2009q3$$
$$+ \underset{(7.970)}{0.969}\,(TAX\_OTHER\_CRO_{-1} - TAX\_OTHER\_CRO_{-5})$$
$$+ \underset{(2.990)}{0.026}\,(GDP\_CRO - GDP\_CRO_{-4}) - \underset{(-2.651)}{362.160}\, DUM2003q3 + \underset{(3.249)}{449.979}\, DUM2004q2$$

Adjusted R^2: 0.646 LM(2): 2.420

$$\log(REV\_OTHEREXP\_CRO/REV\_OTHEREXP\_CRO_{-4}) = \underset{(-3.118)}{-11.085} + \underset{(3.952)}{2.074}\, DUM2001q4$$
$$- \underset{(-8.349)}{0.865}\,\log(REV\_OTHER\_CRO_{-1}) + \underset{(4.662)}{1.528}\,\log(GDP\_CRO_{-4}) + \underset{(3.326)}{1.742}\, DUM2003q4$$

Adjusted R^2: 0.715 LM(2): 1.012

By definition, the budget balance is calculated as the difference between government revenues and expenditures:

$$BUD\_BALANCE\_CRO_t = TOTALREV\_CRO_t - TOTALEXP\_CRO_t.$$

From this, the budget balance ratio, i.e. the budget balance in relation to nominal GDP, can be derived.

Theoretically, the change in the debt level should be identical to the fiscal balance, i.e. a budget surplus should result in an equivalent reduction in the level of public debt. In the reality of economic accounting, however, certain operations only affect either the budget balance or the debt level. Therefore, the model includes an exogenous variable representing the change in the level of public debt, denoted DELTA_DEBT_CRO. The total level of Croatian debt outstanding is then computed as:

$$DEBT\_CRO_t = DEBT\_CRO_{t-1} - BUD\_BALANCE\_CRO_t + DELTA\_DEBT\_CRO_t.$$

The debt ratio is then computed as the current debt level over nominal GDP. This is approximated in the following way:

$$DEBTRATIO\_CRO_t = 100 \cdot DEBT\_CRO_t/(GDP\_CRO_t + GDP\_CRO_{t-1} + GDP\_CRO_{t-2} + GDP\_CRO_{t-3})$$

Note that this equation is not based on GDP for a calendar year, but on the sum of economic activity of four consecutive quarters, i.e. $GDP\_CRO_t + GDP\_CRO_{t-1} + GDP\_CRO_{t-2} + GDP\_CRO_{t-3}$. This is due to the fact that the model – like the sub-models for the other former Yugoslav republics in the model – is quarterly. Hence, the above formula gives the debt ratio for each quarter, but only the ratio for the fourth quarter of each year is identical to the annual value of the debt-to-GDP ratio.

Identities

bud_balance_cro = totalrev_cro – totalexp_cro

bud_ratio_cor = (bud_balance_cro/gdp_cro)*100

capitalstock_cro = capitalstock_cro $_{-1}$ * (1-(1.47/ 100)) + ifix_cro

debt_cro = debt_cro$_{-1}$ – bud_balance_cro + delta_debt_cro

debt_ratio_cro = (debt_cro / (gdp_cro + gdp_cro $_{-1}$ + gdp_cro $_{-2}$ + gdp_cro $_{-3}$)) * 100

demand_cro = consumr_cro + gr_cro + exr_cro + investr_cro

r_cro = (g_cro / p_g_cro) * 100

gdpr_cro = investr_cro+consumr_cro+gr_cro+exr_cro–imr_cro

gdp_cro = (gdpr_cro * p_gdp_cro) / 100

gross_wager_cro = (gross_wage_cro/cpi_cro)*100

inctaxcorp_cro = (inctaxratecorp_cro*gdp_cro)/100

inctaxpers_cro = (inctaxrate_cro*gross_wage_cro*emp_cro)/100000

inctax_cro = inctaxpers_cro + inctaxcorp_cro

INFL_CRO = (CPI_CRO / CPI_CRO$_{-4}$ - 1) * 100

INVESTR_CRO = IFIXR_CRO + INVENTR_CRO

IR_LR_CRO = I_LR_CRO - INFL_CRO

NET_WAGE_CRO = GROSS_WAGE_CRO-TAXWEDGE_CRO

NET_WAGER_CRO = (NET_WAGE_CRO / CPI_CRO) * 100

OILHRK = OIL / EURUSD * HRKEUR

PROD_CRO = GDPR_CRO / EMP_CRO * 100

SOCIALCONT_CRO = (SOCCONTRATE_CRO*GROSS_WAGE_CRO*EMP_CRO)/100000

TAXWEDGE_CRO =
(AV_TAXRATE_CRO*GROSS_WAGE_CRO)/ 100

TOTALEXP_CRO = G_CONS_CRO + G_SUBSIDIES_CRO +
G_TRANSFER_CRO+ G_OTHEREXP_CRO+INTEREST_CRO

TOTALREV_CRO = TAX_VAT_CRO + INCTAX_CRO +
SOCIALCONT_CRO+TAX_OTHER_CRO+REV_OTHER_CRO

TRENDEMP_CRO = LFORCE_CRO * (1 - (NAIRU_CRO / 100))

ULC_CRO = GROSS_WAGE_CRO / PROD_CRO

UN_CRO = LFORCE_CRO - EMP_CRO

UR_CRO = UN_CRO / LFORCE_CRO * 100

UTIL_CRO = (GDPR_CRO / YPOT_CRO) * 100

YD_CRO = GDP_CRO + G_TRANSFER_CRO
+ G_SUBSIDIES_CRO - INCTAX_CRO
- SOCIALCONT_CRO - TAX_OTHER_CRO

YDR_CRO = (YD_CRO / CPI_CRO) * 100

log(YPOT_CRO) = 0.67 * log(TRENDEMP_CRO)
+ 0.33 * log(CAPITALSTOCK_CRO) + log(TRENDTFP_CRO)

exr_cro = exr_crobih + exr_crosrb
+ exr_croslo + exr_crorow

imr_cro = exr_bihcro/1.95583*hrkeur
+ exr_srbcro/dineur*hrkeur
+ exr_slocro/1.95583*hrkeur + imr_crorow

inventr_CRO=moving avarage(INVENTR_CRO_CRO, 8)

lforce_cro = partrate_cro * pop_cro

interest_cro = debt_cro$_{-1}$ * i_debt_cro / 100

consum_cro = consumr_cro * p_consum_cro / 100

tax_vat_cro = (consum_cro * vatrate_cro / 100)

MODEL EVALUATION

To evaluate the constituent country models in the multi-country model, a dynamic ex post simulation over the period 2005q1 to 2010q4 was performed. Some time series, in particular for Bosnia and Herzegovina, only start in 2005, and the dataset used for the estimations ends in 2010 for both Bosnia and Herzegovina and Serbia. Although the model relies on quarterly data, the evaluation is based on annual data. This is more appropriate since many quarterly series were derived from their annual aggregates or had to be calculated with the aid of related indicators. The evaluation of the ability of the model to replicate the development of the endogenous variables is based on the following three statistical measures:

Mean absolute percent error (MAPE). The MAPE is calculated according to the following formula:

$$\text{MAPE} = \frac{1}{n}\sum_{t=1}^{n}\left|\frac{Forecast_t - Actual_t}{Actual_t}\right| * 100$$

The difference between the actual and the forecast values is divided by the actual values. The absolute value of this calculation is summed for every forecast point in time and divided by the number of forecasted realisations *n*. This makes it a percentage error so that the error of forecasted series that differ in levels can be compared.

Root mean squared error (RMSE), calculated as illustrated below:

$$\text{RMSE} = \sqrt{\frac{1}{n}\sum_{t=1}^{n}(Forecast_t - Actual_t)^2}$$

The RMSE is the square root of the squared deviation of the forecasted data realisations from the observed ones. It indicates the absolute fit of the model to the data, i.e. how close the observed data points are to the values predicted by the model. The RMSE is an absolute measure. It can be interpreted as the standard deviation of the unexplained variance. It has the useful property of being measured in the same unit as the dependent variable. The RMSE is a good measure of how accurately the model predicts the endogenous variables. It is the most important criterion for fit if the main purpose of the model is to supply a forecast.

Theil's inequality coefficient U2. Theil's inequality coefficient U2 compares the model forecast with a naïve no-change forecast. Hence the benchmark for measuring the accuracy of the forecast is the value observed in the previous period. The U2 statistic takes the value of 1 under the naïve forecasting method. Values less than 1 indicate better forecasting accuracy than the naïve forecasts while values larger than 1 indicate the opposite. Theil's inequality coefficient is calculated according to the following formula:

$$THEIL = \sqrt{\frac{\sum_{t=1}^{n}\left(\frac{Forecast_t - Actual_t}{Actual_t}\right)^2}{\sum_{t=1}^{n}\left(\frac{Actual_t - Actual_{t-1}}{Actual_{t-1}}\right)^2}}$$

For important endogenous variables, the values of the forecast accuracy measures are summarised in the following tables. In each table, the values of the statistical measures are shown for each of the four countries in the model. The last column depicts the arithmetic average over the four sub-models. Table 1 depicts the mean absolute percent error (MAPE). In those cases where the variable is measured in percent (i.e. the GDP growth rate, the inflation rate, the unemployment rate and the budget balance to GDP ratio), the mean absolute error (MAE) is taken instead of the mean absolute *percent* error. Table 2 shows the root mean squared error, while Theil's inequality coefficient is displayed in Table 3.

Table 1: Mean absolute percent error (MAPE)

Variable	*Bosnia*	*Croatia*	*Serbia*	*Slovenia*	*Average*
Real GDP growth rate	5.08	3.17	2.94	2.69	3.47
Real GDP	9.37	10.53	5.11	3.89	7.22
Private consumption	5.82	6.25	5.17	2.90	5.03
Public consumption	8.57	1.95	7.56	1.56	4.91
Fixed investment	12.88	20.03	12.74	11.49	14.28
Exports	14.50	12.13	12.85	5.63	11.28
Imports	11.40	13.61	13.06	4.51	10.65
Nominal GDP	8.67	14.57	11.21	3.04	9.37
Inflation rate	0.90	2.85	4.96	1.24	2.49
Employment	1.99	2.35	1.17	3.66	2.29
Unemployment	8.70	15.16	8.67	13.26	11.45
Unemployment rate	1.85	1.83	1.77	1.54	1.75
Budget balance ratio	2.17	3.88	2.41	1.41	2.47

Source: author's own calculations.

Table 2: Root mean squared error (RMSE)

Variable	Bosnia	Croatia	Serbia	Slovenia	Average
Real GDP growth rate	5.98	3.93	3.80	3.20	4.23
Real GDP	727	6472	20286	366	6963
Private consumption	367	2743	19561	140	5703
Public consumption	117	319	5819	30.51	1571
Fixed investment	2267	3173	10853	265	3629
Exports	401	3134	17922	33	5447
Imports	488	4871	39222	318.	11225
Nominal GDP	862	12098	96451	333	27437
Inflation rate	1.06	3.56	5.70	1.41	2.93
Employment	20551	45.1	29381	32144	20530
Unemployment	27031	40.8	80059	14574	30426
Unemployment rate	2.03	2.31	2.04	1.89	2.07
Budget balance ratio	3.42	5.28	2.90	1.81	3.35

Source: author's own calculation

Table 3: Theil's inequality coefficient

Variable	Bosnia	Croatia	Serbia	Slovenia	Average
Real GDP growth	0.37	0.45	0.37	0.36	0.39
Real GDP	0.07	0.06	0.03	0.02	0.04
Private consumption	0.04	0.04	0.04	0.02	0.03
Public consumption	0.05	0.01	0.05	0.01	0.03
Fixed investment	0.09	0.11	0.08	0.07	0.09
Exports	0.11	0.06	0.08	0.03	0.07
Imports	0.08	0.08	0.11	0.03	0.07
Nominal GDP	0.07	0.08	0.07	0.02	0.06
Inflation rate	0.12	0.52	0.22	0.21	0.27
Employment	0.01	0.01	0.01	0.02	0.01
Unemployment	0.04	0.10	0.05	0.08	0.07
Unemployment rate	0.04	0.09	0.03	0.00	0.04
Budget balance ratio	0.30	0.50	0.49	0.22	0.38

Source: author's own calculations.

Taking all three goodness-of-fit measures into account, the model for Slovenia generally performs best, while the sub-model for Serbia delivers the worst fit for the endogenous variables. In terms of the mean absolute percent error (MAPE), the models for Croatia and for Bosnia and Herzegovina perform about equally well. Regarding the root mean squared error (RMSE), out of the three other sub-models, excluding Slovenia, the model for Bosnia and Herzegovina performs best, closely followed by the model for Croatia, while the Serbian one is clearly worst. Finally, in terms of Theil's inequality coefficient, the best-performing sub-model for Slovenia is followed by Bosnia and Herzegovina, Serbia and finally Croatia. In all cases, i.e. for all sub-models and for all the variables considered here, Theil's inequality coefficient is below 1, indicating that the structural models unambiguously beat the naïve no-change forecast. All sub-models and the entire multi-country model can therefore be regarded as suitable for forecasting purposes.

Within each country sub-model, the variables which can be tracked best are employment, unemployment, the budget balance-to-GDP ratio and, with the exception of Serbia, inflation. Among the GDP demand components, gross fixed capital formation is tracked worse. This can be explained by the fact that fixed capital formation is the demand component with the largest volatility. On the other hand, exports and imports can be tracked quite well. This is remarkable insofar as foreign trade contains the bilateral export and import relations between the four former Yugoslavian countries, together with foreign trade with the rest of the world. Bilateral exports between each pair of countries depend on the relevant real exchange rate and on final demand in the importing country. Hence, obviously, real demand in each country as well as the components of the real exchange rates (i.e. the nominal exchange rates and the price ratio between each pair of countries) can be reproduced reasonably well by the model(s).

In addition to the previously described evaluation of the structural macro model itself, a sound model evaluation should also include a comparison of the structural model with alternative approaches. Such alternative models are pure time series models. In the following, for three important macroeconomic variables (GDP growth, inflation, unemployment), the forecasting accuracy of the structural multi-country model is compared to single-equation time series models for each variables (autoregressive models – AR) and a multi-equation model of all three variables (a vector-autoregressive model – VAR). The evaluation is again based on the measures Mean Absolute Error (MAE), Root Mean Squared Error (RMSE) and Theil's inequality coefficient. The results, which have been taken from Weyerstrass (2015), are summarised in Table 4, Table **5**, and Table 6.

Table 4: Mean absolute error (MAE)

		Macromodel	ARMA	VAR
Slovenia	GDP growth	2.69	4.45	3.94
	Unemployment rate	1.54	1.29	1.42
	Inflation	1.24	1.24	1.60
Serbia	GDP growth	2.94	2.72	3.07
	Unemployment rate	1.77	2.60	1.78
	Inflation	4.96	3.13	7.90
Croatia	GDP growth	3.17	2.71	3.97
	Unemployment rate	1.83	3.32	1.24
	Inflation	2.85	1.40	1.37
Bosnia-Herz.	GDP growth	5.08	4.26	3.87
	Unemployment rate	1.59	1.52	1.58
	Inflation	0.90	2.15	2.14

Source: Weyerstrass (2015).

Table 5: Root mean squared error (RMSE)

		Macromodel	ARMA	VAR
Slovenia	GDP growth	3.20	5.35	5.11
	Unemployment rate	1.89	1.77	1.92
	Inflation	1.41	1.67	1.84
Serbia	GDP growth	3.80	3.16	3.86
	Unemployment rate	2.04	3.24	2.05
	Inflation	5.70	3.65	10.72
Croatia	GDP growth	3.93	3.26	5.08
	Unemployment rate	2.31	3.70	1.58
	Inflation	3.56	1.75	1.89
Bosnia-Herz.	GDP growth	5.98	4.98	4.52
	Unemployment rate	1.77	1.83	1.74
	Inflation	1.06	2.70	2.79

Source: Weyerstrass (2015).

Table 6: Theil's inequality coefficient

		Macromodel	ARMA	VAR
Slovenia	GDP growth	0.357	0.758	0.632
	Unemployment rate	0.090	0.084	0.091
	Inflation	0.214	0.270	0.262
Serbia	GDP growth	0.371	0.363	0.382
	Unemployment rate	0.034	0.053	0.034
	Inflation	0.223	0.168	0.359
Croatia	GDP growth	0.449	0.505	0.658
	Unemployment rate	0.104	0.154	0.076
	Inflation	0.516	0.258	0.284
Bosnia-Herz.	GDP growth	0.372	0.451	0.371
	Unemployment rate	0.021	0.021	0.020
	Inflation	0.121	0.339	0.382

Source: Weyerstrass (2015).

For Bosnia and Herzegovina, the structural macromodel deliveers the best inflation forecast, while the VAR model is better regarding GDP growth and the unemployment rate. For Croatia, the VAR model gives the best forecasts of the unemployment rate. For GDP growth and inflation, the VAR model is better. For Slovenia, the structural macroeconometric model has the best fit in terms of all three statistical tests for GDP growth and inflation, while the ARMA model is best for the unemployment rate. For Serbia, the opposite is true, i.e. the ARMA model gives the best forecasts of GDP growth and inflation, while the structural model is best regarding the unemployment rate. Overall, only for Slovenia, i.e. the country with the longest available time series, the structural model gives the best forecasts, while for the other countries in the model the time series models give better ex post forecasts for the evaluation period.

Overall, the ability of the multi-country model and the sub-models to reproduce the endogenous variables can be regarded as satisfactory. Hence, the model seems suitable for forecasting and simulation exercises. The choice of structural macroeconometric models as the suitable model type for the multi-country model for the former Yugoslavia instead of theoretically more sophisticated models like Dynamic Stochastic General Equilibrium (DSGE) models thus seems well justified. Estimated macroeconometric models are almost exclusively based on estimated parameters and thus avoid any problems associated with the calibration of deep structural parameters like consumer preferences. Previous studies have documented that more rigorous aggregate demand / aggregate supply models like the multi-country model for the former Yugoslavia described in this book are superior to sophisticated DSGE models (see, e.g., Crespo Cuaresma et al. 2009, Colander et al. 2008, Rubaszek and Skrzypczynski 2008, Wang 2008).

Furthermore, when comparing the forecasting accuracy of different model types, it has to be kept in mind that structural models have their virtues which cannot be captured by analysing the forecasting performance alone. Structural models enable the analysis of macroeconomic consequences of policy measures as well as exogenous shocks. When using VAR and ARMA models, this is not so straightforward, since these time series models do not include explicitly truly exogenous variables or policy instruments. Furthermore, the results of the statistical tests have to be interpreted with caution given the shortness of the time series for the former Yugoslav countries contained in the model. Insofar the results for Slovenia are promising since this is the country with the longest history of reliable time series.

POLICY SIMULATIONS

The multi-country model for four successor states of the former Yugoslavia has been developed with the purpose of serving as a tool for generating macroeconomic forecasts and, in particular, for the analysis of economic policies. Hence, in this chapter some policy experiments are described:

Firstly, it is evaluated how an isolated fiscal policy implemented in only one of the four countries differs from coordinated action in all four countries.

Secondly, the budgetary effects of the demographic development in Slovenia are explored along with different strategies of coping with these effects.

Thirdly, different budget consolidation strategies for Slovenia are investigated, including a derivation of optimal fiscal policies in the aftermath of the severe economic crisis.

Fourthly, the results of simulations undertaken with the sub-models for Serbia and Slovenia regarding the macroeconomic effects of different scenarios of future developments in the euro area are presented.

Finally, trade and general macroeconomic effects of Croatia's EU accession on the other countries in the region are investigated.

ISOLATED VERSUS COORDINATED FISCAL POLICIES

International coordination of macroeconomic policies has attracted much attention in recent years. Discussions have included, in particular, whether economic performance can be improved by coordination. Although this is still a controversial issue, many economists have argued that coordination positively affects economic performance. Tanzi (2008) analyses the requirements for successful fiscal coordination, concluding that the best fiscal policies each country can pursue are those aimed at putting its own house in order. Such policies are also most beneficial in an international policy coordination context.

Not least due to the impacts of the severe economic crisis, many countries in Europe and beyond are confronted with high budget deficits and debt levels. In the EU, the Stability and Growth Pact (SGP) prescribes that the budget deficit shall not exceed 3 percent in relation to GDP, and public debt should remain below 60 percent of GDP. Since many countries are currently breaking at least one of these criteria, they have to pursue restrictive fiscal policies. On the other hand, Keynesian macroeconomic theory predicts that reducing government expenditures or raising taxes in an economy without full employment will increase unemployment and negatively affect economic growth; hence there may be undesirable spillovers of budgetary consolidation policies. Applying a macroeconomic multi-country model with sub-models for all important countries in the world economy in general and in the EU in particular, Weyerstrass et al. (2006) analyse international spillovers resulting from reducing the public deficit by (a) decreasing public consumption and (b) increasing lump-sum taxes. This study finds that economic policy coordination in the euro area would create considerable gains. The simulations in Weyerstrass et al. (2006) were performed with the MSG3 model, the most recent version of the McKibbin-Sachs Global Model. This is a dynamic, intertemporal, general-equilibrium model of a multi-region world economy. The MSG3 model is a two-sector version of the twelve-sector G-Cubed multi-country by McKibbin and Wilcoxen (1998). In many ways the aggregation results in a model similar to the McKibbin and Sachs' (1991) MSG2 model except that there is substantial estimation of key parameters in the MSG3 model.

Taking empirical evidence on international spillovers of national fiscal policies as well as the high interdependencies and the small size of the open economies of the former Yugoslavia into account, this section analyses differences between fiscal policy measures undertaken in each of the considered countries separately as opposed to coordinated action. In a nutshell, this culminates in the comparison of fiscal policy multipliers from isolated and joint policy measures. In particular, a reduction in public consumption and a reduction in transfers to private households are considered.

For the calculation of government spending multipliers, the equations determining public consumption endogenously in the models are switched off, rendering public consumption exogenous. Then, a baseline simulation is performed over the period 2005 to 2010. As this is an ex post simulation, the actual realisations of public consumption are used in this baseline run. Then, five alternative simulations are performed. In each of the first four simulations, in only one country public consumption is permanently reduced (as compared to the baseline) by one million units of the respective national currency per annum. In the fifth simulation, public consumption in all country-models is permanently reduced by one million units of the relevant national currencies.

For the simulations with transfer payments as the policy instrument, the annual nominal personal disposable income of private households is permanently reduced (as compared to the baseline) by one million units of each country's national currency. In these simulations, public consumption is determined endogenously by the relevant behavioural model equations, as in the baseline. Similarly to the case of public consumption, a baseline run is compared to scenarios in which disposable income is reduced, first separately in each country model, and finally in all sub-models simultaneously.

Figure 1 shows the government spending multipliers, while the transfer multipliers are illustrated in Figure 2. These multipliers are the outcome of the isolated fiscal policy measures, i.e. when public consumption or transfer payments, are reduced in one country at a time only. Positive numbers are shown in the figures, i.e. if a reduction in a fiscal policy instrument results in a decrease of GDP, this is shown as a positive multiplier. In other words, if the fiscal policy instrument and GDP change in the same direction, the multiplier will be positive.

Figure 1: Government consumption multipliers – isolated policy measures

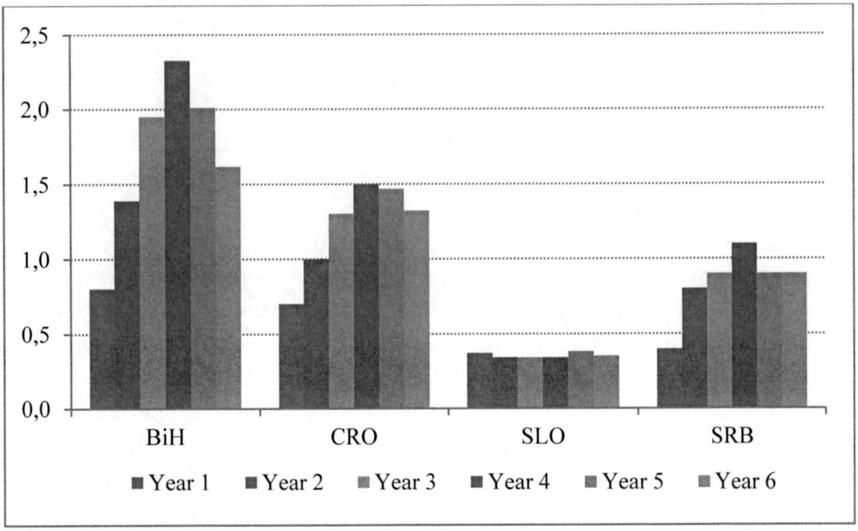

BiH: Bosnia and Herzegovina; CRO: Croatia; SLO: Slovenia; SRB: Serbia.

Source: author's own calculations

Figure 2: Transfer multipliers – isolated policy measures

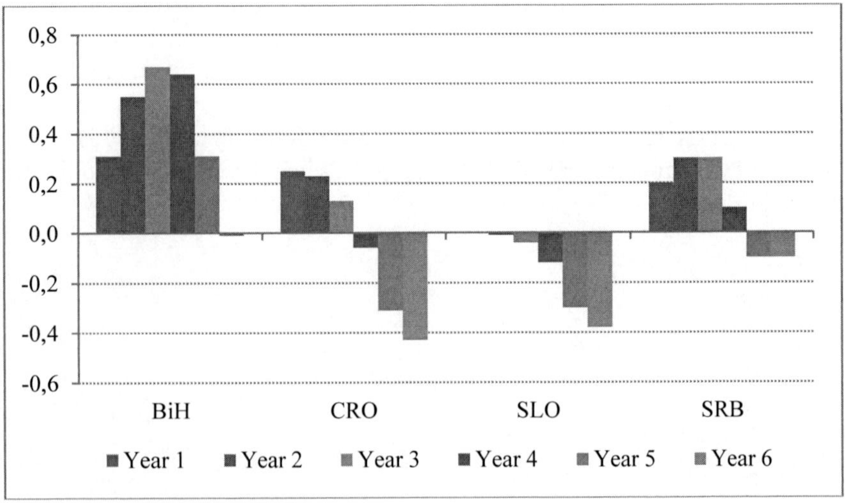

BiH: Bosnia and Herzegovina; CRO: Croatia; SLO: Slovenia; SRB: Serbia.

Source: author's own calculations

Fiscal policy multipliers turn out to be largest for Bosnia and Herzegovina. In this country, the maximum spending multiplier reaches the value of 2.3. At the other end of the spectrum, in Slovenia, the government consumption multiplier is clearly below 1 (and even below 0.5), and in Serbia it exceeds 1 only in one year. Among the countries considered here, Slovenia has already transformed its economic and institutional structures to the largest extent to resemble the traditional or "core" EU Member States. Hence, in this country, fiscal policy is able to influence the real economy as little as has been commonly found for industrialised countries, at least in the absence of a severe economic crisis. According to the OECD (2009), government spending multipliers are, on average, between 1.1 and 1.3, while income tax multipliers reach 0.5 to 0.8. On the other hand, Bosnia and Herzegovina lags behind the most in achieving economic and institutional reforms, and in addition the country is confronted with the highest unemployment rate in the countries contained in the multi-country model. According to the 2013 progress report by the European Commission, the reform process has stalled in Bosnia and Herzegovina, while the other countries in the region are making progress (European Commission 2013a). This might be an explanation for the comparatively high effectiveness of demand-side fiscal policy measures in this country.

In the following, the extent of fiscal policy spillovers is estimated. To this end, the impact of isolated fiscal policy measures in each of the four countries of the multi-country model is compared to the impacts of joint fiscal policy measures. Figure 3 shows the percentage deviation of real GDP from the baseline of no discretionary government consumption reductions compared to the effects of public consumption reductions undertaken in all countries simultaneously. As before, in each country nominal public consumption is decreased by 1 million units of the national currency per year. To account for the different magnitudes of the fiscal policy impulses due to the different currencies, the effects are evaluated with respect to percentage changes rather than absolute deviations in real GDP. Similarly, the effects of reductions in transfers on real GDP are displayed in Figure 4.

In both figures, for each country the fiscal policy impacts on real GDP that result from isolated actions are denoted by the country acronym alone, while coordinated fiscal policies are denoted by the country acronym plus "all".

Figure 3: Changes in government consumption – isolated versus coordinated policy measures

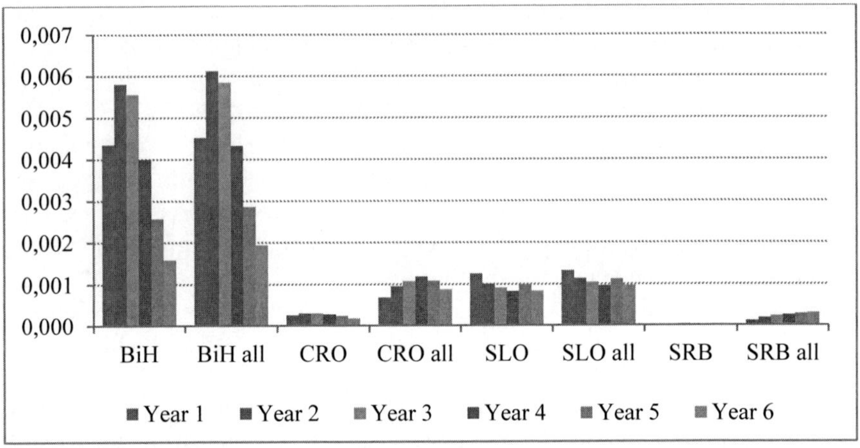

BiH: Bosnia and Herzegovina; CRO: Croatia; SLO: Slovenia; SRB: Serbia. Country acronym without "all": isolated policy, country acronym plus "all": coordinated policy

Source: author's own calculations

Figure 4: Changes in transfers – isolated versus coordinated action

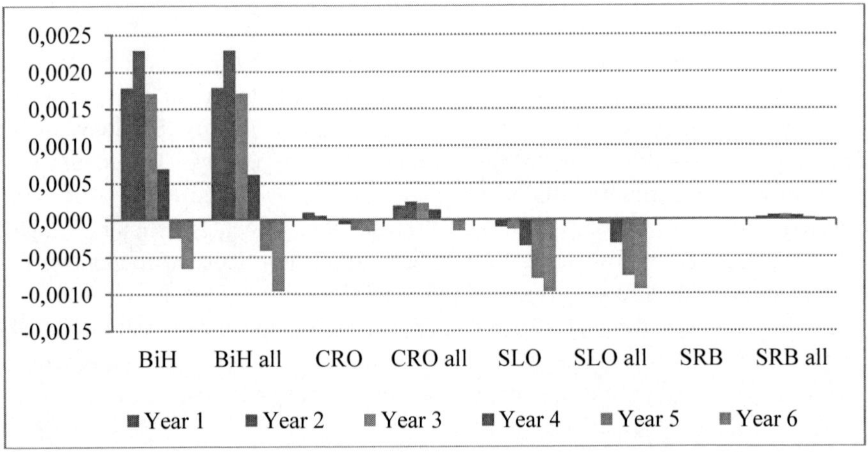

BiH: Bosnia and Herzegovina; CRO: Croatia; SLO: Slovenia; SRB: Serbia. Country acronym without "all": isolated policy, country acronym plus "all": coordinated policy

Source: author's own calculations

Both for public spending and transfers, the effects of coordinated policies are clearly larger than the effects of isolated policy actions. In terms of relative changes in real GDP, fiscal policy is most effective in Bosnia and Herzegovina and least effective in Serbia. The difference between isolated and coordinated policies is smallest for Slovenia and largest for Croatia. Hence, Croatia benefits the most from expansionary policy measures undertaken in its neighbouring countries, but on the other hand suffers the most from restrictive policies enacted abroad.

Transfer multipliers are almost zero for Serbia, no matter whether only Serbia or all four countries adopt changes in transfer payments. For the other countries transfer multipliers (in the sense of effects on real GDP) become negative after a certain period of time. For Bosnia and Herzegovina as well as Croatia, this happens in the fifth year, while for Slovenia this is already the case in the first year. This implies that the cut in transfers simulated here even stimulates those two economies in the medium or even in the short run. The negative effect of transfer cuts on real GDP in Slovenia warrant some explanation. The reader might recall that cuts in transfers have been simulated here. This results in a debt reduction. The model contains a fiscal rule which relates public consumption to changes in the level of debt. Hence, if public consumption is endogenously determined, which is the case in the transfer scenarios considered here, the decline in debt allows higher public consumption, which counteracts the negative demand effect from the reduced transfer payments. In the other countries such effects are either absent or the elasticity of public consumption to changes in the debt level is not large enough.

The analyses presented in this section have clearly shown that there are significant cross-country spillovers from national fiscal policies. This supports current initiatives to foster policy coordination in the European Union within the "European Semester", as laid down in the "Six Pack", the "Two Pack" and the "Treaty on Stability, Coordination and Governance in the Economic and Monetary Union (TSCG)" (for details see European Commission 2013b).

HOW TO COPE WITH POPULATION AGEING IN SLOVENIA

The model for Slovenia has already been used for several policy simulations in the past. In a recent paper (Weyerstrass and Neck 2013), the model was simulated over the period 2012 to 2060 so as to determine the budgetary and macroeconomic consequences of population ageing and to analyse the effects of possible strategies to cope with this phenomenon.

Not only in the aftermath of the severe financial and economic crisis but in many industrialised countries, particularly in Europe, concerns have been raised about the consequences of demographic development for the fiscal stance and economic outlook. The "Great Recession" of 2007 to 2009 resulted in declining GDP and increasing unemployment in nearly all industrialised countries, irrespective of their initial situation. This aggravated the budgetary problems in addition to already high and rising government debt before the crisis. Some countries were hit particularly hard, which was partly due to government failures and structural problems. This is also true for Slovenia, whose economic situation deteriorated very strongly during the last few years.

Slovenia was the only successor state of the former Yugoslavia to enter the European Union in 2004, together with most former socialist countries from Central and Eastern Europe, and Slovenia even joined the euro area as early as 2007. Its economic development was successful in terms of the main macroeconomic indicators before the "Great Recession". However, the impact of the recession was especially deep in Slovenia, with a decline in GDP by almost 8 percent in 2009 and an increase in unemployment to the level of the year before Slovenia joined the euro area (2006). Until now, economic development in Slovenia has been very subdued. In 2012 and 2013, aggregate production decreased by 2.5 percent and 1.1 percent respectively. In its Spring 2014 forecast, the European Commission projected a gradual recovery of GDP growth in 2014 (0.8 percent) and 2015 (1.4 percent) (European Commission 2014).

A substantial part of the problem results from the enormous fiscal deficits and the resulting increase in public debt over the last few years. After having achieved a balanced budget in 2007, Slovenia had a deficit of about 2 percent in relation to GDP in 2008. In the following years, this deficit widened considerably, reaching about 6 percent in relation to GDP in the period 2009 to 2011. After declining to 3.8 percent in 2012, the deficit ratio widened again substantially to almost 14 percent in 2013. For 2014 and 2015, it is expected to decline to 4.3 percent and 3.1 percent respectively (European Commission 2014). As a consequence of this budgetary development, the debt-to-GDP ratio increased to 47 percent in 2011, more than twice the figure of 2008. In the following years, the debt ratio continued its sharply rising trend to 54.4 percent in 2012 and even to almost 72 percent in 2013. A large part of this increase was caused by capital which the government had to inject into the banking system as some banks faced severe capital losses due to the bursting of a housing bubble which had contributed to the high economic growth prior to 2009. Such bank recapitalisations were also mainly responsible for the very high budget deficit in 2013. According to the Spring 2014 forecast of the European Commission, the debt ratio will rise further in the coming years, reaching 81 percent in 2015 (European Commission 2014).

The stock of government debt which Slovenia had already accumulated prior to the economic and financial crisis indicates long-run problems as causes in addition to the short-run effects of the "Great Recession". One of these problems is the pension issue, which is prominent on the government's agenda but far from a solution. In a recent paper (Weyerstrass and Neck 2013), potential effects of the demographic development projected for Slovenia on the country's public finances and on the labour market and general macroeconomic development were analysed, with special emphasis on the pension problem. There, a long-run projection of the age composition of the Slovenian population was used as the basis of several alternative policy scenarios.

In the coming decades, the demographic development will put considerable pressure on public finances in Slovenia, as in most European countries. For the simulations documented in this section, the population projection EUROPOP2010 by Eurostat was used.[17] The EUROPOP2010 population projections are based on assumptions of fertility, mortality and migration. They assume convergence of socio-economic and cultural factors between EU countries over time. Therefore, the realisations of the demographic components on which the projections are based are assumed to be the same in all countries in the convergence year (2150). This implies that in 2150 no net migration will take place in the countries considered, and that the fertility rate as well as life expectancy at birth will be equalised by that year. According to these projections, the population of Slovenia will continue to grow quite quickly to approximately 2.155 million inhabitants in 2025. Afterwards the population is projected to decline slowly. The projected demographic development in Slovenia will lead to a marked increase in the proportion of people aged 65 and above. This will result in a sharp rise in the dependency

[17] Details on the EUROPOP2010 projections in general can be found on the EU website: http://epp.eurostat.ec.europa.eu/statistics_explained/index.php/Population_projections. Details for Slovenia are available from the website of the Slovenian Statistical office: http://www.stat.si/eng/novica_prikazi.aspx?id=3989.

ratio, i.e. the relation between people of working age and those in retirement. The share of people aged 65 years and above is projected to almost double to 31.5 percent between 2011 and 2060. Due to a low fertility rate, the ratio between people of retirement age (65 and older) and those of working age (15 to 64 years) is projected to rise dramatically from slightly below 24 percent in 2011 to almost 58 percent in 2060.

For the 2012 update of the Slovenian Stability Programme, the consequences of this projected demographic development for public finances were assessed (Slovenian Ministry of Finance 2012). According to these projections, age-related public expenditures will increase from about one quarter to more than one third of GDP. This is mainly caused by the increase in pensions. As a consequence, the budget balance will deteriorate dramatically. The high budget deficit will push up public debt. As a result, interest payments will rise sharply, contributing to a further increase in the budget deficit. According to these projections by the Slovenian government, in 2060 the primary budget deficit (i.e. the budget deficit excluding interest payments) will amount to 13.4 percent in relation to nominal GDP. Due to the high public debt, which is projected to reach nearly 550 percent in relation to GDP, interest expenditures will account for almost one quarter of GDP. Hence, by 2060 the overall budget deficit-to-GDP ratio would increase to as much as 36.5 percent.

This sharp deterioration in public finances is caused by two factors. First, the rising number of the elderly pushes pension payments up. At the same time, the size of the working-age population decreases, hence funds flowing into the pension system which are financed by employees' and employers' contributions and which are thereby linked to the number of employed people declines unless contribution rates are raised. Higher contributions reduce the purchasing power of employees and raise production costs for companies. Furthermore the production potential is restricted by a declining labour force. This can only partly be compensated for by increasing capital intensity and technical progress.

The projections in the Slovenian Stability Programme clearly show that Slovenian public finances are far from being sustainable in the long run if no corrective measures are implemented. Hence adaptations of the pension system to the ageing of the population are of utmost importance. At present, the statutory retirement age is 63 years for men and 61 for women. The minimum insurance period required for retirement at these ages is 20 years. Early retirement is possible at the age of 58 with 40 years of insurance for men and 38 years of insurance for women. In the past, annual pension increases were related to the rise in nominal wages. Since the pension reform introduced in 1999, in February of each year pensions are increased by the growth rate of nominal wages in the previous year minus 0.6 percentage points. Currently, negative accrual rates for early retirement are rather small and do not exceed 3.6 percent per year. Similarly, additional accrual rates for postponing retirement are also rather low. They are digressive and do not exceed 3.6 percent per year either. The 1999 pension reform has resulted in a stabilisation of the effective retirement age as well as pension expenditures in relation to GDP. In 2010, the effective retirement age was 61 years and 10 months for men and 58 years and 5 months for women. The average old-age pension amounted to about 65 percent of the average net wage, and pension expenditures made up 11 percent of GDP (Stanovnik et al. 2012).

These considerations show the need for corrective measures and an assessment of their budgetary and macroeconomic consequences. The model for Slovenia was applied to run the following policy scenarios:

- Baseline scenario: first, a baseline run with the assumption of no policy change was run over the period 2012 to 2060. In this baseline, the policy instruments were projected on the basis of their actual 2011 values, as were all other exogenous variables. As policy instruments relevant for the pension system, the average retirement rate (not that this is a direct instrument, but rather the result of legislative initiatives), the average pension replacement rate and the average contribution rate to the pension system were considered.
- "Higher pension age" scenario: Increase in pension age: in this scenario, the average pension age was raised from the actual level of about 60 years in 2011 to 63 years from 2015 onwards and 65 years from 2018. The scenario was further divided into two sub-scenarios: in the first sub-scenario it was assumed that 75 percent of all people who were retired in the baseline scenario and were now not eligible for retirement were employed. In contrast, for the second sub-scenario it was assumed that the Slovenian labour market was only capable of absorbing 25 percent of the additional labour force. Hence, the majority of those older people who had to remain in the labour force for another three to five years were now assumed to be unemployed. Although in Slovenia older employees are protected by law from being dismissed, it is reasonable to assume that not all older people would be able to find an adequate job. Even though the demographic development will probably cause skills shortages in certain sectors and for certain

qualifications, it is sensible to assume that a skills mismatch between labour demand and supply will remain, in particular with regard to older people.

- Scenario with reduced gross pension replacement rate: here the average pension replacement rate, i.e. the average pension as a percent of the gross wage, was reduced by 5 percentage points from 2012 onwards. In 2011, the average pension replacement rate amounted to about 45 percent.
- Scenario with increased social security contribution rate: in this scenario, from 2012 onwards the average social security contribution rate (including both employers' and employees' contributions) was increased by 1 percentage point to about 22 percent of the average gross wage.

The simulation results show that lowering the pension replacement rate is the most effective policy measure for limiting the increase in the budget deficit and, hence, public debt, without having strong negative effects on the labour market (see Table 7).

Table 7: Budgetary and macroeconomic indicators in the different scenarios

	2010	**2020**	**2030**	**2040**	**2050**	**2060**
		Baseline				
Pensions (% of GDP)	11.2	14.8	16.5	17.9	18.3	17.9
Primary budget balance (% of GDP)	-4.0	-3.3	-5.4	-6.0	-5.1	-2.3
Overall budget balance (% of GDP)	-5.3	-6.8	-11.9	-16.5	-20.4	-22.7
Government debt (% of GDP)	38.6	71.2	131.0	210.3	302.2	399.5
Unemployment rate	11.9	10.8	9.2	7.5	5.9	5.2

Table 7 (continued)

Higher pension age, 75 percent find employment						
Pensions (% of GDP)	11.2	13.4	15.2	16.4	17.0	16.8
Primary budget balance (% of GDP)	-4.0	-1.7	-3.7	-4.2	-3.5	-1.1
Overall budget balance (% of GDP)	-5.3	-4.8	-8.9	-12.2	-15.0	-16.1
Government debt (% of GDP)	38.6	62.7	102.7	160.0	226.3	293.8
Unemployment rate	11.9	12.9	11.3	10.1	8.4	7.3
Higher pension age, 25 percent find employment						
Pensions (% of GDP)	11.2	13.1	14.8	16.0	16.6	16.5
Primary budget balance (% of GDP)	-4.0	-3.3	-5.1	-5.7	-4.8	-2.1
Overall budget balance (% of GDP)	-5.3	-6.9	-11.5	-16.0	-19.6	-21.7
Government debt (% of GDP)	38.6	72.9	129.1	205.2	292.5	383.3
Unemployment rate	11.9	17.5	16.0	15.4	13.3	11.4
Lower gross replacement rate						
Pensions (% of GDP)	11.2	13.2	14.8	16.0	16.4	16.0
Primary budget balance (% of GDP)	-4.0	-1.8	-3.8	-4.3	-3.3	-0.6
Overall budget balance (% of GDP)	-5.3	-4.7	-8.8	-12.1	-14.6	-15.2
Government debt (% of GDP)	38.6	57.9	99.5	156.9	222.1	285.1
Unemployment rate	11.9	10.8	9.2	7.6	6.0	5.3
Higher social security contribution rate						
	2010	2020	2030	2040	2050	2060
Pensions (% of GDP)	11.2	14.8	16.6	17.9	18.4	17.9
Primary budget balance (% of GDP)	-4.0	-2.5	-4.7	-5.3	-4.4	-1.7
Overall budget balance (% of GDP)	-5.3	-5.7	-10.5	-14.7	-18.0	-19.7
Government debt (% of GDP)	38.6	64.9	116.4	186.7	268.2	352.1
Unemployment rate	11.9	10.5	8.9	7.2	5.6	5.0

Source: Weyerstrass and Neck (2013)

Raising the average retirement rate can have similar effects on the fiscal position of the country, but only if most of the additional older workers find employment. If, on the contrary, most of the additional persons in the labour force are unemployed, public debt rises nearly as much as in the baseline of no policy change. An increase in the social security contribution rate is less effective at coping with the fiscal consequences of population ageing than a lower pension replacement rate. What is more, with respect to the macroeconomic performance, the scenario with a lower pension replacement rate also gave the best results.

None of the analysed measures is sufficient to stabilise the debt ratio at values below, or even close to, the reference level of 60 percent set in the Maastricht treaty and in the Stability and Growth Pact. Hence, even more drastic reforms than the relatively moderate options considered in Weyerstrass and Neck (2013) will be required to fully offset the pressure on public finances from an ageing population.

OPTIMAL FISCAL POLICIES FOR SLOVENIA AFTER THE CRISIS

Introduction

As a result of the severe financial and economic crisis that began in 2007, which has since been dubbed the "Great Recession", many countries have been faced with high budget deficits and hence rising public debt. Budget deficits were caused by the working of automatic stabilisers and as a result of discretionary fiscal policy measures aiming at supporting aggregate demand. Furthermore, many countries were forced to inject large amounts of money into the banking sector so as to strengthen their capital basis. Banks had liquidity and, in some cases also, solvency problems as the value of public bonds held by them decreased as a result of rising risk premiums on these bonds. Furthermore, in some countries large numbers of bank loans became non-performing due to the economic crisis which sent many companies into insolvency. Not only those countries which entered the crisis with already high public debt were affected, but also some fiscally sound economies faced the problem of unsustainable sovereign debt. In the European Union, the government debt issue is felt particularly hard for two reasons: on the one hand, the EU set itself the goal of reducing national debt levels to 60 percent of GDP and government deficits to 3 percent of GDP or below in the Maastricht Treaty and has attempted to enforce these targets through the Stability and Growth Pact, albeit with only limited success. On the other hand, some EU Member States which benefited from reduced interest rates through membership in the monetary union were tempted to pursue expansionary policies until financial markets recognised the danger of their debt becoming unsustainable and began to fear that these countries might be confronted with sovereign default. As a result, interest rates increased and some EU countries (especially some southern countries like Greece, Portugal, Spain, Italy and Cyprus) were caught in a trap of high and increasing public debt and decreasing national income (see, for example, Neck et al. 2013; Fenz et al. 2012).

Fiscal policy-makers in those EU countries are confronted with a trade-off between two goals which are equally important, namely consolidating public finances on the one hand and stimulating domestic demand on the other hand. The strategy of the European Commission and the other members of the "Troika" (the International Monetary Fund [IMF] and the European Central Bank [ECB] alongside the EU) which provided financial support under the strict supervision of experts, aims to fulfil both tasks simultaneously. While fiscal policies have to focus strictly on consolidating the budget by reducing public spending and raising taxes, the task of stimulating demand – at least in the medium term – is assigned to structural measures reforming the labour and goods markets. This is facing increasing criticism from the public, politicians and also many economists, who claim that an expansionary course of fiscal policy is required to return to a growth path in the weak economies of the EU periphery. According to this view, the present austerity prescriptions are not remedies but are paving the way to an even deeper crisis, and an expansionary policy through additional government expenditures, especially investment, is called for (Neck et al. 2013).

The effects of the "Great Recession" on the Slovenian economy and its public finances have been analysed in several studies. Like other small open economies (for instance, Austria), Slovenia was hit by the worldwide economic and financial crisis mainly via exports and fixed capital formation. In 2009, real GDP slumped by almost 8 percent. The unemployment rate rose sharply from about 4.5 percent to 6 percent, which was the level that had been reached in 2006, i.e. the last year before Slovenia's euro area accession. As already mentioned earlier, the public debt to GDP ratio increased from 22.0 percent of GDP in 2008 to 72 percent in 2013, with a further increase being expected for the near-term future, mainly on account of the expected subdued macroeconomic development. This sharp deterioration in public finances has three main reasons. Firstly, rising unemployment resulted in higher expenditure on unemployment benefits, while at the same time tax revenues and social security contributions declined on account of decreasing employment (i.e. the working of the automatic stabilisers). Secondly, the government tried to counteract the decline in private demand by introducing some expansionary fiscal policy measures. Thirdly, the government had to inject capital into the banking system as some banks faced severe capital losses due to the bursting of a housing bubble which had contributed to high economic growth prior to 2009. This real estate bubble had been fuelled by the decrease in long-term interest rates on the prospect of euro area membership. This section presents different budget consolidation strategies, with the aim of identifying those strategies which are least harmful to aggregate demand and employment.

Similar analyses have been performed in the past with other versions of the Slovenian model. As a recent example of such a study, Neck et al. (2013) investigate the trade-off between the needs for budget consolidation and the desirability of supporting demand by expansionary fiscal policies. The simulations show that for the Slovenian economy, an expansionary fiscal policy is neither feasible nor desirable as it results in unsustainable government debt and only has weak (positive) effects on income and employment. Therefore it seems that the Slovenian Stability Programme and the related policy prescriptions of the EU are not only more realistic but also more desirable than the proposals of some Keynesian economists. The simulations in Neck et al. (2013) with the Slovenian model support Taylor's (2009) recommendation of sticking to the automatic stabilisers instead of pursuing discretionary fiscal policies.

Simulations of different budget consolidation policies

By means of simulations of a stand-alone version of the Slovenian part of the multi-country model, this section investigates how public finances and the general macroeconomic performance in Slovenia are affected by different budget consolidation strategies. In the next section, the results of these simulations are compared to "optimal" fiscal policies. The algorithm which is used to derive these optimal policies, and which has been described earlier in this book is quite complex and therefore not able to handle the large multi-country model. This has the disadvantage that possible impacts of the different Slovenian budget consolidation strategies on Serbia, Bosnia and Herzegovina and Croatia cannot be assessed directly. However, such impacts on the other countries in the multi-country model may be assessed on the basis of the spillovers derived above.

The version of the model used for the simulations in this section and the optimisations in the next section is based on data until the end of 2013. The simulations are performed over the 5-year period 2014 to 2018. For *ex ante* simulations, i.e. simulations for a period in the future, plausible paths have to be specified for the exogenous variables and policy instruments. Using these time paths for the exogenous variables and policy instruments, a baseline run is performed. The alternative scenarios are then defined in terms of deviations from the baseline. "Truly" exogenous variables, i.e. those out of the control of domestic policy-makers are, in particular, international variables. In the version of the Slovenian model used here, these comprise world trade, the exchange rate between the euro and the US dollar, the short-term interest rate, which is mainly determined by the European Central Bank, and the average long-term interest rate, i.e. the yield on 10-year government bonds, in the euro area. Regarding world trade, it is expected to grow by 4.5 percent in 2014 and to reach an annual growth rate of 6 percent thereafter, which approximates its long-term average prior to the "Great Recession". Similarly, it is assumed that the euro area short- and long-term interest rates will normalise in the coming years, or more concretely, that the 3-month Euribor will rise from 0.25 percent in 2014 to 0.5 percent in 2015, 1.0 percent in 2016, 1.5 percent in 2017 and finally 2.0 percent in 2018. Following the term structure of interest rates and due to the assumed normalisation of European financial markets, the average euro area long-term interest rate is set to rise gradually from 3.0 percent in 2014 to 4.5 percent in 2018.

For the fiscal policy instruments, it is assumed that government consumption, public investment and transfer payments to private households will increase by 4 percent per year over the entire simulation period, with the average personal income tax rate being held constant at its 2013 level.

The following strategies to reduce the high public deficit and debt are then implemented:

- Scenario 1: reduction in government consumption by 10 percent relative to the baseline;
- Scenario 2: reduction in public investment by 60 percent relative to the baseline;
- Scenario 3: reduction in transfers by 10 percent relative to the baseline;
- Scenario 4: increase in the personal income tax rate by 4 percentage points (to 16.65 percent); the income tax rate is defined as personal income tax revenues divided by the tax base, i.e. the number of employed persons multiplied by the average gross wage; hence, tax brackets and deductions are implicitly but not explicitly taken into account.

In scenario 1, government consumption is reduced by 10 percent with respect to the baseline. This results in a debt ratio of 77.9 percent in 2018 (compared to 83.1 percent in the baseline). Then, in the other scenarios the policy instruments are adjusted in such a way that in the final year of the simulation period almost the same debt ratio as in scenario 1 is achieved. The aim of these analyses is to identify the budget consolidation strategy that is less harmful to economic growth and employment while reaching the same debt target. This approach results in the setting of the policy instruments as specified above.

The large reduction in public investment compared to government consumption results from its relatively small size. In 2013, the share of public consumption in nominal GDP was 20 percent while public investment only accounted for less than 3 percent of GDP. Although these two instruments directly influence both the public budget and GDP, transfers to households act indirectly via their impact on disposable income. Finally, income taxes are deducted from the gross wage. However, a rising income tax rate affects the economy indirectly as well as trade unions claim higher wages so as to compensate for a larger wedge between gross and net wages. This, in turn, is harmful to employment, and hence too sharp an increase in the income tax rate may erode the tax base, and in an extreme case even result in declining tax revenues, as prescribed by the Laffer curve.

Table 8 shows the results of the baseline simulation. Due to the assumed revival of world trade, real GDP growth recovers slightly in 2014 and gains more momentum from 2015 onwards. This positive development is accompanied by a substantial growth in employment and a reduction in unemployment. Despite the rising real net wages, the labour force declines. This is particularly caused by the decline in the population of working age. Hence, the reduction in unemployment is more pronounced than the increase in employment. Due to this positive development on the labour market, wage growth and thus inflation picks up after 2014.

Table 8: Budget consolidation strategies – baseline

	2014	**2015**	**2016**	**2017**	**2018**
GDP growth	0.9	2.4	2.8	3.0	2.8
Inflation rate	1.5	2.0	1.9	2.1	2.0
Employment (persons)	809,651	816,662	823,410	827,190	828,232
Unemployment (persons)	105,816	96,894	87,338	80,442	76,810
Unemployment rate	11.6	10.6	9.6	8.9	8.5
Budget balance ratio	-3.5	-4.1	-3.8	-3.0	-2.0
Debt ratio	70.1	76.8	82.5	86.9	90.4

Unemployment and the unemployment rate refer to registered persons and deviate from the internationally harmonised definition; debt level does not include very recent data revisions.

Source: author's own calculations

Due to the positive real economic development, the budget deficit is gradually reduced, but according to these simulations it is not until 2018 that the Slovenian budget deficit falls below the 3 percent threshold laid down in the Stability and Growth Pact. Accordingly, the debt ratio rises further from 70 percent in 2014 to 90.4 percent in 2018. Therefore, the four budget consolidation scenarios delineated above are performed, and their impacts on the budget, but also on the real economy are explored below. For the different scenarios, the following figures show the deviations of important macroeconomic and budgetary variables from their baseline trajectories. In the figures, "G" denotes scenario 1 (reduction in public consumption), "Invest" denotes scenario 2 (reduction in public investment), "Transfers" is the name for scenario 3 (reduction in transfers to private households), and scenario 4 (increase in the average personal income tax rate) is named "Tax_rate".

Figure 5: Budget balance ratio (simulation results)

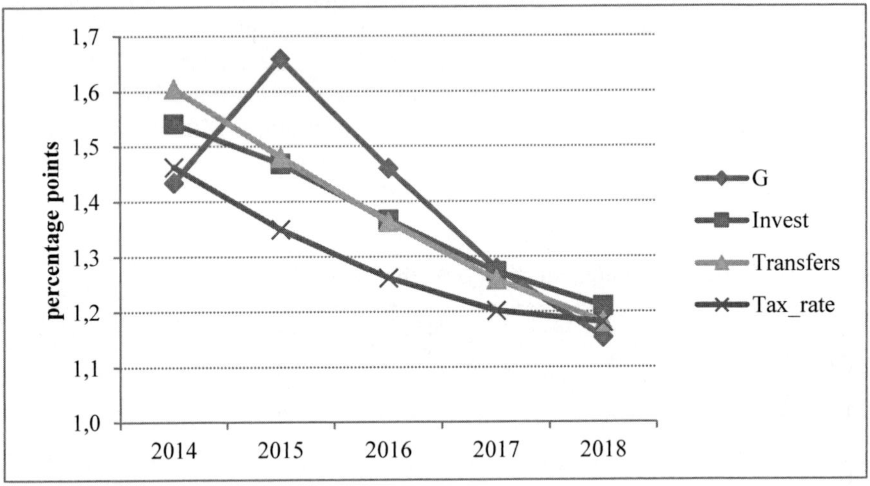

Source: author's own calculations

Figure 6: Public debt ratio (simulation results)

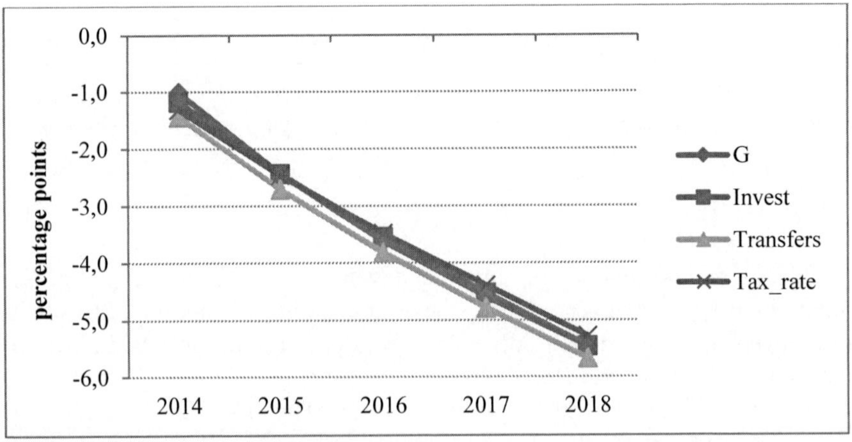

Source: author's own calculations

Figure 7: Real GDP growth (simulation results)

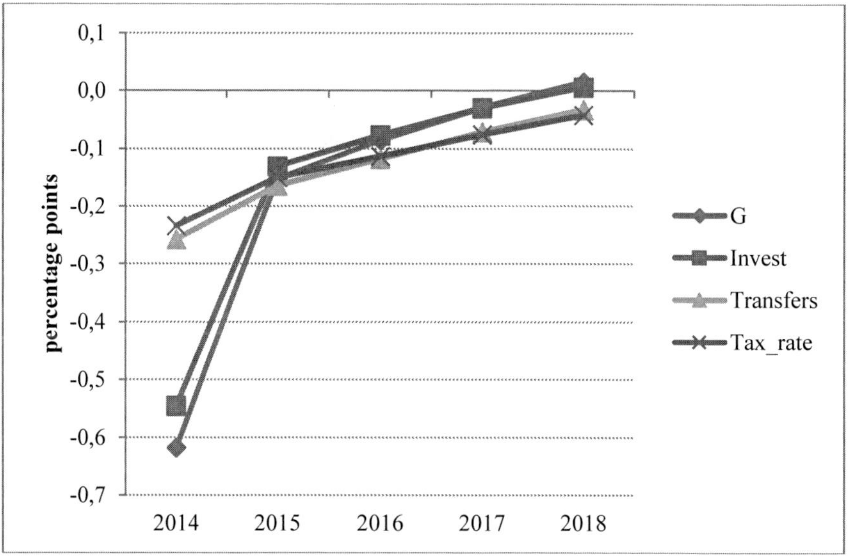

Source: author's own calculations

Figure 8: Real GDP level (simulation results)

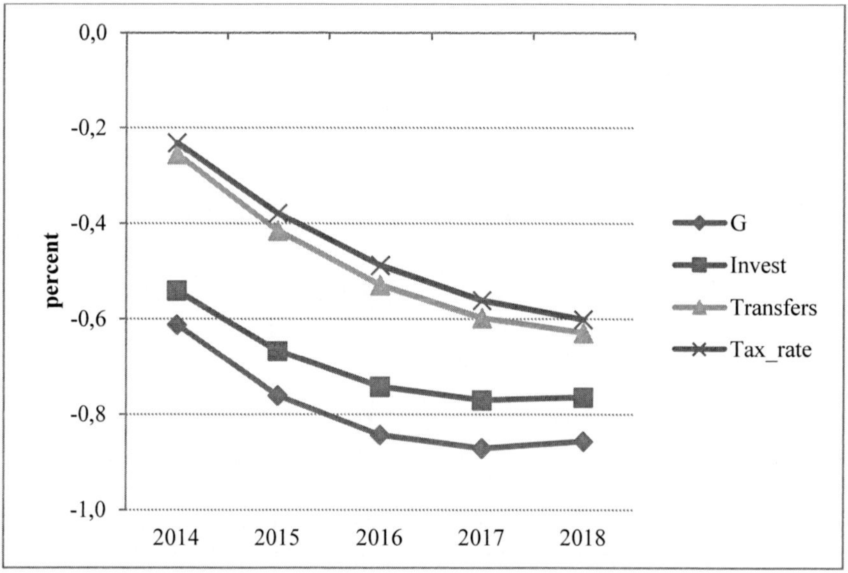

Source: author's own calculations

Figure 9: Level of potential GDP (simulation results)

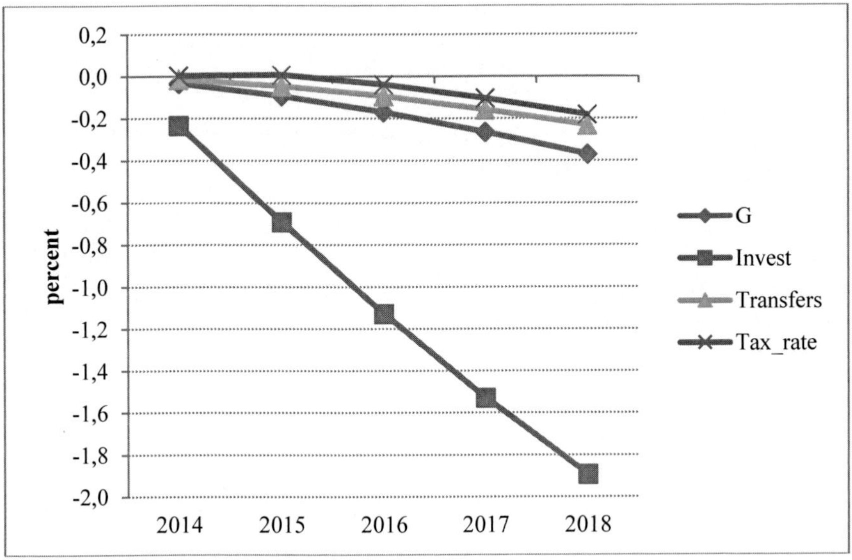

Source: author's own calculations

Figure 10: Inflation rate (simulation results)

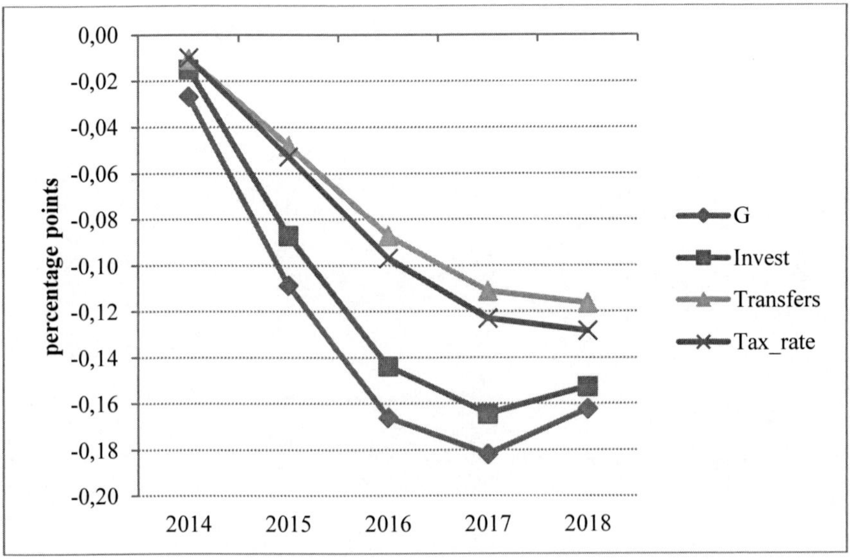

Source: author's own calculations

Figure 11: Number of employed persons (simulation results)

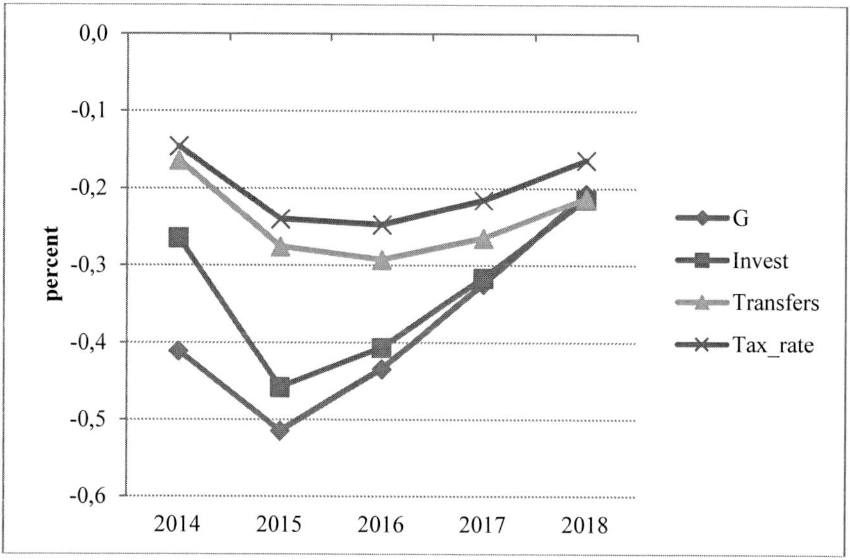

Source: author's own calculations

Figure 12: Number of unemployed persons (simulation results)

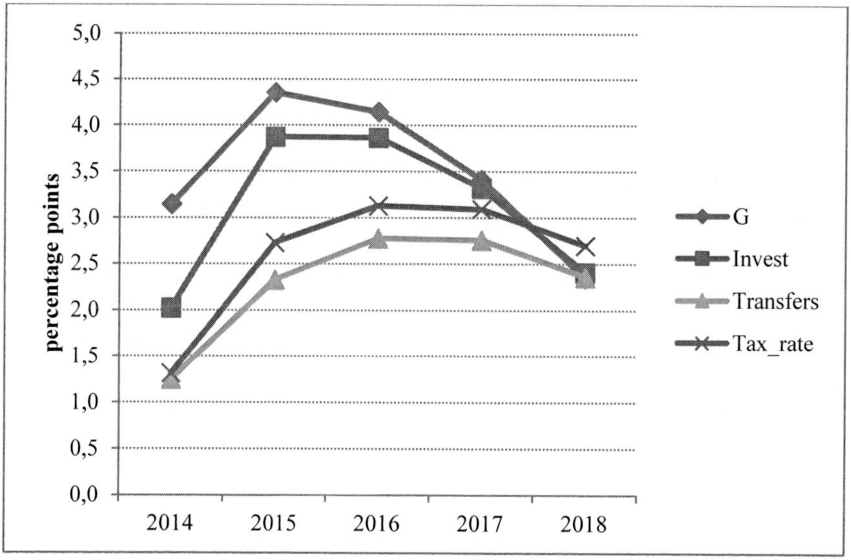

Source: author's own calculations

Figure 13: Unemployment rate (simulation results)

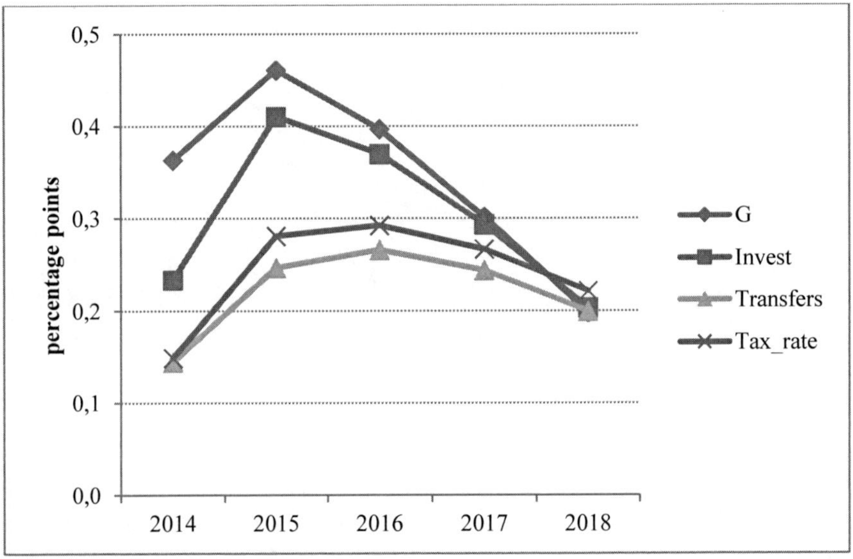

Source: author's own calculations

The budget balance ratio improves in all four scenarios, but the improvement decreases over time from between 1.4 and 1.6 percentage points in 2014 to about 1.2 percentage points in 2018. One exception is the first scenario (reduction in government consumption) in which the improvement in the budget balance ratio first increases and then declines. As noted above, all scenarios were designed in such a way that towards the end of the simulation period the reduction in the debt ratio is almost identical across the scenarios. Hence, in all four cases in 2018 the debt ratio is about 5.5 percentage points below the baseline.

In all scenarios, real GDP growth is lower than in the baseline but approaches the baseline trajectory over time. When government consumption or public investment is reduced, the immediate impact on GDP growth is the largest, but in these two scenarios the negative impacts becomes smaller over time. In the other two scenarios (reduction in transfers or raising the tax rate) the growth rate stays below the baseline over the entire period. Due to the large initial impact on GDP growth, in the case of a reduction in public consumption, the level of GDP also deviates the most from the baseline. The strategy of reducing public investment also has a substantial and durable negative impact on the level of output, while the strategies of cutting transfers or raising taxes are somewhat less harmful in this respect. A different picture emerges when the long-run production possibilities as measured via potential GDP are considered. In this regard, cutting public investment is by far the most harmful strategy to consolidate the budget, as investment is undertaken to renew and expand the capital stock, and the capital stock is one of the main determinants of potential GDP. Hence, while reducing public investment may be a successful strategy to reduce a budget deficit in the short run, in the long run such a policy undermines the growth opportunities of an economy, and hence future tax revenues would be negatively affected.

The reduction in aggregate demand also results in lower inflation. Again, the largest effect can be observed in the cases of decreasing public consumption or investment. Finally, the negative deviation of real GDP from the baseline results in lower employment and higher unemployment. Again, cutting transfers or raising the income tax rate are less problematic budget consolidation strategies than reducing government consumption or public investment.

Summing up the simulation results, it turns out that in all cases the budget deficit can be reduced, but the policies considered here are not sufficient to reach a balanced budget. However, while the policies assumed in the baseline, i.e. expenditure growth of 4 percent p.a. and unchanged tax rates, will result in a reduction of the budget deficit to 2.0 percent by 2018, the alternative fiscal policies analysed in the other scenarios would be sufficient to reduce the deficit to 0.8 percent by 2018. The debt ratio would continue to rise to 85 percent in 2018 as compared to 90 percent in the baseline.

The simulations show that even more drastic restrictive fiscal policy measures would be required to stabilise and eventually reduce the debt ratio. Such policies would negatively affect production and employment in the short to medium run, but consolidating the public budget is necessary to secure access to the financial markets to finance public expenditures and also to secure fiscal policy leeway. Among the budget consolidation strategies explored here, cutting public consumption or public investment has a larger immediate negative effect on aggregate production, while the negative effects of reducing transfer payments to households or higher income taxes are less harmful. Cutting public investment is the most problematic strategy since it not only affects actual demand but also reduces the long-run growth potential.

OPTIMAL FISCAL POLICIES – CONSOLIDATION OR INCREASED SPENDING?

Simulations like those described in the previous section are the most common method of analysing the effects of fiscal policies with macroeconometric models. However, simulations suffer from the subjective and somewhat random choice of policy instruments and scenario assumptions. As an alternative, "optimal" policies may be determined. Many theoretical (e.g. Petit 1990) and empirical (e.g. Chow 1975, 1981; Kendrick 1981) studies have used optimum control theory to obtain recommendations concerning economic policies.

The determination of "optimal" policies requires the specification of an objective function containing the desired time paths of objective variables. These objectives are those endogenous variables which are most relevant for policy-makers in the considered country, i.e. variables that are high on the political agenda. The desired time paths of the policy instruments also have to be specified, but it is then left to the optimisation algorithm to determine the actual time paths of the instruments, i.e. the realisations of the policy instruments that are required to come as close as possible to the desired values of the target variables. As the theory underlying the formulation of such an objective function is much less developed than the theory used for constructing the econometric model, it is advisable to experiment with various specifications of the objective function to check whether the optimal policies determined under one particular objective function are robust with respect to alternative specifications of that function (Neck et al. 2011).

The optimisation algorithm

To obtain optimal economic policies for the Slovenian model, the OPTCON2 algorithm is used here which was developed based on previous work by Chow (1975, 1981) and Kendrick (1981); see Blueschke-Nikolaeva et al. (2012). The original version of the OPTCON algorithm was developed and implemented in GAUSS by Matulka and Neck (1992).

As is usual in economic policy applications, a quadratic intertemporal objective function is assumed involving deviations of the values of the respective variables from some pre-specified "ideal" paths. The objective function has the following form:

$$L = \frac{1}{2}\sum_{t=1}^{T}\begin{bmatrix}\mathbf{x}_t - \tilde{\mathbf{x}}_t \\ \mathbf{u}_t - \tilde{\mathbf{u}}_t\end{bmatrix}\mathbf{W}_t\begin{bmatrix}\mathbf{x}_t - \tilde{\mathbf{x}} \\ \mathbf{u}_t - \tilde{\mathbf{u}}_t\end{bmatrix}$$

$$\mathbf{W}_t = \alpha^{t-1}\,\mathbf{W}\,,\ ,\ \mathrm{t} = 1,\ldots,\mathrm{T}.$$

x_t denotes the vector of state variables, u_t denotes the vector of control variables, $\tilde{x}_t$ and $\tilde{u}_t$ are the desired values of the state and control variables, W_t is the matrix of the weights given to the deviations of the state and control variables from their desired values and α denotes the discount factor. The intertemporal nature of the optimisation problem is considered, i.e. deviations of the actual from the desired values of the target variable over the entire optimisation horizon are taken into account.

The objective function *L* has to be minimised subject to the set of constraints given by the econometric model. With the nonlinear Slovenian macroeconometric model, this results in a multivariable nonlinear-quadratic optimal control problem. An exact solution to such a problem is not possible; only approximations are. Although this algorithm allows for stochastic extensions, the following analysis is confined to deterministic optimal control solutions, assuming the model parameters and the model equations are known exactly. The main reason for this restriction is that only limited reliable information is available about the stochastics of the model. Furthermore, previous studies have shown that stochastic control results often come close to the deterministic solutions (see, for example, Neck et al. 2010).

Optimisation results

Slovenian policy-makers are currently confronted with low economic growth on the one hand and increased public debt on the other. Policy-makers in such a position might be tempted to increase public spending further with the aim of supporting growth and reducing unemployment. However, this would raise the debt level still further, which might eventually cut Slovenia off from the financial markets. During the financial crisis, the risk premium on Slovenian government bonds (defined as the difference between 10-year government bond yields for Slovenia and for Germany) increased sharply, and came down only after Slovenia had managed to issue a bond denominated in US dollars in May 2013. Hence, instead of trying to support demand, it might be preferable to reduce the debt level so as to secure low long-term interest rates and to create leeway for future fiscal policies. Generally, the increase in fiscal deficits and public debt caused by fiscal expansions during the crisis has led to a discussion of the perception of financial markets as to fiscal sustainability. Both Ardagna (2009) and Afonso and Strauch (2004) show that financial markets value fiscal discipline since interest rates on long-term government bonds and stock market prices worsen considerably in periods of fiscal expansion. More generally, contributions in Alesina and Giavazzi (2013) discuss the effectiveness of fiscal policies in the crisis, i.e. the size of fiscal multipliers, as well as the issue of the sustainability of public finances and alternative means of debt reduction.

Against this background, the Slovenian model will be used together with the optimisation algorithm OPTCON to investigate whether a better overall macroeconomic and fiscal performance can be reached with a more expansionary fiscal policy or with a stricter consolidation strategy. For the optimisations, the same model for Slovenia as described above has been used so as to make the results comparable to the simulations above. Hence, the model is a stand-alone one without the trade and exchange rate links to the other country blocs of the multi-country model, but the Slovenian model used here was updated to include data until the end of 2013.

The optimisations complement those documented in Neck et al. (2011).[18] There, the focus lay on the question as to which way the Slovenian government – or any government of a small open economy – should react to a severe drop in private demand due to an external shock, taking the negative impacts of higher public demand on fiscal solvency into account. In this section, the issue addressed is whether the government should continue to promote growth by increased public spending with the aim of generating tax revenues, or whether an active budget consolidation strategy is preferable. Based on a version of the Slovenian model without the links to the other countries in the multi-country model described here, Neck et al. (2011) find that even without expansionary fiscal policies the budget deficit would further increase in the medium term, reaching 9 percent of GDP in 2015. In this paper, different fiscal policy reactions to the financial and economic crisis of 2007 to 2009 in Slovenia are investigated. To this end, first the effects of the global crisis under the assumption of no-policy reactions, i.e. assuming that macroeconomic policies are conducted without trying to mitigate the effects of the crisis, are simulated. Next, the possibilities of fiscal policy to compensate for the lack of private demand during the crisis by increasing public demand are explored. It turns out that a full compensation for the decline in exports, private consumption and investment by increasing public consumption would require an extremely

---

[18] Thanks go to Dmitri Blueschke from Klagenfurt University for integrating the Slovenian model in the optimisation algorithm OPTCON2, which itself is implemented in MATLAB, and for conducting the optimisations.

expansionary fiscal policy, resulting in a drastic deterioration of public finances, with a budget deficit of 40 percent of GDP over several years. Partial compensation for the lack of private demand by means of fiscal policies, supported by an expansionary monetary policy by the ECB, could mitigate the GDP contraction and narrow the budget deficit to about 20 percent of GDP, which is still non-sustainable and violates the Stability and Growth Pact. "Optimal" fiscal policies are not as strongly expansionary and countercyclical as one would expect, given the rather "Keynesian" character of the underlying model with adaptive expectations and the possibility of persistent disequilibria on the goods and labour markets, as well as sticky wages and prices. Instead, optimal policies are only modestly active, taking the strong trade-offs between countercyclical fiscal policies and the requirements of fiscal solvency into account.

For the following optimisations, three policy scenarios are distinguished. In each scenario it is assumed that the policy-maker has one main target variable. The main target is either the budget debt ratio (scenario "*sc_debt*"), the growth rate of real GDP (scenario "*sc_grgdpr*"), or the level of real GDP (scenario "*sc_gdpr*"). Differentiating between one scenario with the focus on the *growth rate* and another scenario with the *level* of GDP is meant to reveal whether one of these scenarios calls for a more active fiscal policy than the other. The hypothetical policy-maker tries to come as close as possible to specified 'ideal' values for these main targets. In addition, some minor target variables are included. These are the inflation rate, the unemployment rate, the current account balance and the budget balance ratio. To achieve the targets, the policy-maker may use two control variables (policy instruments): public consumption and transfers to private households. Target paths are also specified for these control variables so that there is a trade-off between using the instruments to achieve the desired targets and the costs of using these instruments, in addition to the various trade-offs implied by the underlying Slovenian model.

The ideal paths for the main and minor target variables imply smooth real GDP growth, low values for the unemployment rate and inflation, a balanced current account and a balanced public budget. In each optimisation, all main and minor target variables are included but with varying weights. As an example, the level of real GDP is given the same weight as the minor variables, except for the scenario with real GDP as the main target, where real GDP is assigned a higher weight. The weights are normalised to account for the different magnitude of the variables.

The optimisations are compared to a baseline assuming no active policy intervention (*sc_baseline*). Table 9 shows the assumed "ideal" paths of the target variables, and the weights are displayed in Table 10. While the target paths are identical across scenarios, the weights of the "main" and "minor" targets vary. The same weights are assumed in each year of the optimisation period while the target values may differ each year. The target variables of the instruments (government consumption and transfers to households) are identical to the assumed paths of these variables in the baseline simulation above. The "ideal" realisations of these two fiscal policy instruments then deviate from the paths of the baseline simulation since the optimisation aims to set these instruments in such a way that the weighted targets, i.e. the weighted deviations of all target variables from their desired values over the entire optimisation period, is minimised.

Table 9: "Ideal" values of the target variables in the different scenarios

	Target values				
	2014	2015	2016	2017	2018
Target variables					
Current account (% of GDP)	0	0	0	0	0
GDP growth rate	3	3	3	3	3
Unemployment rate	12	11	10	9	8
Inflation rate	2	2	2	2	2
Level of GDP	Compatible with 3% growth rate				
Budget balance ratio	0	0	0	0	0
Debt ratio	60	60	60	60	60
Policy instruments					
Public consumption	4% p.a. growth				
Transfer payments	4% p.a. growth				

Table 10: Weight matrix in the different scenarios

	Scenarios			
	baseline	debt	grgdp	gdp
Target variables				
Current account (% of GDP)	1	1	1	1
GDP growth rate	1	1	10	1
Unemployment rate	1	1	1	1
Inflation rate	1	1	1	1
Level of GDP	1	1	1	10
Budget balance ratio	1	1	1	1
Debt ratio	1	10	1	1
Policy instruments				
Public consumption	1	1	1	1
Transfers	1	1	1	1

The following figures show the optimisation results for the four scenarios. Although the model is quarterly, only annual results are reported, as before. The quarterly data show a strong seasonal pattern which is irrelevant from the point of view of policy-making and conceals the relevant results. Figure 14 to Figure 20 depict the target or "state" variables, and the resulting paths of the fiscal policy instruments are shown in Figure 21 and Figure 22.

Figure 14: Budget balance ratio (optimisation results)

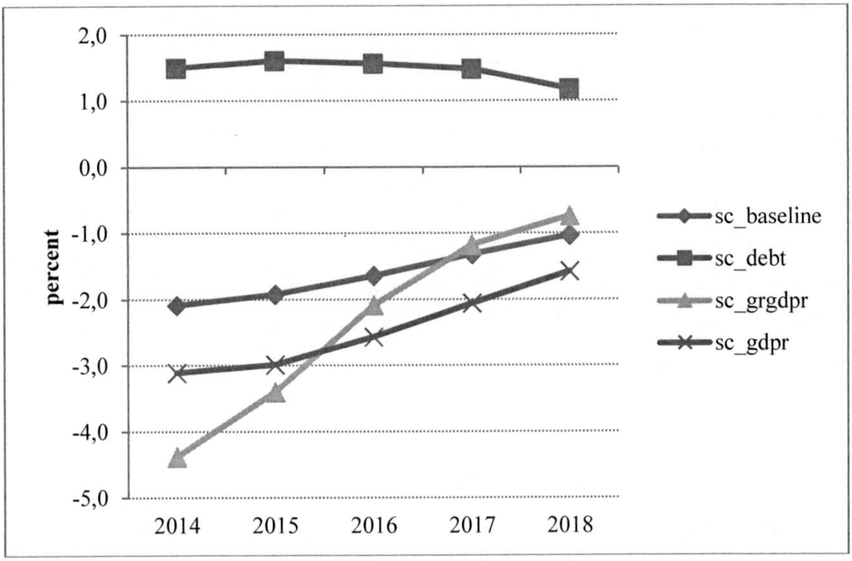

Source: author's own calculations

Figure 15: Public debt ratio (optimisation results)

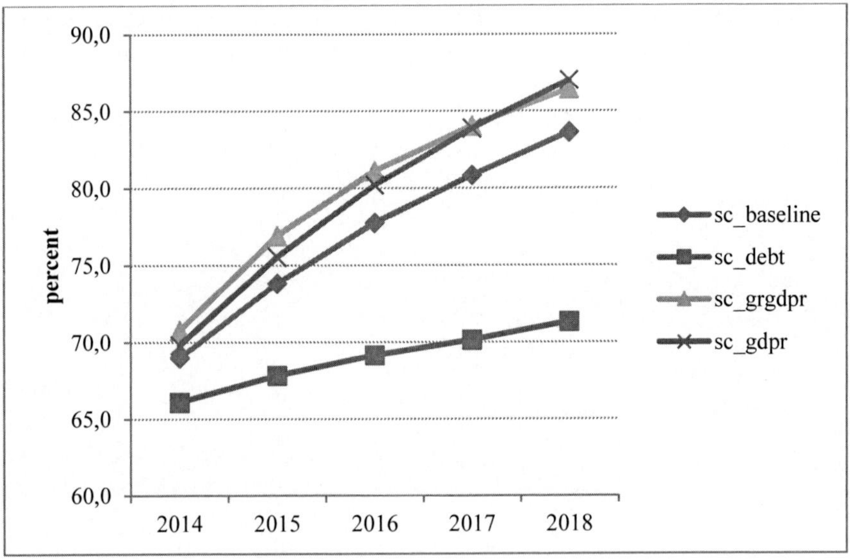

Source: author's own calculations

Figure 16: Real GDP growth rate (optimisation results)

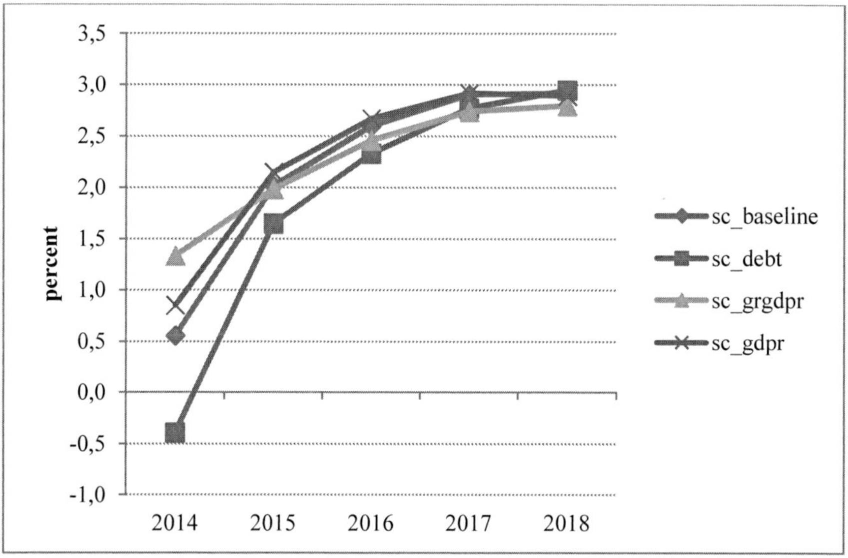

Source: author's own calculations

Figure 17: Real GDP level (optimisation results)

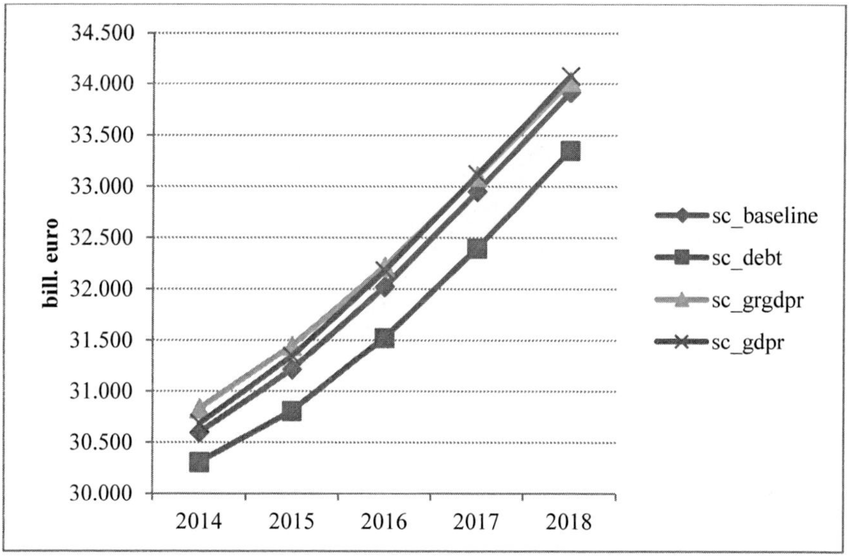

Source: author's own calculations

Figure 18: Number of employed persons (optimisation results)

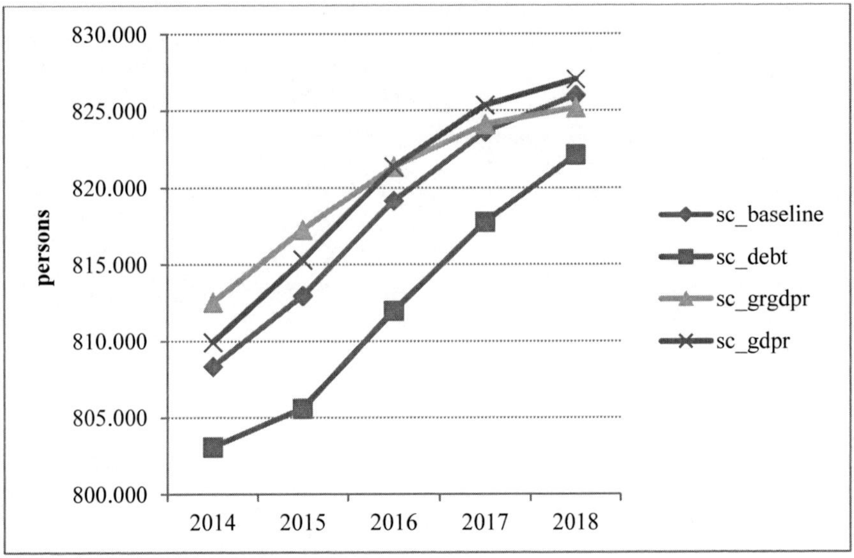

Source: author's own calculations

Figure 19: Unemployment rate (optimisation results)

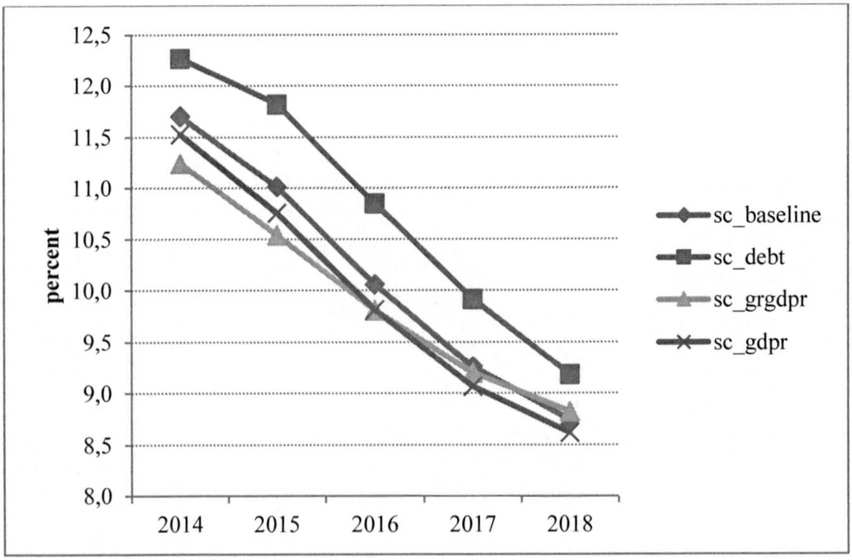

Source: author's own calculations

Figure 20: Inflation rate (optimisation results)

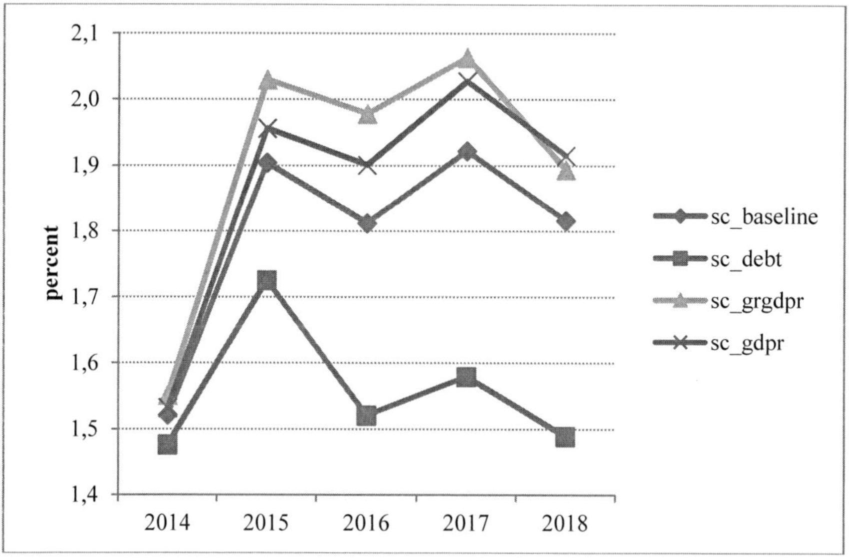

Source: author's own calculations

Only in the scenario with a high weight given to budget consolidation is a budget surplus achieved in each year of the optimisation period. On the other hand, in this scenario real GDP and inflation are very low due to a public spending restraint, and hence the ratio between the debt level and nominal GDP increases further, although very modestly in comparison with the other scenarios and with the simulation. The other extreme case is the scenario with the focus on a high GDP growth rate. In this case, fiscal policies are very expansionary, pushing the deficit ratio to 4½% in the first year and to 3½% in the second year. Interestingly, in all other scenarios, including the one with a high weight attached to the GDP level, the deficit ratio remains below the threshold of 3% specified in the Maastricht Treaty and in the Stability and Growth Pact. In the scenarios aiming at high GDP growth, the debt ratio reaches more than 85% by 2018, clearly showing that such a strategy is unsustainable and would certainly not be tolerated by the financial markets.

The real GDP growth rate converges towards the 3% target value over time, but in the scenario aimed at consolidating the budget fast, the necessary restrictive fiscal policy results in declining real GDP in the first year. Hence, the path of the real GDP level stays clearly lower in this case compared to all other scenarios, which in turn are quite close to each other. Due to the worse macroeconomic performance in the scenario with a high weight attached to consolidating public finances, employment is significantly lower and hence unemployment higher than in the other scenarios. In all other optimisation scenarios, unemployment declines quite substantially. This is not only achieved by sustained employment growth, but also by the decreasing labour supply due to demographic developments.

Figure 21: Government consumption (optimisation results)

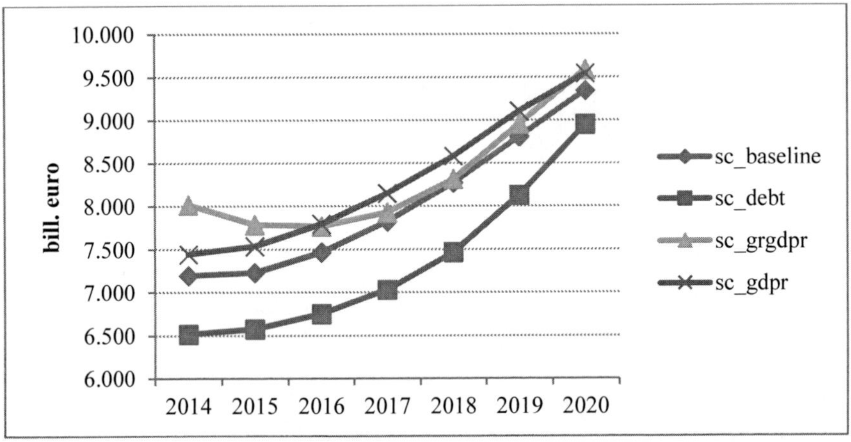

Source: author's own calculations

Figure 22: Transfer payments (optimisation results)

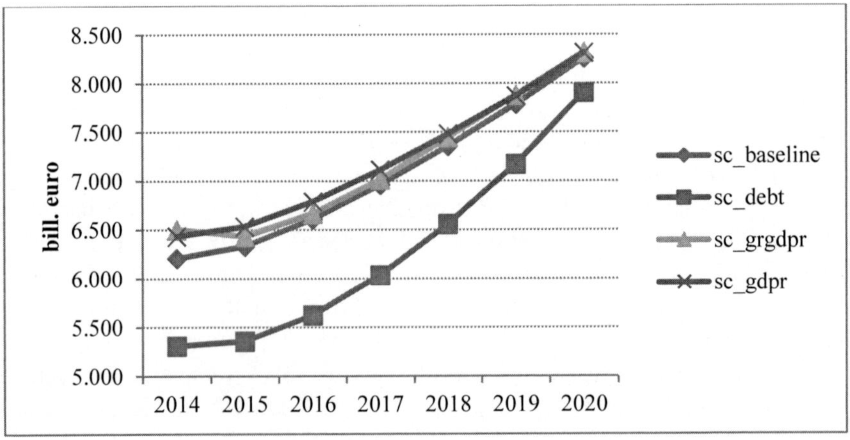

Source: author's own calculations

In the baseline optimisation, both government consumption and transfers grow at an average annual rate of 3%, compared to 4% in the simulation. The 4% annual average growth rate was also the target in the optimisations. This shows that even in the baseline optimisation, the actual paths of the instruments deviate from the desired paths as the algorithm adjusts the instruments so as to meet the other targets as well. In the baseline, government consumption increases by less than 1% in 2014 and in 2015, but afterwards the growth rate increases, eventually reaching 5.7% in 2018. In this scenario, transfers even decrease in the first year, before accelerating as well.

As would be expected, if a high weight is attached to consolidating the budget, the optimisation results advise policy-makers to use public spending very cautiously. In this scenario, government consumption and transfers to households are significantly reduced in the first year, and their average annual growth rates over the entire five-year period amount to only 0.9% and 0.7% respectively. On the other hand, in the cases with a high weight given to the growth rate or the level of GDP, public spending is more expansionary than in the baseline. Interestingly enough, if the policy-maker is particularly concerned about achieving the desired GDP level, fiscal policies should be even more expansionary than in the case of specifically trying to achieve the desired GDP growth rate.

Summing up the results, the short-run trade-off between rapid budget consolidation and sustaining significant GDP growth is clearly confirmed. On the one hand, a very restrictive fiscal policy may delay an economic recovery. On the other hand, very expansionary public spending endangers fiscal solvency. Hence, it might be concluded that after the financial crisis, which pushed up debt levels, the focus should lie on consolidating the budget, but growth and employment should be impaired as little as possible, not least as increasing employment, income and profits generate public revenues. Hence, economic growth is the foundation for successful and sustainable budget consolidation.

This conclusion is in line with recent policy advice issued by the IMF according to which most advanced economies should adjust their fiscal policies at a gradual pace, within a credible medium-term plan, to limit the short-run impact of fiscal tightening on growth. However, delaying the adjustment too much would entail the risk that investors lose confidence in a government's willingness to put fiscal policy on a sound footing and begin to demand higher interest rates, which can quickly lead to debt dynamics that spiral out of control, particularly if debt levels and hence the interest burden are already very high (IMF 2013).

THE FUTURE OF THE EURO AREA AND IMPACTS ON SLOVENIA AND SERBIA

After the foundation of the European Economic and Monetary Union (EMU) in 1999, the diverging competitiveness of the peripheral and the core countries resulted in the accumulation of sizeable current account imbalances. At the same time, some countries built up large stocks of public debt. The countries which lost international price competitiveness now have to undergo painful reforms aimed at restoring their competitiveness. During this reform period, domestic demand is declining, spilling over to other countries via the trade channel. As the deficit countries became unable to finance their public budgets via capital markets, the other euro area countries, the European Central Bank (ECB) and the International Monetary Fund (IMF) established financial rescue plans and new institutions, in particular the European Stability Mechanism (ESM). While financial assistance was conditional on deep structural reforms in the recipient countries, the other EU countries assumed large claims and guarantees. If the recipient countries failed to repay the loans, public debt in the donor countries would increase, necessitating restrictive fiscal policies with negative short-run effects on domestic demand in these countries as well. Furthermore, banks would be affected by a write-down on their holdings of public bonds if the yields of these bonds rose sharply due to the unsound fiscal policies of the issuing countries. As a result, banks may be forced to reduce their credit supply. As many banks operate internationally, credit supply in countries other than the home markets of the respective banks would also be affected. Should the reform programmes underway in the peripheral countries fail to restore international competitiveness and the sustainability of public finances, one or more of the affected countries might eventually have to leave the euro area in order to devalue its currency so as to increase its international competitiveness in this way.

In Weyerstrass and Grozea-Helmenstein (2013b), different scenarios for future euro area development are delineated, and their macroeconomic consequences for Slovenia and Serbia are determined by means of simulations with the macroeconometric models for these economies. This section summarizes the assumptions and results of the simulations in that paper.

The choice of Slovenia and Serbia for the simulations allows interesting insights. On the one hand, both countries are successor states of the former Yugoslavia; hence they share common characteristics and a common economic and political heritage. However, already in the 1980s and early 1990s they followed different reform paths, which materialised in a higher degree of economic openness and stronger trade relations with Western countries in Slovenia. For Serbia on the other hand, Russia was traditionally the main trading partner. Major differences between the two countries relate to their size in terms of territory and population, as well as their level of economic and social development (GDP per capita and unemployment) (Mencinger 2001). On the other hand, Slovenia already became a member of the European Union in 2004, and in 2007 it was the first country from Central and Eastern Europe to introduce the euro as legal tender. Being a euro area Member State, Slovenia assumed obligations within the ESM, and via its capital share it participates in the ECB bond purchase programmes and in the payment system Target2. However, Slovenia itself got into trouble as the bursting of a housing and real estate bubble caused many loans to become non-performing, pushing Slovenian banks into liquidity problems. Due to the low capitalisation, the liquidity problem turned into severe solvency problems, and ultimately the government had to inject large amounts of capital into the banking sector, which pushed public debt up. Serbia, on the other hand, is only an EU candidate country. Hence, Serbia is still outside the fiscal policy and financial architecture of the EU in general and the euro area in particular. In both countries, a lax credit policy by private banks, fuelled by substantial cross-border funding in the period preceding the economic and financial crisis which started in 2007, led to a sharp rise in the indebtedness of companies and private households. Debtors are now facing difficulties to service the loans, resulting in a rising share of non-performing loans and debt write-offs. In Weyerstrass and Grozea-Helmenstein, the following four scenarios of the future euro area development were considered.

- "Baseline": the baseline scenario is based on the assumption that those countries that are currently confronted with structural problems will manage to solve these problems by implementing painful structural reforms. This implies that investor confidence can be restored with the support of ESM programmes and implicit ECB guarantees through the commitment to buy any amount of government bonds necessary to secure reasonable interest rates and risk premia. Under these conditions, the crisis countries will manage to reduce their unit labour costs substantially thanks to structural reforms. This internal devaluation will help restore international price competitiveness. In addition, regaining the confidence of international investors will help decrease public deficits and reduce the wealth losses which resulted from the financial crisis.

Furthermore, the capitalisation of the banking sector will gradually be strengthened. However, since it takes time for structural reforms to become fully effective, in the crisis countries growth will remain subdued and unemployment will remain elevated for many years. The following, more pessimistic scenarios will be defined as deviations from this baseline.

- "Greek exit": In this scenario, Greece leaves the euro area while the other countries solve their problems and stay in the common currency area. In this case, the new Greek currency would be drastically devalued. Accordingly, the value of Greek debt would rise substantially since it is denominated in euro. Hence, a further haircut on Greek public bonds would be inevitable. Since Slovenia participates in the ESM and in the ECB bond purchase programmes, its public debt would increase, since the guarantees and loans given to Greece have to be written off. As neither Slovenian nor Serbian banks are significantly engaged in Greece, no substantial losses for Slovenian or Serbian banks would be likely in this scenario. Hence, from this perspective there is no reason to expect reductions in credit supply in Slovenia or Serbia. However, Greek banks are engaged in Serbia with a share of 15 percent of total assets. If Greece left the euro area, it can be expected that Serbian banks would come under pressure due to the write-off on their Greek sovereign bonds. Hence, it is assumed that on Greece's exit from the euro area Greek banks would reduce their exposure abroad, resulting in a decrease in credit availability in Serbia. For Slovenia, such consequences would not occur since Greek banks are not engaged in Slovenia. But other Western European banks are also present in Central and Eastern Europe. These banks would have to write down their Greek debt as well. This may affect credit availability in the countries in which they are engaged.
- "GIIPS exit". In a highly pessimistic and also rather unlikely scenario, it is assumed that all peripheral countries with structural problems, i.e. the so-called GIIPS countries – Greece, Ireland, Italy, Portugal and Spain – leave the euro area. The remaining countries keep the common currency. In this scenario, the exiting countries would be unable to repay large parts of their public debt, since their new currencies would devalue drastically, pushing up their euro denominated public debt. Investors would claim significantly higher risk premia to compensate for the increased risk of default by these countries. Regarding the economic consequences for Slovenia and

Serbia, it is not relevant whether each of the exiting countries introduced its own currency or whether they formed a "Southern euro area", since the new currency or currencies would drastically devaluate against the "Northern euro" in any case. The impact of Italy and Spain leaving the euro area would be considerable for Slovenia. These two countries alone account for four fifths of the total amount of debt securities of the GIIPS countries owned by Slovenian residents. Moreover, according to the 2012 Financial Stability Review of the Bank of Slovenia, Slovenian residents (mainly insurance companies and banks) held 8.5 percent of their total investment in foreign debt securities.

- "Euro area break-up". Finally, in the fourth and extremely pessimistic scenario it is assumed that the euro area totally breaks up and all countries introduce their own currencies. This implies that Slovenia would return to the tolar, its currency prior to its euro area accession in 2007.

An exit of one or more countries from the euro area would affect the economies of Slovenia and Serbia via several transmission channels, of which reduced exports and credit constraints might be considered the most important ones. Investment may, in addition, be affected by reducing the value of collateral available to back credits. In a business cycle expansion, the ratio of debt to asset values may rise to such a high level that a business cycle turning point could set in motion a spiralling decline in the price and quantity of collateral assets and hence in credit access. Output and investment would then decline because the collateral constraint limits access to working capital financing (Mendoza 2008). In addition, private consumption would probably be affected by negative wealth effects as in the financial crisis, the value of real estate and financial wealth decreased substantially. The decline of real estate prices was particularly severe in Slovenia where a housing bubble burst which had been fuelled by very low real interest rates in the period after joining the euro area until the outbreak of the crisis. As a euro area member state participating in the European Stability Mechanism and via its capital subscriptions in the ECB bond purchase programmes, Slovenia would suffer from irrecoverable loans and guarantees given to the crisis countries.

Based on a meta study of existing analyses with different methodologies, Born et al. (2012) conclude that most studies estimate the depreciation which is necessary to induce a sizeable improvement in Greece's current account to 20 to 30 percent. Based on the historical experiences of other countries, the required real depreciation could reach as much as 50 percent (Alcidi et al. 2012). If Greece stays in the euro area, wages and prices would have to decrease by this amount. If Greece leaves the euro area and prices and wages remain constant, the new Greek currency would depreciate in nominal terms. Based on these considerations, in the scenario of a Greece exit from the euro area, the ensuing nominal depreciation of the new Greek currency is assumed to be 30 percent. Although the current account deficits of the other crisis countries are smaller, it is assumed that their new currencies would also depreciate by 30 percent against the euro in the scenario of all GIIPS countries exiting. The implementation of the reduced import demand on Slovenia and Serbia in the simulations takes the different trade links of the two countries into account. Greece accounts for 0.26 percent of Slovenia's exports and for 1.7 percent of Serbia's exports. Hence, as a direct effect, an export reduction of 30 percent of 0.26 percent for Slovenia, and 30 percent of 1.7 percent for Serbia is assumed in the Greek exit scenario. The total export share to all GIIPS countries (Greece, Ireland, Italy, Portugal, and Spain) adds up to 13.6 percent for both Slovenia and Serbia. Accordingly, the direct effect is set to an export reduction of 30 percent of 13.6 percent for both countries in the scenario of a euro area exit of the GIIPS countries. For the scenario of a euro area break-up, it is assumed that the direct impacts on exports are three times as large as in the GIIPS exit scenario. As other trading partners of the countries leaving the euro area would also experience a decline in economic activity, they would need fewer imports as well, which also affects Slovenia's and Serbia's exports. This additional indirect effect is assumed at 50 percent of the direct effects. This assumption of 50 percent is, of course, rather arbitrary, and any larger or smaller indirect effect could also be conceivable. However, a larger effect seems less likely since more distant regions of the world economy would be affected to a lesser extent, and hence exports to these regions would only decline slightly. It is furthermore assumed that the largest negative effect of a euro area exit of one or more countries would last for two years. For the third year of the simulation period, 75 percent of the original effect is assumed. For the fourth year, a further reduction to 50 percent of the original impact is taken, and for the final year a return to the baseline path is assumed.

In addition to the impact on exports, the exit of one or more countries from the euro area can be expected to influence investments in the other countries as well. First and foremost, companies would invest less in reaction to the decline in final demand. But in addition to this demand effect, supply effects on investment are also plausible. As banks incur losses of their wealth since they have to write-down on public bonds of the exiting countries, they might be forced to reduce their credit exposure. This lower credit availability would impair those investment projects that are financed by bank loans. According to data from the Slovenian and the Serbian National Banks, about 40 percent of all company investment is financed by bank loans. Regarding credit supply, it is assumed that availability in Slovenia and Serbia would decline by 5 percent and 10 percent respectively if only Greece leaves the euro area. In the GIIPS exit scenario, credit rationing is assumed to reach 20 percent in Slovenia and 30 percent in Serbia respectively. Finally, for the most dramatic scenario of a total euro area break-up, the corresponding figures are 30 percent in Slovenia and 50 percent in Serbia. For Serbia, larger impacts on credit supply are assumed so as to account for the larger engagement of banks from the crisis countries in Serbia. Following these calculations and assumptions, investment is additionally reduced by the assumed decline in credit supply, multiplied by the share of bank financing of investments (i.e. 40 percent).

For Slovenia as a euro area Member State, a third transmission channel of the euro area crisis is taken into account in addition to a reduction in exports and credit constraints. Slovenia participates in the financial assistance programmes that the euro area countries established for Greece, Portugal, Ireland and the Spanish banking sector – and later on also for Cyprus, but this has not been taken into account in the simulations, as the programme was initiated much later. Furthermore, Slovenia is part of the Eurosystem, and hence participates in the Target2 system. Based on calculations made by the German ifo Institute for Germany, Slovenian exposure to the GIIPS countries amounts to 5.60 billion euros for Greece alone, and to 12.53 billion euros for all countries under consideration. For the simulations it is assumed that on the exit of a country from the euro area, the Slovenian government would have to write down all its claims to the country concerned. This would push up Slovenia's public debt level by 5.60 billion euros if only Greece left the euro area and by 12.53 billion euros if all GIIPS countries exited or if the euro area broke up completely. It is further assumed that this would happen at once, before the start of the simulation period. The additional public debt would then be repaid by reducing public consumption linearly by one fifth of the additional debt in each of the five simulation years. This implies that additional interest payments for this part of public debt that is repaid later and not immediately in the first year are not taken into account. Hence, in the Greek exit scenario, public consumption is reduced by 1.12 billion euros per year and by 2.51 billion euros p.a. in the other two scenarios. It should be noted that these assumptions do not imply that Slovenia's public debt level would return to the baseline scenario by the end of the simulation period. Additional debt would instead be accumulated due to the working of the automatic stabilisers, i.e. additional unemployment benefits and reduced tax revenues.

The following figures show the macroeconomic and budgetary consequences of the different scenarios regarding the future development of the euro area. The figures depict deviations from the baseline scenario in which no current member state leaves the euro area. For all variables, assumptions regarding the most important exogenous variables (world trade, oil price, exchange rates and fiscal policy instruments) have been chosen in such a way that the baseline simulation results come close to the most recent forecasts of the European Commission, the OECD and the IMF for the economies of Slovenia and Serbia. The baseline results themselves are not reported here since the interest lies exclusively on the deviations from the baseline in the different euro area scenarios. The simulations were run over the period 2013 to 2017.

Figure 23: Real GDP in the euro area scenarios

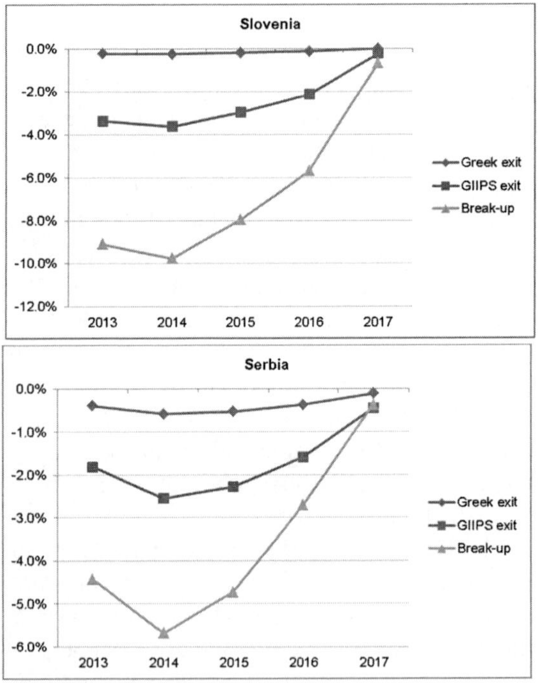

Deviations from baseline in percent

Source: Based on Weyerstrass and Grozea-Helmenstein (2013b)

Figure 24: Real investment in the euro area scenarios

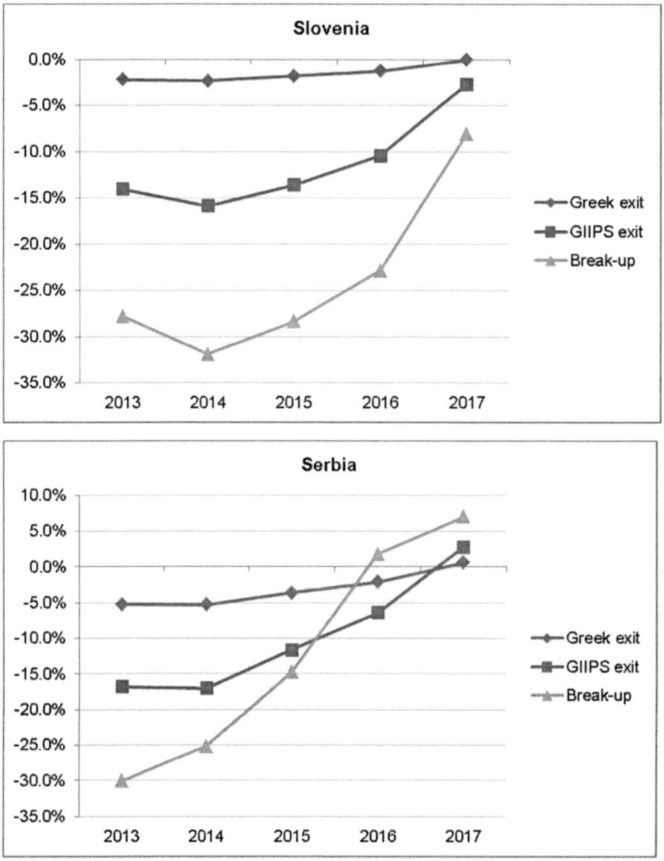

Deviations from baseline in percent

Source: Based on Weyerstrass and Grozea-Helmenstein (2013b)

Figure 25: Real exports in the euro area scenarios

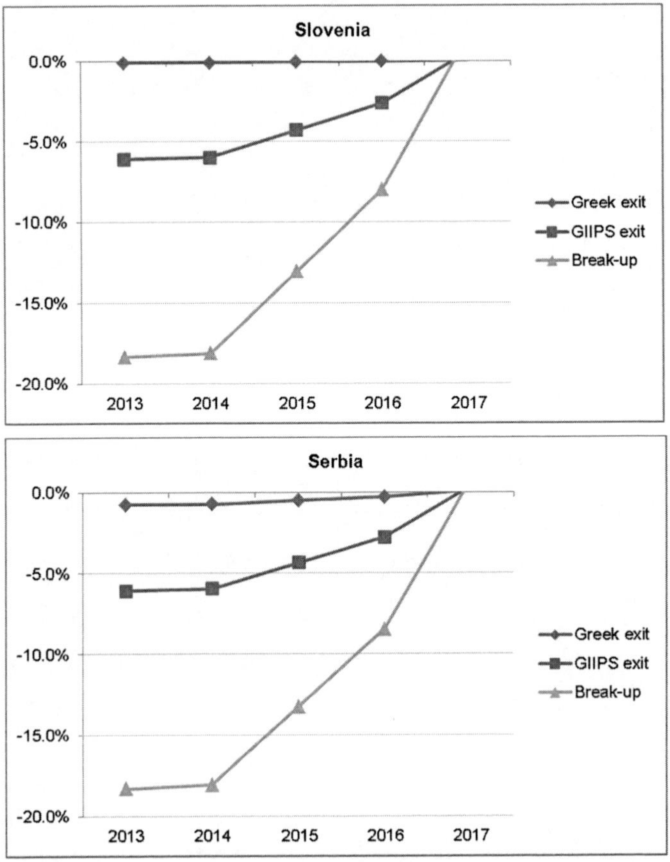

Deviations from baseline in percent

Source: Based on Weyerstrass and Grozea-Helmenstein (2013b)

Figure 26: Employment in the euro area scenarios

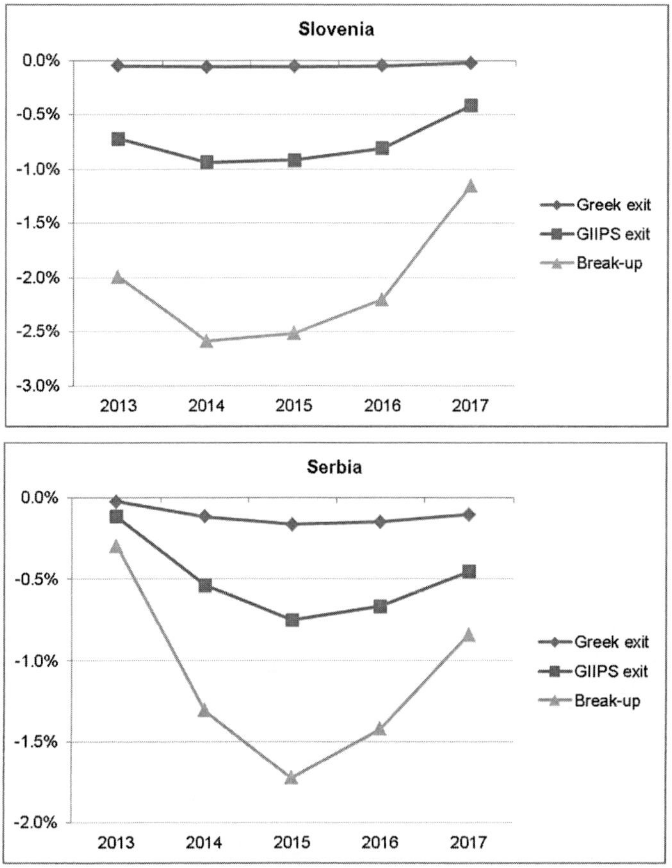

Deviations from baseline in percent

Source: Based on Weyerstrass and Grozea-Helmenstein (2013b)

Figure 27: Unemployment rate in the euro area scenarios

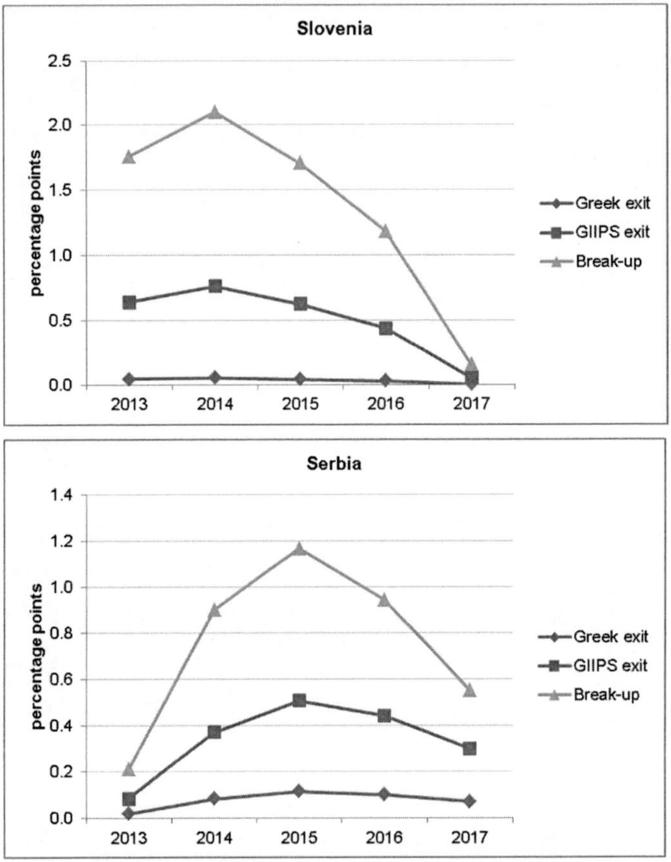

Deviations from baseline in percentage points

Source: Based on Weyerstrass and Grozea-Helmenstein (2013b)

Figure 28: Inflation rate in the euro area scenarios

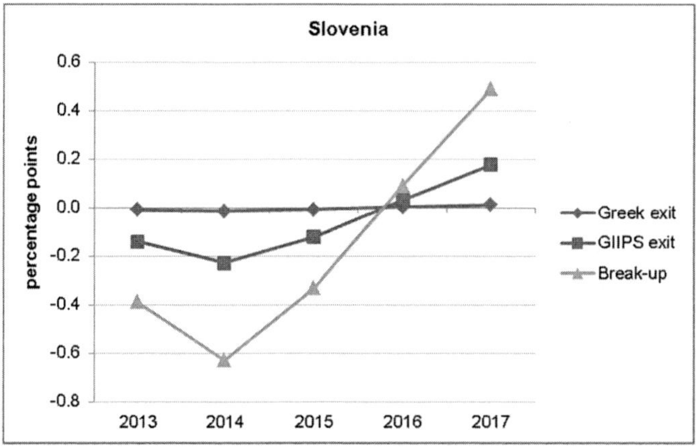

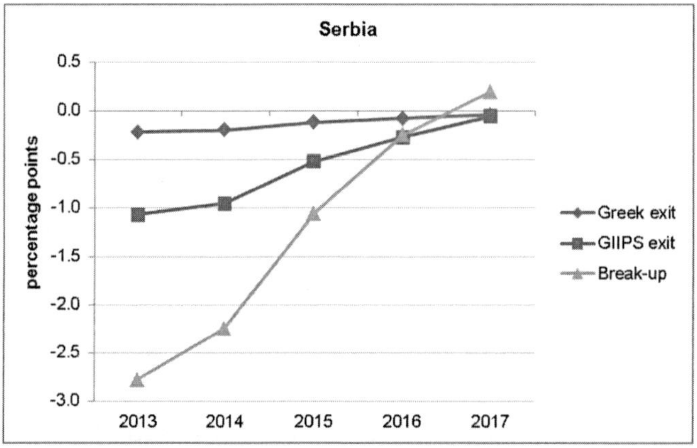

Deviations from baseline in percentage points

Source: Based on Weyerstrass and Grozea-Helmenstein (2013b)

Figure 29: Budget balance ratio in the euro area scenarios

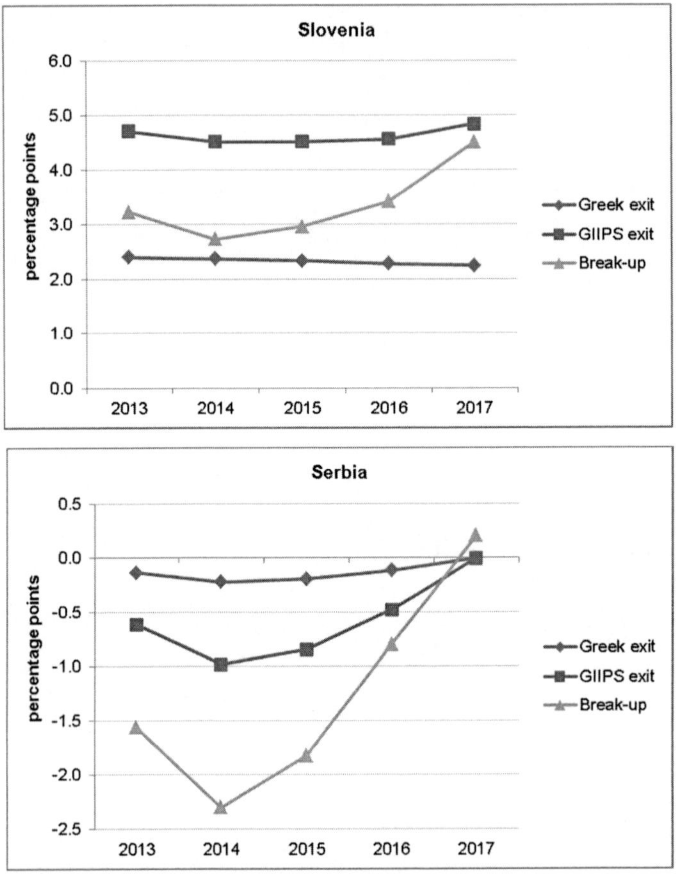

Deviations from baseline in percentage points

Source: Based on Weyerstrass and Grozea-Helmenstein (2013b)

Figure 30: Public debt ratio in the euro area scenarios

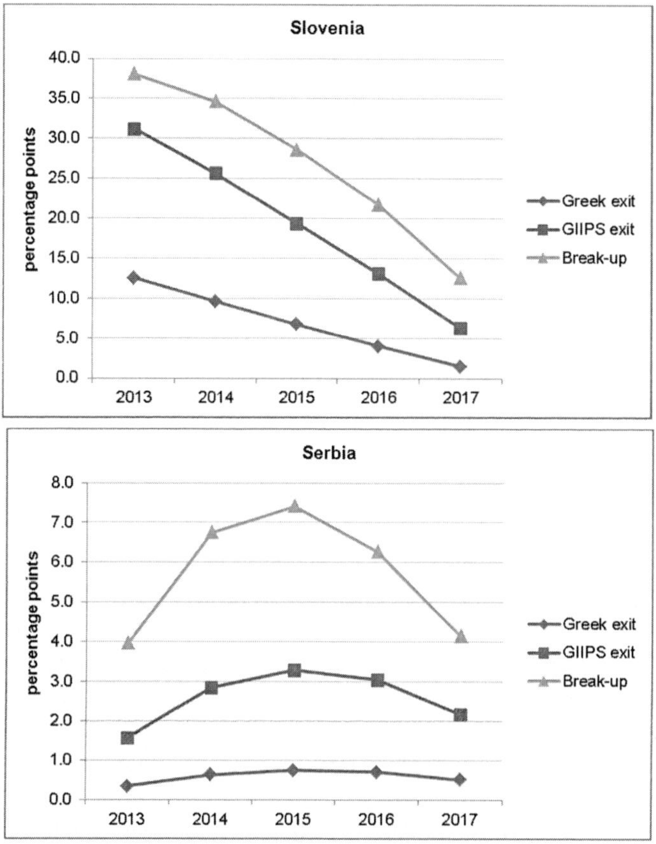

Deviations from baseline in percentage points

Source: Own illustration, based on Weyerstrass and Grozea-Helmenstein (2013b)

The simulations in Weyerstrass and Grozea-Helmenstein (2013b) show that a euro area exit of Greece alone would affect the economies of Slovenia and Serbia only marginally. If, in addition to Greece, Italy, Ireland, Portugal and Spain left the euro area too (GIIPS exit) or if the euro area even broke up completely, the negative economic impacts on Slovenia and on Serbia would be dramatic. In the worst case, real GDP might shrink by almost 10 percent in Slovenia and by 6 percent in Serbia. This is caused by a collapse in exports of more than 18 percent and in investment of around 30 percent. In the case of an exit by Greece, Ireland, Italy, Portugal and Spain, employment would decline by up to 0.9 percent in Slovenia and 0.8 percent in Serbia, compared to the baseline of a successful resolution of the euro area crisis. As a consequence, the unemployment rate would be 0.8 and 0.5 percentage points higher respectively. Should the euro area break up totally, employment might decline by up to 2.6 percent in Slovenia and 1.7 percent in Serbia. This would push up the unemployment rate by 2.1 percentage points in Slovenia and 1.2 percentage points in Serbia. The larger effects in Slovenia compared to Serbia are caused by the additional fiscal consolidation aimed at reducing the higher public debt incurred by the write-down on the fiscal assistance. Interestingly, at the end of the simulation period, investment in Serbia is even higher than in the baseline. This is brought about by the assumed return of credit availability to the baseline in the final year. Hence, companies are then able to undertake investments postponed during the crisis. This recovery is less evident in Slovenia as in this country the collapse in investment in the first three years of the simulation period is also less pronounced. Real exports also recover and exceed their baseline level in the final year of the simulation period. This is due to a real devaluation of the Slovenian and Serbian currencies as a result of the decline in wages and prices relative to the baseline.

Obviously, the scenario of a successful resolution of the problems would be preferable to any scenario involving the exit of one or more countries from the euro area. If the financial assistance from the international community indeed helps the peripheral countries to restore their competitiveness by implementing structural reforms, the loans given to them will be fully repaid. In this sense, the ESM loans and ECB interventions may be viewed as an investment in the ability of the countries to repay their loans. Should, on the other hand, the crisis countries fail to implement the necessary structural reforms successfully, the weaker economic growth and high unemployment would make fiscal consolidation nearly impossible. As the simulations have shown, this would have dramatic consequences for their trading partners and creditor countries like Slovenia and Serbia. These results and conclusions are also relevant for any other small open economy in the euro area, including Austria.

THE EFFECTS OF CROATIA'S EU ACCESSION ON EXTERNAL TRADE WITH ITS NEIGHBOURING COUNTRIES

Trade effects of EU integration

On 1 July 2013, Croatia joined the European Union as its 28th Member State. This can be expected to have significant effects on Croatia's, but also on Bosnia and Herzegovina's, Serbia's and Slovenia's external trade. This chapter aims to estimate potential effects on trade and general macroeconomic indicators like real GDP growth, unemployment and inflation in Croatia, Slovenia, Serbia and Bosnia and Herzegovina that can be expected from Croatia's EU accession.

In order to assess the macroeconomic effects of the EU enlargement process, it is essential to analyse how trade between old and new members and among old members is affected. The gross trade effects of a country's accession to the EU can be divided into trade creation, trade diversion and trade displacement (Wilhelmsson 2006). Positive effects arise as new members replace expensive domestic production with cheaper imports from other EU Member States because trade barriers for intra-EU trade have been eliminated. To this extent, trade creation is taking place, which improves the allocation of resources in the economy. On the other hand, there is also a negative effect as new members replace previous cheaper imports from the rest of the world by imports from other Member States because tariffs on goods from the rest of the world have not been eliminated. This effect is called trade diversion whereby resource allocation in the economy deteriorates. Finally, trade displacement may take place. In this case, increased trading by a new EU Member State to third markets replaces the exports of other countries to these markets.

The EU Eastern enlargement rounds of 2004 and 2007 integrated ten countries from Central and Eastern Europe (CEEC) into the EU: in 2004, eight countries from this region joined the EU (the Czech Republic, Slovakia, Estonia, Latvia, Lithuania, Hungary, Poland, and Slovenia), followed in 2007 by Bulgaria and Romania. Croatia, which followed in 2013, was thus only the second country from the former Yugoslavia to join the EU, nine years after Slovenia's accession. The EU enlargements towards the CEEC region were preceded by extensive efforts to integrate them into the European market. Important steps in this process were the gradual liberalisation of trade between the incumbent EU members and the CEECs, as laid down in the Europe Agreements (EAs), and the promotion of trade integration among the CEECs (the Central European Free Trade Agreement CEFTA, and the Baltic Free Trade Agreement BFTA). CEFTA and the BFTA were established with the intention of increasing trade among the Central European and the Baltic countries respectively. These trade agreements aimed at creating a free trade area for industrial goods. In the case of the BFTA, free trade was eventually extended to include agricultural products. CEFTA resulted in free trade in industrial goods between its original members as of 1 January 1997. However, the liberalisation of trade in agricultural products has not advanced much. When CEFTA came into force on 1 March 1993, the founding members were Poland, the Czech Republic, Slovakia, Poland and Hungary. It expanded with the accession of Slovenia in 1996, Romania in 1997 and Bulgaria in 1999. Estonia, Latvia and Lithuania implemented the BFTA in April 1994, introducing free trade in industrial goods. The integration of trade was advanced further in 1997 when the agreement on free trade in agricultural products came into force. Croatia joined the Central European Free Trade Agreement in 2003 (Wilhelmsson 2006).

When most CEFTA members joined the EU in 2004 and 2007, they left CEFTA again. The only country to join the free trade agreement during this period was Macedonia, in 2006. Afterwards, in 2007, Albania, Bosnia and Herzegovina, Moldova, Serbia and Montenegro as well as Kosovo became CEFTA members. In the past the Central European Free Trade Agreement mainly served as a waiting room for the period until EU membership. This was also the case for Croatia (Holzner 2013).

Upon its EU accession in July 2013, Croatia naturally withdrew from CEFTA. All countries joining the EU have to apply EU trade rules to their former CEFTA partners as well. Hence, since its EU accession Croatia has been applying EU rules to Bosnia and Herzegovina and Serbia too. This might divert Croatia's trade away from these countries, while trade between Croatia and Slovenia should benefit as both countries are now EU members, and hence trade between them is now completely free of tariffs. However, Slovenia's exports and imports are probably only marginally affected since Slovenia has already been an EU Member State since 2004, and its foreign trade has traditionally been orientated towards its "Western" neighbours Austria and Italy, as well as towards Germany as the largest EU economy.

Wilhelmsson (2006) finds that the EU enlargement process until 2004 resulted in significant gross trade creation, both in trade between the EU and the CEECs and among the CEECs. Trade creation, trade diversion and trade displacement could be detected. Trade diversion only took place to a small extent, largely limited to the 1995 enlargement involving Austria, Finland and Sweden. Furthermore, Wilhelmsson (2006) could not detect any trade displacement, but this might be due to the fact that this study did not control for factors increasing intra-EU trade (the Single Market Programme and the Economic and Monetary Union). However, this lack of evidence of trade displacement can be interpreted as an indication that this possible integration effect has not been significant. All this suggests that the enlargement process has resulted in significant net trade creation.

According to Papazoglou et al. (2006), the 2004 Eastern EU enlargement not only generated additional foreign trade but also resulted in some re-direction of trade flows. All accession countries experienced increases in both exports and imports, but imports to each accession country rose more than exports. The rise in accession countries' exports in general accrued with the "old", i.e. pre-2004 EU-15 members, which benefited from a rising share of the accession economies' exports, while trade by the accession countries with the rest of the world decreased, particularly in North America and the Far East. The relative trade balance of the incumbent EU members vis-à-vis the CEECs has improved, since most of the created trade has been due to EU exports to the CEECs. Hence, while international trade of all accession countries rose, in terms of the trade balance, the incumbent EU members could improve their positions vis-à-vis the accession countries, while the opposite is true for the new Member States.

In a recent assessment of the potential macroeconomic and trade effects of Croatia's EU accession, Holzner (2013) estimates that the share of Croatian exports to the EU will increase by 2.2 percentage points, while the share of exports to the CEFTA countries and to the rest of the world is expected to drop by 0.7 and 1.5 percentage points respectively. According to Holzner's (2013) estimations, Croatia's exports to Serbia will decline by 71 million US dollars as a result of Croatia's EU accession. Croatia's exports to Bosnia and Herzegovina are estimated to drop by 18.2 million US dollars, while exports to the EU should increase by 104 million US dollars. On the other hand, Croatia's exports to the rest of the world are estimated to drop by about 180 million US dollars. In terms of nominal changes in imports, Holzner's (2013) simulation results suggest a drop in Croatian imports from Bosnia and Herzegovina (by about 10 million US dollars) and an increase in imports from Serbia (by about 22 million US dollars). The shifts in the value of imports from the EU (an increase in excess of 110 million US dollars) and the rest of the world (an increase of 190 million US dollars) are more substantial. Separate estimations for Slovenia are not included in Holzner (2013). Hence, for the subsequent simulations, the effects on exports to and imports from Slovenia have to be derived from the effects that Holzner (2013) estimates for the entire

EU and from the actual shares of the entire EU and Slovenia in Croatia's foreign trade.

Table 11 shows that in 2012 and in the first half of 2013 both Slovenia and Bosnia and Herzegovina accounted for slightly less than 7 percent of Croatia's foreign trade, while Serbia made up 2 ½ percent. It is striking that there is a large discrepancy between Bosnia's share in Croatia's exports (12.5 percent in 2013) compared to its import share (3.5 percent). Already before Croatia's EU accession on 1 July 2013, about 60 percent of the country's exports were directed to the other 27 EU Member States, and the EU-27 were also responsible for about 60 percent of Croatia's imports.

Table 11: Share EU27, Slovenia, of Bosnia and Herzegovina and Serbia in Croatia's foreign trade

		2012		I.-VI.2013	
		Mill. US$	%	Mill. US$	%
TOTAL	Exports	12,369.0		5,725.5	
	Imports	20,834.3		10,667.7	
	TOTAL	33,203.2		16,393.2	
EU27	Exports	7,194.5	58.2%	3,540.3	61.8%
	Imports	13,031.0	62.5%	6,368.6	59.7%
	TOTAL	20,225.5	60.9%	9,908.8	60.4%
SLOVENIA	Exports	1,064.6	8.6%	570.5	10.0%
	Imports	1,217.6	5.8%	560.0	5.3%
	TOTAL	2,282.3	6.9%	1,130.5	6.9%
BOSNIA AND HERZEGOVINA	Exports	1,577.5	12.8%	717.5	12.5%
	Imports	728.7	3.5%	377.9	3.5%
	TOTAL	2,306.2	6.9%	1,095.5	6.7%
SERBIA	Exports	537.4	4.3%	209.8	3.7%
	Imports	362.4	1.7%	176.2	1.7%
	TOTAL	899.8	2.7%	385.9	2.4%

Source: Croatian Bureau of Statistics; author's own calculations

Simulating trade effects of Croatia's EU accession

For the simulations of the impact on Croatia's and its neighbours' macroeconomic developments resulting from the trade effects of Croatia's EU accession, the estimations of Holzner (2013) have to be transformed into inputs to the multi-country model. The trade effects are modelled as exogenous changes to Croatia's exports to and imports from the other countries contained in the model and the rest of the world. Holzner's (2013) estimates imply changes in Croatia's external trade as shown in Table 12.

Table 12: Impacts of Croatia's EU accession on Croatia's foreign trade

Croatian exports to and imports from		2012 Value [mill. US$]	Change due to EU accession Value [mill. US$]	%
TOTAL	Exports	12,369.0	-196.2	-1.6%
	Imports	20,834.3	311.6	1.5%
	TOTAL	33,203.2	115.4	0.3%
EU27	Exports	7,194.5	104.2	1.4%
	Imports	13,031.0	110.5	0.8%
	TOTAL	20,225.5	214.7	1.1%
SLOVENIA	Exports	1,064.6	15.4	1.4%
	Imports	1,217.6	10.3	0.8%
	TOTAL	2,282.3	25.7	1.1%
BOSNIA AND HERZEGOVINA	Exports	1,577.5	-18.2	-1.2%
	Imports	728.7	-10.2	-1.4%
	TOTAL	2,306.2	-28.4	-1.2%
SERBIA	Exports	537.4	-71.0	-13.2%
	Imports	362.4	21.8	6.0%
	TOTAL	899.8	-49.2	-5.5%
REST OF THE WORLD	Exports	3,059.5	-179.7	-5.9%
	Imports	6,712.2	190.5	2.8%
	TOTAL	9,771.7	10.8	0.1%

Source: Croatian Bureau of Statistics; Holzner (2013);author's own calculations

While Croatia's trade with Serbia and Bosnia and Herzegovina are directly mentioned in Holzner (2013), the impacts on exports to and imports from Slovenia have to be derived from the estimated effects on Croatia's trade with the entire EU and Slovenia's share relative to the EU share in Croatia's exports and imports. The macroeconomic multi-country model was simulated over a period of 5 years. First a baseline run is performed, counterfactually assuming that Croatia did not join the European Union. Then, Croatia's bilateral trade with the other countries in the model and with the rest of the world is changed exogenously – with respect to the baseline – according to the estimates shown in the last column in Table 12. Those fields which are relevant for the model inputs are shaded in grey. After having run the model, the final trade effects will differ from the model inputs as shown in Table 12, since there will be macroeconomic feedback effects from the changes in trade to income and back again to foreign trade.

Simulation results

The simulations are performed over the period 2013 to 2017. To be more precise, the actual simulation started in 2012 since for many time series the database ends in 2011. However, as Croatia joined the EU in 2013, the simulation results are only interpreted from that year onwards. Furthermore, although the multi-country data which have been used for the simulations are quarterly, only the annual aggregates are shown and interpreted, as many quarterly time series had to be constructed due to missing data; in addition the quarterly series are distorted since seasonally non-adjusted data were used. The simulations were performed in such a way that Croatia's exports and imports as determined endogenously by the relevant model equations were altered with add factors. However, since the export and import equations take demand in the importing country and the real exchange rates into account, any changes in these explanatory variables caused by the first-round trade effects also feed back into exports and imports. Therefore, already in the first year of the simulation period, the effects deviate somewhat from the model inputs which are based on Holzner (2013) (see Table 12).

Table 13: Effects of Croatia's EU accession (% deviations from baseline)

	2013	2014	2015	2016	2017
			Croatia		
Exports total	-2.80	-4.78	-4.90	-4.97	-5.04
Exports to BiH	-0.70	-1.33	-1.45	-1.57	-1.82
Exports to SRB	-7.49	-12.93	-12.87	-12.74	-12.48
Exports to SLO	0.63	0.68	0.60	0.87	1.12
Exports to ROW	-3.49	-5.92	-6.17	-6.52	-6.96
Imports total	-0.97	-2.07	-2.16	-1.63	-0.79
Imports from BiH	-2.32	-5.82	-6.81	-8.23	-10.25
Imports from SRB	-0.02	-2.50	-5.55	-7.34	-8.07
Imports from SLO	-1.49	-5.82	-7.02	-5.96	-5.23
Imports from ROW	-0.91	-1.75	-1.70	-1.06	-0.02
Real GDP	-1.74	-3.38	-3.74	-3.87	-3.74
Employment	-0.25	-0.62	-0.67	-0.69	-0.66
CPI	-0.04	-0.61	-1.54	-2.63	-3.66
			Bosnia and Herzegovina		
Exports total	-0.24	-0.52	-0.56	-0.71	-1.06
Exports to CRO	-2.32	-5.82	-6.81	-8.23	-10.25
Exports to SRB	0.10	0.34	0.33	0.40	0.42
Exports to SLO	-0.09	-0.55	-0.88	-0.75	-0.44
Exports to ROW	0.00	0.06	0.17	0.26	0.33
Imports total	-0.07	-0.33	-0.39	-0.29	-0.22
Imports from CRO	-0.70	-1.33	-1.45	-1.57	-1.82
Imports from SRB	-0.02	-0.11	-0.59	-1.12	-1.86
Imports from SLO	-0.03	-0.06	-0.09	-0.21	-0.57
Imports from ROW	-0.20	-0.33	-0.32	-0.29	-0.57
Real GDP	0.05	0.01	-0.15	-0.42	-1.00
Employment	0.01	0.01	-0.02	-0.08	-0.17
CPI	0.00	0.00	0.00	-0.07	-0.16

Table 13 (continued)

	2013	2014	2015	2016	2017
			Slovenia		
Exports total	-0.11	-0.41	-0.46	-0.36	-0.28
Exports to CRO	-1.49	-5.82	-7.02	-5.96	-5.23
Exports to SRB	0.06	0.28	0.40	0.30	0.12
Exports to BiH	-0.03	-0.06	-0.09	-0.21	-0.57
Exports to ROW	0.00	0.01	0.03	0.06	0.10
Imports total	-0.07	-0.33	-0.39	-0.29	-0.22
Imports from CRO	0.63	0.68	0.60	0.87	1.12
Imports from SRB	-0.16	-0.65	-1.26	-1.69	-2.05
Imports from BiH	-0.09	-0.55	-0.88	-0.75	-0.44
Imports from ROW	-0.12	-0.45	-0.56	-0.53	-0.52
Real GDP	-0.07	-0.20	-0.25	-0.30	-0.36
Employment	-0.01	-0.04	-0.06	-0.07	-0.09
CPI	0.00	-0.01	-0.02	-0.03	-0.03
		Serbia			
Exports total	-0.01	-0.12	-0.37	-0.66	-0.98
Exports to CRO	-0.02	-2.50	-5.55	-7.34	-8.07
Exports to BiH	-0.02	-0.11	-0.59	-1.12	-1.86
Exports to SLO	-0.16	-0.65	-1.26	-1.69	-2.05
Exports to ROW	0.00	0.00	-0.06	-0.14	-0.22
Imports total	-0.56	-0.78	-1.04	-1.05	-1.20
Imports from CRO	-7.49	-12.93	-12.87	-12.74	-12.48
Imports from BiH	0.10	0.34	0.33	0.40	0.42
Imports from SLO	0.06	0.28	0.40	0.30	0.12
Imports from ROW	0.26	0.69	0.38	0.36	0.08
Real GDP	0.56	1.07	1.22	1.38	1.63
Employment	0.04	0.11	0.10	0.13	0.18
CPI	0.01	0.76	0.95	1.07	1.19

Note: CRO: Croatia, BiH: Bosnia and Herzegovina; SLO: Slovenia; SRB: Serbia, ROW: rest of the world

Source: Author's own calculations

Since the simulation was run over a period in the future, assumptions had to be made for the future development of the exogenous variables. For world trade as well as the domestic fiscal policy variables, the average pattern of the past was extrapolated over the 5 year simulation horizon. For the exchange rate between the euro and the US dollar it was assumed that it remains constant. The exact settings of the exogenous variables might be disputed, but in such simulation analyses differences between the scenarios are relevant while the absolute realisations of the variables are not of immediate interest. For the same reason the actual realisations of the endogenous variables will not be interpreted, the focus lying on deviations of the scenario with Croatia's EU accession from the counterfactual alternative of no EU accession.

For Croatia, both the trade and total macroeconomic effects are substantial. The magnitude of the negative trade effects increases over time. The decline in real exports rises from 2.8 percent in the first year to 5 percent in the final year of the 5 year simulation horizon. On the other hand, the decline in imports also becomes more substantial until the third year (2015) but decreases afterwards. This is caused by the decline in real domestic demand which, together with the decrease in exports, is reflected in a negative deviation of real GDP from the baseline. This result is in line with Holzner (2013), who estimates that as a result of Croatia's EU accession, its domestic output will decline. In contrast to the model simulations shown here, Holzner (2013) provides no information on the development over time since he performed a comparative static analysis. Furthermore, Holzner (2013) confines himself to the direct trade effects. According to the model simulations as shown in Table 13, in the final year real GDP decreases by 3.7 percent, but the extent of the decrease is slightly smaller than in the fourth year. This indicates that the negative effects of Croatia's EU accession will not become ever larger over time, but will at least stabilise in the medium run. This is partly due to the decrease in domestic prices which makes Croatia's goods and services more competitive on the world markets. As implemented in the model inputs, Croatia's exports to Bosnia and Herzegovina and to Serbia (no EU Member States), as well as to the rest of the world decline, while Croatia's exports to Slovenia (an EU Member State) are positively influenced by its EU accession. Croatia's imports from all other countries in the multi-country model are negatively affected. The same applies to Croatia's imports from the rest of the world, but due to the decreasing domestic demand this negative deviation from the baseline decreases over time, and in the final year imports from the rest of world lie only marginally below the baseline.

Due to macroeconomic feedback effects, not only trade between Croatia and the other countries in the multi-country model is affected by Croatia's EU accession, but also trade among the other countries changes, although these effects are relatively small. Bosnia and Herzegovina's exports to Slovenia decline, while exports to Serbia and to the rest of the world rise. Total exports are negatively affected due to the large negative impact on Bosnia and Herzegovina's exports to Croatia. For Slovenia, exports to Croatia and Bosnia and Herzegovina decrease with respect to the baseline, while exports to Serbia and the rest of the world are positively affected. Finally, Serbia's exports decrease to all other countries in the multi-country model as well as to the rest of the world.

Bosnia and Herzegovina's real GDP first increases, but then declines from the third year onwards. Employment follows the same profile, while consumer prices are almost identical to the baseline until the third year, decreasing somewhat in the last two years. In Slovenia, real GDP, employment and the consumer price index are negatively affected over the entire simulation period. The opposite is true for Serbia; in this country the largest macroeconomic effects outside Croatia can be observed. In the final year of the simulation period, Serbian GDP is 1.6 percent higher than in the counterfactual scenario of Croatia staying outside the EU, and the consumer price index is 1.2 percent higher than in the baseline.

The simulations in this section have shown that the EU accession triggers not only trade creation and trade diversion effects for the accession country, but also affects the macroeconomic performance of other countries and trade between other countries, in particular if the accession country had belonged to another free trade area like the CEFTA before joining the EU. Furthermore, as a result of macroeconomic feedback effects as well as cross-country spillovers, not only trade but all macroeconomic indicators like real GDP, employment and the price level in the accession country, but also in other countries, are affected.

CONCLUSIONS

Economic policy decisions should be based on a sound assessment of their potential costs and benefits. The qualitative impacts of fiscal and monetary policy measures or of external events can often be derived from economic theory, but only a comprehensive representation of the economic interdependencies enables the quantification of these effects. Furthermore, policy-makers as well as private households and companies require forecasts of economic developments in the short and medium-term future. Hence, it is desirable to have a tool at hand that facilitates the evaluation of different economic policy measures as well as the generation of economic forecasts. As for any other country, this also applies to the successor states of the former Yugoslavia.

A macroeconomic model is such a tool, especially if it is an econometric model based on sound theoretical foundations and estimated with actual data from the economy under consideration. In this book, a multi-country model for important successor states of the former Yugoslavia is described alongside with the application of this model to different policy simulations. The multi-country model consists of sub-models for Bosnia and Herzegovina, Slovenia, Serbia and Croatia. The countries became independent only in the 1990s. Hence, reliable data are only available for a very short period. Therefore, the model is based on quarterly data. Unfortunately, for many macroeconomic indicators only annual data are available. Hence, as described in the book, for many aggregates quarterly time series had to be constructed. Furthermore, due to the ongoing transformation process of the countries under consideration, economic data are frequently revised after their first release. Notwithstanding these data limitations, the model is capable to track the endogenous variables reasonably well in an ex post simulation.

The model has been used (a) to evaluate how an isolated fiscal policy implemented in only one of the four countries differs from coordinated action in all four countries; (b) to explore the budgetary effects of the demographic development in Slovenia along with different strategies of coping with these effects; (c) to investigate different budget consolidation strategies for Slovenia, including a derivation of optimal fiscal policies in the aftermath of the severe economic crisis; (d) to simulate the macroeconomic effects of different scenarios of future developments in the euro area for Serbia and Slovenia; and (e) to investigate trade and general macroeconomic effects of Croatia's EU accession on the other countries in the region.

The simulations represent examples of the ample range of applications of the macroeconometric multi-country model in future consultancies of economic policy-making in the former Yugoslavia.

REFERENCES

Afonso, A. and R. Strauch (2004), Fiscal Policy Events and Interest Rate Swap Spreads: Evidence from the EU, European Central Bank Working Paper Series No. 303.

Alcidi, C., A. Giovannini, and D. Gros (2012), Grexit: Who would pay for it?, CEPS Policy Brief No. 272, 23 May 2012.

Alesina, A. and F. Giavazzi, eds. (2013), Fiscal Policies after the Financial Crisis, National Bureau of Economic Research Conference Report.

Ardagna, S. (2009), Financial markets' behavior around episodes of large changes in the fiscal stance, European Economic Review, Vol.53 (January), 37–55.

Behrens, D., G. Haber and K. Weyerstrass (2011), European Economic Integration of the Successor States of the former Yugoslavia. Development of a Macroeconomic Model, Institute for Advanced Studies (IHS), Vienna. Research Report.

Berrer, H., D. Grozea-Helmenstein and K. Weyerstrass (2009), Macroeconomic Model for Serbia. Data, Estimation and Evaluation. Institute of Economic Research, Vienna, and Institute for Advanced Studies (IHS), Vienna. Research Report.

Blueschke-Nikolaeva, V., D. Blueschke and R. Neck (2012), Optimal control of nonlinear dynamic econometric models: An algorithm and an application. Computational Statistics & Data Analysis, Vol. 56(11), 3230-3240.

Born, B., T. Buchen, K. Carstensen, Ch. Grimme, M. Kleemann, K. Wohlrabe and T. Wollmershäuser (2012), Austritt Griechenlands aus der Europäischen Währungsunion: historische Erfahrungen, makroökonomische Konsequenzen und organisatorische Umsetzung. Memo, ifo Institute, Munich.

Brainard, W.C., J. Tobin (1968), Pitfalls in Financial Model Building, American Economic Review 58(2), 99-122.

Chow, G.C. (1975), Analysis and Control of Dynamic Economic Systems. John Wiley & Sons, New York.

Chow, G.C. (1981), Econometric Analysis by Control Methods. John Wiley & Sons, New York.

Christoffel, K., G. Coenen and A. Warne (2008), The New Area-Wide Model of the euro area. A micro-founded open-economy model for forecasting and policy analysis, ECB Working Paper Series, No. 944.

Colander, D., P. Howitt, A. Kirman, A. Leijonhufvud and P. Mehrling (2008), Beyond DSGE Models: Towards an Empirically-Based Macroeconomics. Paper for presentation at the 2008 American Economics Association Meeting. http://www.econ.brown.edu/fac/Peter_Howitt/publication/complex percent20macro6.pdf.

Crespo Cuaresma, J., M. Feldkircher, T. Slacik and J. Wörz (2009), Simple but Effective: The OeNB's Forecasting Model for Selected CESEE Countries. Oesterreichische Nationalbank. Focus on European Economic Transition Q4/09, 84-95.

D'Auria, F., C. Denis, K. Havik, K. Mc Morrow, C. Planas, R. Raciborski, W. Röger and A. Rossi (2010), The production function methodology for calculating potential growth rates and output gaps. European Commission Economic Papers 420. Brussels.

Dees, S., F. di Mauro, M.H. Pesaran, V.L. Smith (2007), Exploring the international linkages of the euro area: a global VAR analysis, Journal of Applied Econometrics 22, 1-38.

Deutsche Bundesbank (2001), Unsicherheit, Handlungsfreiheit und Investitionsverhalten – ein empirischer Befund für Deutschland, Monatsbericht September 2001, 71-88.

Dickey, D.A. and W.A. Fuller (1979). Distribution of the Estimators for Autoregressive Time Series with a Unit Root. Journal of the American Statistical Association, 74, 427-431.

Engle, R.F. and C.W.J. Granger (1987), Co-integration and error correction: Representation, estimation and testing. Econometrica, Vol. 55, No. 2, 251-276.

European Commission (2014), European Economic Forecast. Spring 2014. European Economy 3/2014. Brussels.

European Commission (2013a), Bosnia and Herzegovina. 2013 Progress Report. Brussels.

European Commission (2013b), The EU's economic governance explained. Memo. Brussels.

European Commission (2008a), Bosnia and Herzegovina. 2008 Progress Report. Enlargement Strategy and main challenges 2008-2009. Brussels.

European Commission (2008b), Enlargement Strategy and Main Challenges 2008-2009. Communication from the Commission to the Council and the European Parliament. Brussels.

Fair, R.C. (1992), The Cowles Commission Approach, Real Business Cycle Theories, and New Keynesian Economics, NBER Working Paper Series, No. 3990.

Fenz, G., I. Moder and M. Silgoner (2012), Sovereign debt crisis delays economic recovery, Monetary Policy and the Economy Q3, 5-22.

Godfrey, L.G. (1978), Testing Against General Autoregressive and Moving Average Error Models when the Regressors Include Lagged Dependent Variables, Econometrica, 46, 1293-1302.

Granger, C.W.J. (1997), On Modelling the Long Run in Applied Economics, The Economic Journal 107, 169-177.

Grozea-Helmenstein, D., K. Weyerstrass, H. Berrer and V. Ivanic (2009), Economic Forecast for Serbia 2009 and 2010. Slow recovery follows sharp slowdown. Research Report, Center for Strategic Economic Studies "Vojvodina-CESS", Novi Sad.

Grozea-Helmenstein, D., K. Weyerstrass, V. Ivanic, M. Sokic, D. Scepanovic and L. Aleksic (2010), Economic Forecast for Serbia 2010 and 2011. Economy on the recovery path. Research Report, Center for Strategic Economic Studies "Vojvodina-CESS", Novi Sad.

Grozea-Helmenstein, D., K. Weyerstrass, V. Ivanic, M. Sokic, D. Scepanovic, L. Aleksic and T. Karaulac (2011), Economic Forecast for Serbia 2011 and 2012. Recovery underway, but challenges for economic policy remain topical. Research Report, Center for Strategic Economic Studies "Vojvodina-CESS", Novi Sad.

Haber, G., R. Neck and K. Weyerstrass (2002), Optimal Fiscal and Monetary Policies for Slovenia under Different Exchange Rate Regimes and Targets. In: Welfe, W. (ed.), Macromodels 2001, Lodz, 269-281.

Hall, S. (1995), Macroeconomics and a bit more Reality, The Economic Journal 105, 974-988.

Holzner, M. (2013), Impact of Croatian EU Accession on Regional Trade Patterns, WIIW Policy Notes and Reports, No. 10.

International Monetary Fund (2013), Deficits & Debt. Crisis Offers Preliminary Lessons on Fiscal Policy, IMF Survey, Washington, D.C.

Jorgensen, D.W. (1963), Capital Theory and Investment Behavior, American Economic Review, Papers and Proceedings 53.

Kendrick D.A.(1981), Stochastic Control for Economic Models, 2nd ed. McGraw-Hill, New York. www.eco.utexas.edu/faculty/Kendrick.

Keynes, J.M. (1936), The General Theory of Employment, Interest, and Money. London.

Kokanović, M. (1999), Croatian Labour Realities, 1990-1999, South-East Europe Review for Labour and Social Affairs 2(3), 185-208.

Kwiatkowski, D., P.C.B. Phillips, P. Schmidt and Y. Shin (1992), Testing the Null Hypothesis of Stationarity against the Alternative of a Unit Root, Journal of Econometrics 54, 159-178.

Kydland, F.E. and E.C. Prescott (1982), Time to Build and Aggregate Fluctuations, Econometrica, 50, 1345-1370.

Layard, R., S. Nickell, and R. Jackman (1991), Unemployment: Macroeconomic Performance and the Labour Market, Oxford University Press, Oxford.

Lucas, R. (1976), Econometric Policy Evaluation: A Critique. In: Brunner K. and A. Meltzer (eds.), The Phillips Curve and Labor Markets, Carnegie-Rochester Conference Series on Public Policy, 1. American Elsevier, New York, pp 19-46.

Mankiw, N.G. and D. Romer, eds., (1991), New Keynesian Economics. Vol. 1: Imperfect competition and sticky prices; Vol. 2: Coordination Failures and Real Rigidities. MIT Press.

Matulka, J. and R. Neck (1992), OPTCON: An algorithm for the optimal control of nonlinear stochastic models. Annals of Operations Research, 37, 375-401.

McKibbin, W.J. and J.D. Sachs (1991), Global Linkages, Washington, DC: Brookings Institution.

McKibbin, W.J. and P. Wilcoxen (1998), The Theoretical and Empirical Structure of the G-Cubed model, Brookings Discussion Paper in International Economics no. 118.

Mendoza, E.G. (2008), Sudden Stops, Financial Crises and Leverage: A Fisherian Deflation of Tobin's Q, NBER Working Paper 14444, The National Bureau of Economic Research, Cambridge, MA.

Moore, D. and A. Vamvakidis (2007), Economic Growth in Croatia: Potential and Constraints, IMF Working Papers WP/07/198.

Neck, R., D. Blueschke and K. Weyerstrass (2013), Trade-Off of Fiscal Austerity in the European Debt Crisis: The Case of Slovenia. International Advances in Economic Research 19, 367-380.

Neck, R., D. Blueschke and K. Weyerstrass (2011), Optimal macroeconomic policies in a financial and economic crisis: A Case Study for Slovenia, Empirica 38, 435-459.

Neck, R., G. Haber and K. Weyerstrass (2010), Optimal Deterministic and Stochastic Macroeconomic Policies for Slovenia: An Application of the OPTCON Algorithm, Computational Economics, 36, 37-45.

Neck, R. and K. Weyerstrass (2003), Optimal Economic Policies for Slovenia with Different Sets of Policy Instruments. Dynamics of Continuous, Discrete and Impulsive Systems, Series B: Applications and Algorithms 10, 165-180.

Neck, R., K. Weyerstrass and G. Haber (2004), Policy Recommendations for Slovenia: A Quantitative Economic Policy Approach. In: Böhm, B., H. Frisch and M. Steiner (eds.), Slovenia and Austria: Bilateral Economic Effects of Slovenian EU Accession, Graz, 249-271.

Neck, R., K. Weyerstrass and G. Haber (2005), Optimal Macroeconomic Policies for Slovenia: An Optimal Control Analysis. In: Kopacek, P. (ed.), Advanced Control Strategies for Social and Economic Systems, Oxford, 87-92.

OECD (2009), The Effectiveness and Scope of Fiscal Stimulus. OECD Economic Outlook, Interim Report, Chapter 3, Paris.

OECD (2001), Measuring Capital. OECD Manual. Measurement of Capital Stocks, Consumption of Fixed Capital and Capital Services, Paris.

OECD (1997), Flows and Stocks of Fixed Capital 1971 – 1996, Paris.

Papazoglou, Ch., E.J. Pentecost and H. Marques (2006), A Gravity Model Forecast of the Potential Trade Effects of EU Enlargement: Lessons from 2004 and Path-dependency in Integration, The World Economy, Vol. 9, Issue 8, 1077-1089.

Pesaran, M.H., T. Schuermann, S.M. Weiner (2004), Modeling Regional Interdependencies Using a Global Error-Correcting Macroeconometric Model, Journal of Business and Economic Statistics, Vol. 22, Issue 2, 129-162.

Petit, M.L. (1990), Control theory and dynamic games in economic policy analysis. Cambridge University Press, Cambridge.

Phillips, P.C.B and P. Perron (1988), Testing for a Unit Root in Time Series Regression. Biometrika, 75, 335–346.

Rubaszek, M. and P. Skrzypzynski (2008), On the forecasting performance of a small-scale DSGE model, International Journal of Forecasting 24, 498-512.

Roberts, B.V. (2002), An analysis of Macedonian economic growth during 1997 - 2001. Republic of Macedonia, Ministry of Finance, Bulletin 11-12/2002.

Sargan, J.D. (1964), Wages and Prices in the United Kingdom. A study in econometric methodology. In: Hart, P.E., G. Mills and J.K. Whitaker (eds.), Econometric analysis for national economic planning. Butterworth, London, 25–59.

Sims, Ch.A. (1980), Macroeconomics and Reality, Econometrica 48, 1-48.

Slovenian Ministry of Finance (2012), Stability Programme, Republic of Slovenia, 2012 update. Mimeo, Ljubljana.

Stanovnik, T., E. Turk, and V.P. Rupel (2012), Annual National Report 2012. Pensions, Health Care and Long-term Care. Slovenia. March 2012. Report on behalf of the European Commission, DG Employment, Social Affairs and Inclusion.

Tanzi, V. (2008), International Coordination of Fiscal Policies, Journal of Public Policy, Volume 8, Issue 02 111-124.

Taylor, J.B. (2009), The lack of an empirical rationale for a revival of discretionary fiscal policy. American Economic Review, 99, 250-255.

Taylor, J.B. (1993), Macroeconomic Policy in a World Economy. From Econometric Design to Practical Operation, New York, London.

Tinbergen, J. (1939), Statistical Testing of Business Cycle Theories, Geneva: League of Nations.
Tobin, J. (1978), Monetary Policies and the Economy: The Transmission Mechanism, Southern Economic Journal 44(3), 421-431.
Tobin, J. (1969), A General Equilibrium Approach to Monetary Theory, Journal of Money, Credit, and Banking 1(1), 15-29.
Wang, M.-Ch. (2008), Comparing the DSGE model with the factor model: an out-of-sample forecasting experiment. Deutsche Bundesbank Discussion Paper Series 1: Economic Studies No. 04/2008.
Weyerstrass, K. (2015), Forecasting accuracy of a multi-country macroeconometric model for the former Yugoslavia, Estudios de Economia Aplicada (Applied Economic Studies), Vol. 33-2, 1-24.
Weyerstrass, K. (2011), SLOPOL. A macroeconometric model of the Slovenian economy, IB Revija 1-2 / 2011, 57-66.
Weyerstrass, K. (2009), A Macroeconometric Model for Bosnia and Herzegovina, Eastern European Economics 47(5), 63-92.
Weyerstrass, K. and D. Grozea-Helmenstein (2013a), A macroeconometric model for Serbia, International Advances of Economic Research, Volume 19, Issue 2 (May), 85-106.
Weyerstrass, K. and D. Grozea-Helmenstein (2013b), Euro Area Scenarios and their Economic Consequences for Slovenia and Serbia, Managing Global Transitions, Vol. 11, No. 4 (Winter).
Weyerstrass, K., G. Haber and R. Neck (2001), SLOPOL1: A Macroeconomic Model for Slovenia, International Advances in Economic Research 7, 20-37.
Weyerstrass, K., J. Jaenicke, R. Neck, G. Haber, B. van Aarle, K. Schoors, N. Gobbin and P. Claeys (2006), Economic spillover and policy coordination in the Euro Area, European Commission, Economic Papers, No. 246. Brussels.
Weyerstrass, K., R. Neck and G. Haber (2000), Optimal Monetary and Fiscal Policies for Slovenia under Flexible and Fixed Exchange Rates. Central European Journal of Operations Research 8, 209-223.
Weyerstrass, K., R. Neck and G. Haber (2002), Towards an Objective Function for Slovenian Fiscal Policy-Making: A Heuristic Approach. In: Tangian, A.S. and J. Gruber (eds.), Constructing and Applying Objective Functions, Berlin et al., 366-389.
Weyerstrass, K. and R. Neck (2013), A young EU member's ageing: budgetary and macroeconomic consequences of Slovenia's demographic prospects, Empirica, Vol. 40, issue 3, 427-456.
Weyerstrass, K. and R. Neck (2011a), Macroeconomic Effects of the Adoption of the Euro in Serbia. Research Report, Klagenfurt University.
Weyerstrass, K. and R. Neck (2011b), Macroeconomic Effects of the Adoption of the Euro in Bosnia and Herzegovina. Research Report, Klagenfurt University.
Weyerstrass, K. and R. Neck (2008), Macroeconomic Effects of Slovenia's Integration in the Euro Area, Empirica 35(4), 391-403.
Weyerstrass, K. and R. Neck (2007), SLOPOL6: A Macroeconometric Model for Slovenia, International Business and Economics Research Journal 6(11), 81-94.
Weyerstrass, K., U. Schuh, H. Hofer and D. Grozea-Helmenstein (2009), European Economic Integration of Bosnia and Herzegovina. Development of a Decision Support System, Institute for Advanced Studies, Research Report.

Wilhelmsson, F. (2006), Trade Creation, Diversion and Displacement of the EU Enlargement Process, Discussion Paper, Lund University. Department of Economics.

Woodford, M. (2003), Interest and Prices: Foundations of a Theory of Monetary Policy. Princeton University Press.

APPENDIX

LIST OF VARIABLES

Table 14: Model variables

Variable name	Description
BALANCE_BIH	Overall budget balance
BALANCE_CURR_BIH	Budget balance excl. public investment
BALANCE_CURR _RATIO_BIH	Current budget balance as percent of GDP
BALANCERATIO_BIH	Overall budget balance as percent of GDP
CAPR_BIH	Real capital stock [mill. KM]
COMP_EMP_BIH	Total compensation of employees
CONS_BIH	Consumption of households and NPISH (mill. KM), nom.
CONSR_BIH	Consumption of households and NPISH (mill. KM), real
CPI_BIH	Consumer price index (2005 = 100); until 2004 RPI
DEBT_BIH	Stock of foreign debt of government sector, end of period [mill. KM]
DEBTRATIO_BIH	Public debt as percent of GDP
DELTADEBT_BIH	Debt level adjustment in BiH
DEMANDR_BIH	Real total demand
EMP_ADJ_BIH	Employment, adjusted with LFS
EMP_BIH	Registered employment
EXPOTHER_BIH	Other government expenditures

Variable name	Description
EXPTOTAL_BIH	Total government expenditures
EXR_BIH	Exports of goods and services (mill. KM), real
G_BIH	Government consumption (mill. KM), nom.
GCONS_BIH	Government consumption (fiscal statistics)
GDP_EXP_BIH	GDP, nom., expenditure approach (mill. KM)
GDPR_EXP_BIH	GDP, real, expenditure approach (mill. KM)
GR_BIH	Government consumption (mill. KM), real
GWAGE_BIH	Average quarterly gross wage per employee (KM)
GWAGER_BIH	Real gross wage per employee
IFIXR_BIH	Gross fixed capital formation (mill. KM), real
IL_BIH	Long-term lending rate private enterprises
IL_DEBT_BIH	Implicit interest rate on public debt
ILREAL_BIH	Real long-term interest rate
IMR_BIH	Imports of goods and services (mill. KM), real
INFL_BIH	CPI inflation
INTEREST_BIH	Interest payments on public debt
INVENTR_BIH	Change in inventories (mill. KM), real
INVESTR_BIH	Total investment (mill. KM), real
IS_BIH	Short-term lending rate private enterprises
LFORCE_ADJ_BIH	Adjusted labour force
LFORCE_BIH	Labour force
NAIRU_BIH	Non accelerating inflation rate of unemployment
NEER_BIH	Nominal effective exchange rate (decrease: appreciation of KM)

Variable name	Description
NWAGE_BIH	Average quarterly net wage per employee (KM)
NWAGER_BIH	Real net wage per employee
PARTRATE_BIH	Labour force as percentage of total population
PGDP_EXP_BIH	GDP (expenditure approach) deflator
PROD_BIH	Labour productivity
REER_BIH	Real effective exchange rate (decrease: appreciation of KM)
REMIT_BIH	Remittances from temp. workers and people living abroad
REVOTHER_BIH	Grants and other government revenues
REVTOTAL_BIH	Total government revenues
SOCCONTR_BIH	Social security contributions
SOCCONTREMP_BIH	Social security contributions per employee
SUBSIDIES_BIH	Subsidies
TAXINCOME_BIH	Income and profit taxes
TAXVAT_BIH	Sales taxes; VAT
TRANSFERS_BIH	Social benefits
TRENDEMP_BIH	Trend employment
TRENDTFP_BIH	Trend total factor productivity
UCC_BIH	User cost of capital
UN_ADJ_BIH	Unemployment, adjusted with LFS
UN_BIH	Registered unemployment
UR_ADJ_BIH	Unemployment rate (adjusted)
UR_BIH	Unemployment rate (registered)

Variable name	Description
UTIL_BIH	Capacity utilisation rate
UTIL_SA_BIH	Seasonally adjusted capacity utilisation rate
WEDGE_BIH	Tax wedge on wages in BiH
YD_BIH	Disposable income of private households (current prices)
YDR_BIH	Disposable income of private households (real)
YPOT_BIH	Potential GDP
DEPRATE_BIH	Quarterly depreciation rate of capital stock in BiH
EMPFACTOR_BIH	Ratio between registered employment and LFS data
POP_BIH	Population in Bosnia and Herzegovina
PUBINVEST_BIH	Net acquisition of assets
SOCCONTRATE_BIH	Social security contribution rate
VATRATE_BIH	Value added tax rate in BiH
BUD_BALANCE_CRO	Budget balance in relation to GDP
BUD_RATIO_CRO	General government budget balance
CAPITALSTOCK_CRO	Capital stock, real
CONSUM_CRO	Private household consumption, nominal
CONSUMR_CRO	Private household consumption, real
CPI_CRO	Consumer price index
DEBT_CRO	Level of public debt, end of period
DEBT_RATIO_CRO	Debt level in relation to GDP
DEMANDR_CRO	Total final demand, real
EMP_CRO	Employment
EXR_CRO	Total exports, real

Variable name	Description
G_CONS_CRO	Public consumption (public finance statistics), nominal
G_CRO	Public consumption (national accounts), nominal
G_OTHEREXP_CRO	Other government expenditures
G_SUBSIDIES_CRO	Subsidies
GDP_CRO	GDP, nominal
GDPR_CRO	GDP, real
GR_CRO	Public consumption (national accounts), real
GROSS_WAGE_CRO	Nominal gross wage per employee
GROSS_WAGER_CRO	Real gross wage per employee
I_DEBT_CRO	Implicit interest rate on public debt
I_LR_CRO	Long-term interest rate
I_SR_CRO	Short-term interest rate
IFIXR_CRO	Gross fixed capital formation, real
IMR_CRO	Imports, real
INCTAX_CRO	Total income taxes
INCTAXCORP_CRO	Corporate income taxes
INCTAXPERS_CRO	Personal income taxes
INFL_CRO	Inflation rate
INTEREST_CRO	Interest payments on public debt
INVENTR_CRO	Change in inventories, real
INVESTR_CRO	Total gross capital formation, real
IR_LR_CRO	Real long-term interest rate
LFORCE_CRO	Labour force

Variable name	Description
NAIRU_CRO	Non accelerating inflation rate of unemployment
NEER_CRO	Nominal effective exchange rate of the kuna
NET_WAGE_CRO	Average net wage per employee, nominal
NET_WAGER_CRO	Average net wage per employee, real
P_CONSUM_CRO	Deflator of private consumption
P_G_CRO	Deflator of government consumption
P_GDP_CRO	GDP deflator
PARTRATE_CRO	Labour force as percentage of total population, Croatia
PROD_CRO	Labour productivity
REER_CRO	Real effective exchange rate of the kuna
REV_OTHER_CRO	Other government revenues
SOCIALCONT_CRO	Social security contributions
TAX_OTHER_CRO	Other tax revenues
TAX_VAT_CRO	Value added and excise tax revenues
TAXWEDGE_CRO	Difference between gross and net wage
TOTALEXP_CRO	Total government expenditures
TOTALREV_CRO	Total government revenues
TRENDEMP_CRO	Trend employment
TRENDTFP_CRO	Trend total factor productivity
ULC_CRO	Unit labour cost
UN_CRO	Unemployment
UR_CRO	Unemployment rate
UTIL_CRO	Capacity utilisation rate

Variable name	Description
YD_CRO	Personal disposable income, nominal
YDR_CRO	Personal disposable income, real
YPOT_CRO	Potential GDP
AV_TAXRATE_CRO	Average tax rate
DELTA_DEBT_CRO	Difference between gross and net wage in percent of gross wage
G_TRANSFER_CRO	Transfers to private households
INCTAXRATE_CRO	Average personal income tax rate
INCTAXRATECORP _CRO	Average corporate income tax rate
POP_CRO	Population in Croatia
SOCCONTRATE_CRO	Average social security contribution rate
VATRATE_CRO	Value added and excise tax rate
AVPENSION_SLO	Average pension
AVUNBENEFIT_SLO	Average unemployment benefit
BALANCEGDP_SLO	Budget balance in relation to GDP
BALANCEN_SLO	Budget balance
CAGDP_SLO	Current account balance in percent of GDP
CAN_SLO	Current account balance
CAPR_SLO	Capital stock, real
CDEF_SLO	Private consumption deflator
CN_SLO	Private consumption, nominal
CPI_SLO	HICP for Slovenia
CR_SLO	Private consumption, real

Variable name	Description
DEBT_SLO	Public debt
DEBTGDP_SLO	Debt level in relation to GDP
DEMAND_SLO	Final demand, real
EMP_SLO	Employed persons
EXPDEF_SLO	Export deflator
EXPREST_SLO	Remaining government expenditures
EXR_SLO	Exports, real
FINWEALTH_SLO	Stock of financial assets, total economy
GDEF_SLO	Public consumption deflator
GDPDEF_SLO	GDP deflator
GDPN_SLO	GDP, nominal, mill. euro
GDPR_SLO	GDP, real, mill euro, chained volumes, reference year 2000
GINVR_SLO	Real government investment
GN_SLO	Government consumption, nominal
GNFIN_SLO	Government consumption, financial statistics
GOV10Y_SLO	Yield of 10 year government bonds (before 2002q2 linked with long-term interest rate on loans)
GOV10YR_SLO	Real government bond yield
GR_SLO	Government consumption, real
GRGDPR_SLO	Real GDP growth rate
GRYPOT_SLO	Growth rate of potential GDP
GWAGE_SLO	Average gross wage per employee
GWAGER_SLO	Average gross wage, real

Variable name	Description
IGOVDEBT_SLO	Implicit interest rate on gov. debt (quarterly rate)
IMPDEF_SLO	Import deflator
IMPR_SLO	Imports, real
INCOME_SLO	Disposable income of private households, nominal
INCOMER_SLO	Disposable income of private households, real
INCTAX_SLO	Total income tax revenues
INCTAXCORP_SLO	Corporate taxes on income and profit
INCTAXPERS_SLO	Individual taxes on income and profit
INFL_SLO	Inflation rate
INTEREST_SLO	Interest payments
INVENTR_SLO	Change in inventories (+ statistical discrepancy), real
INVR_SLO	Gross fixed capital formation, real
LFORCE_SLO	Labour force
NAIRU_SLO	Non-accelerating inflation rate of unemployment
NWAGE_SLO	Average net wage per employee
NWAGER_SLO	Average net wage, real
PARTRATE_SLO	Labour force participation rate
PENSIONERS_SLO	Number of pensioners
PENSIONS_SLO	Pensions paid by Pension Fund
POP1564_SLO	Population aged 15 to 64
PRINVR_SLO	Real private investment
PROD_SLO	Labour productivity
REER41_SLO	Real effective exchange rate, 41 partners, CPI based (Eurostat)

Variable name	Description
REVREST_SLO	Remaining government revenues
SOCCOMP_SLO	Social security contributions by companies
SOCEMP_SLO	Employees' social security contributions
SOCTOTAL_SLO	Social security contributions by employers and employees
TRENDEMP_SLO	Trend of employment
TRENDTFP_SLO	Trend of total factor productivity
UCC_SLO	User cost of capital
ULC_SLO	Unit labour cost
UN_SLO	Unemployed persons
UNBENEFIT_SLO	Total unemployment benefit
UR_SLO	Unemployment rate
UTIL_SLO	Capacity utilisation rate
VAT_SLO	VAT and sales tax revenues
WEDGE_SLO	Difference between gross and net wage
YPOT_SLO	Potential output
DEBTADJ_SLO	Diff. between change in public debt level and budget balance
DEPRATE_SLO	Quarterly depreciation rate of capital stock in Slovenia
GINVN_SLO	Government investment, nominal
INCTAXRATE_SLO	Average personal income tax rate
PENSIONERS1549_SLO	Pensioners aged 15 to 49
PENSIONERSxx_SLO	Pensioners aged xx in Slovenia
POP1549_SLO	Population aged 15 to 49 in Slovenia

Variable name	Description
POPxx_SLO	Population aged xx in Slovenia
REPRATE_SLO	Pension replacement rate
RESTTRANSFERS_SLO	Remaining public transfers to private households
SOCEMPRATE_SLO	Average social sec. contr. rate, employees
UNBENEFITRATE_SLO	Unemployment benefit rate
VATAXRATE_SLO	VAT rate in Slovenia
BALANCE_SRB	General budget balance
BALANCERATIO_SRB	Budget balance in relation to GDP
CAPR_SRB	Real capital stock [mill. RSD]
CONS_SRB	Consumption of households and NPISHs, nom.
CONSR_SRB	Consumption of households and NPISHs, real
CPI_SRB	Consumer price index
DEBT_SRB	Public debt [mill. RSD] (end of period)
DEBTRATIO_SRB	Public debt as percentage of GDP
DEMANDR_SRB	Total real demand
EMP_SRB	Persons in employment
EXPREST_SRB	Remaining, unspecified government expenditures
EXR_SRB	Exports of goods and services, real
G_SRB	Public consumption, nom.
GDP_SRB	GDP, nominal [mill. RSD]
GDPR_SRB	GDP, real
GFCFR_SRB	Gross fixed capital formation, real
GOVCONS_SRB	Public consumption (fiscal statistics)

Variable name	Description
GR_SRB	Public consumption, real
GRGDPR_SRB	Real GDP growth rate
GWAGE_SRB	Average gross wage
GWAGER_SRB	Gross real wage rate
IL_DEBT_SRB	Implicit interest rate on public debt
ILEND_SRB	Total lending interest rate
IMR_SRB	Imports of goods and services, real
INFL_SRB	inflation rate
INTEREST_SRB	Interest payment
INVENTR_SRB	Changes in inventories, real
LFORCE_SRB	Labour force
NAIRU_SRB	Non-accelerating inflation rate of unemployment
NBSRATE_SRB	NBS interest rate, open market operations
NEER_SRB	Nominal effective exchange rate
NWAGE_SRB	Average net wage
NWAGER_SRB	Net real wage rate
PARTRATE_SRB	Labour force as percentage of total population
PGDP_SRB	GDP deflator
PROD_SRB	Labour productivity
REER_SRB	Real effective exchange rate
REVREST_SRB	Remaining, unspecified government revenues
SOCBENEFIT_SRB	Social insurance benefits
SOCCONTR_SRB	Social contributions

Variable name	Description
SUBSIDIES_SRB	Subsidies
TAXCORP_SRB	Corporate income tax
TAXINC_SRB	Personal income tax
TRENDEMP_SRB	Trend of employment
TRENDTFP_SRB	Trend of total factor productivity
UCC_SRB	User cost of capital
ULC_SRB	Unit labour costs
UN_SRB	Number of unemployed persons
UR_SRB	Unemployment rate
UTIL_SRB	Capacity utilisation rate
VAT_SRB	Value added tax revenues
YD_SRB	Personal disposable income, nominal
YDR_SRB	Personal disposable income, real
YPOT_SRB	Potential output
AV_TAX_RATE_SRB	Average income tax rate in Serbia
CORPTRATE_SRB	Corporate income tax rate in Serbia
DELTADEBT_SRB	Diff. between change in debt level and budget balance
DEPRATE_SRB	Quarterly depreciation rate of capital stock in Serbia
PINCTRATE_SRB	Personal income tax rate in Serbia
POP_SRB	Population in Serbia
SOCCONTRATE_SRB	Social security contribution rate in Serbia
VATRATE_SRB	Value added tax rate in Serbia
DINEUR	Exchange rate dinar / euro

Variable name	Description
DINUSD	Exchange rate dinar / US dollar
HRKDIN	Exchange rate kuna / dinar
HRKEUR	Exchange rate kuna / euro
HRKUSD	Exchange rate kuna / US dollar
KMDIN	Exchange rate KM / dinar
KMHRK	Exchange rate KM / kuna
KMUSD	Exchange rate KM / US dollar
OILDIN	Oil price in dinar
OILEUR	Oil price in euro
OILHRK	Oil price in kuna
OILKM	Oil price in KM
SLO3M	Interest rate for 3 months, from 2007 on EUROBOR
DUMxxxx	Dummy variable, 1 in the year xxxx
EUR10Y	10 year gov. bond yield, euro area average
EUR3M	3 months EURIBOR
EURUSD	Exchange rate euro / US dollar
OIL	Oil price, USD per barrel Brent
SITEUR	Exchange rate Euro per 100 tolar
WTRADE	World Trade; Source: OECD MEI

Data sources: Statistical offices and national banks of Slovenia, Serbia, Croatia and Bosnia and Herzegovina, Eurostat, OECD.

UNIT ROOT TESTS

Table 15: Results of unit root tests for the model variables (levels)

Variable (level)	ADF		PP		KPSS		Classification
	Mod	Test statistic	Mod	Test statistic	Mod	Test statistic	
AVPENSION_SLO	c	2.785*	c,t	-9.074***	c	1.059***	not stat.
AVUNBENEFIT_SLO	c	-0.346	c,t	-2.241	c	0.935***	not stat.
BALANCE_BIH	*n*	-4.245***	*n*	-6.654***	c,t	0.155**	stat.
BALANCE_CURR_BIH	*n*	-1.141	*n*	-5.555***	c,t	0.247***	not stat.
BALANCE_CURR_RATIO_BIH	*n*	-1.095	*n*	-5.470***	c,t	0.257***	not stat.
BALANCE_SRB	c,t	-5.463***	c,t	-14.069***	c,t	0.247***	stat.
BALANCEGDP_SLO	c	-1.497	c,t	-6.561***	c	0.459*	stat.
BALANCEN_SLO	c,t	-5.437***	c,t	-5.437***	c	0.551**	stat.
BALANCERATIO_BIH	c	-3.749***	c,t	-6.643***	c,t	0.192**	stat.
BALANCERATIO_SRB	c,t	-3.123	c,t	-3.236*	c	0.653**	not stat.
BUD_BALANCE_CRO	c	-1.032	c,t	-5.416***	c,t	0.218***	not stat.
BUD_RATIO_CRO	c	-1.824	c,t	-5.668***	c,t	0.180**	not stat.
CAGDP_SLO	c,t	-7.184***	c,t	-7.191***	c	0.349*	stat.
CAN_SLO	*n*	-2.541**	c,t	-6.052***	c	0.130***	stat.
CAPITALSTOCK_CRO	c,t	-2.263	c,t	-2.345	c	0.796***	not stat.
CAPR_BIH	c,t	-3.502*	c,t	-5.791***	c	0.861***	not stat.
CAPR_SLO	c,t	-2.471	c,t	-2.142	c	1.068***	not stat.
CAPR_SRB	c,t	-2.017	*n*	-1.729	c	0.776***	not stat.
CDEF_SLO	c	-1.877	c	-2.354	c	1.062***	not stat.
CN_SLO	c	-1.065	c,t	-7.348***	c	1.073***	not stat.
COMP_EMP_BIH	c,t	-2.366	c,t	-1.598	c	0.795***	not stat.
CONS_BIH	c,t	-2.699	c,t	-5.793***	c	0.892***	not stat.

Variable (level)	ADF Mod	ADF Test statistic	PP Mod	PP Test statistic	KPSS Mod	KPSS Test statistic	Classification
CONS_SRB	c,t	-4.416***	c,t	-4.317***	c	0.893***	not stat.
CONSR_BIH	c,t	-1.305	c,t	-5.876***	c	0.807***	not stat.
CONSR_SRB	c,t	-2.360	c,t	-7.095***	c	1.000***	not stat.
CONSUM_CRO	c,t	-2.733	c,t	-6.567***	c	0.886***	not stat.
CONSUMR_CRO	c,t	-1.800	c,t	-5.686***	c	0.772***	not stat.
CPI_BIH	c,t	-2.377	c,t	-1.970	c	0.870***	not stat.
CPI_CRO	c,t	-1.774	c,t	-1.897	c	0.910***	not stat.
CPI_SLO	c,t	-0.962	c	-2.480	c	1.005***	not stat.
CPI_SRB	c,t	-2.530	c,t	-1.984	c	0.896***	not stat.
CR_SLO	c,t	-2.097	c,t	-9.464***	c	1.070***	not stat.
DEBT_BIH	c,t	0.408	c,t	-0.094	c	0.499**	not stat.
DEBT_CRO	c,t	-0.606	c,t	-1.322	c	0.887***	not stat.
DEBT_RATIO_CRO	c	-2.106	c	-1.562	c	0.097	not stat.
DEBT_SLO	*n*	-0.247	c,t	-0.081	c	1.004***	not stat.
DEBT_SRB	*n*	-0.297	c,t	0.497	c	0.475**	not stat.
DEBTGDP_SLO	c	0.745	c,t	-0.397	c	0.661**	not stat.
DEBTRATIO_BIH	c	-1.680	*n*	-1.817	c	0.735**	not stat.
DEBTRATIO_SRB	c	-4.434***	c	-9.420***	c	0.655**	stat.
DELTADEBT_BIH	c	-4.940***	c,t	-5.464***	c	0.375*	stat.
DEMAND_SLO	c,t	-1.682	c,t	-4.005**	c	1.031***	not stat.
DEMANDR_BIH	c,t	-2.352	c,t	-9.305***	c	0.833***	not stat.
DEMANDR_CRO	c,t	-0.308	c,t	-2.448	c	0.738**	not stat.
DEMANDR_SRB	c,t	-3.004	c,t	-4.396***	c	0.847***	not stat.
DINEUR	c,t	-2.171	c,t	-2.171	c	0.820***	not stat.

Variable (level)	ADF		PP		KPSS		Classification
	Mod	Test statistic	Mod	Test statistic	Mod	Test statistic	
DINUSD	c,t	-1.960	c,t	-2.013	c	0.654**	not stat.
EMP_ADJ_BIH	c,t	-1.187	c,t	-2.153	c	0.520**	not stat.
EMP_BIH	c,t	-2.708	c,t	-2.619	c	0.698**	not stat.
EMP_CRO	c,t	-1.167	c	-2.661*	c	0.586**	not stat.
EMP_SLO	c,t	-2.693	c	-1.233	c	0.770***	not stat.
EMP_SRB	*n*	-2.150	*n*	-2.311**	c	0.793***	not stat.
EXPDEF_SLO	c	-2.281	c	-1.934	c	1.060***	not stat.
EXPOTHER_BIH	c,t	-3.711**	c,t	-9.916***	c	1.163***	not stat.
EXPREST_SLO	c,t	-1.695	c,t	-8.842***	c	1.035***	not stat.
EXPREST_SRB	c,t	-1.617	c,t	-7.683***	c,t	0.500***	not stat.
EXPTOTAL_BIH	c,t	-1.890	c,t	-6.812***	c	0.793***	not stat.
EXR_BIH	c,t	-3.375*	c,t	-3.587**	c	0.833***	not stat.
EXR_BIHCRO	c,t	-2.172	c,t	-2.332	c	0.756***	not stat.
EXR_BIHROW	c,t	-3.212*	c,t	-3.364	c	0.825***	not stat.
EXR_BIHSLO	c,t	-3.479*	c,t	-2.142	c	0.707**	not stat.
EXR_BIHSRB	c,t	-3.425*	c,t	-4.097**	c	0.780***	not stat.
EXR_CRO	c	-1.933	c,t	-6.883***	c,t	0.147**	not stat.
EXR_CROBIH	c,t	-1.781	c,t	-5.782***	c	0.799***	not stat.
EXR_CROROW	c	-2.018	c,t	-7.404***	c	0.500**	not stat.
EXR_CROSLO	c	-2.162	c,t	-5.318***	c	0.528***	not stat.
EXR_CROSRB	c	-1.673	c,t	-7.853***	c	0.907***	not stat.
EXR_SLO	c	-0.700	c,t	-2.383	c	1.029***	not stat.
EXR_SLOBIH	c	-3.729***	c	-3.599***	c	0.179	stat.
EXR_SLOCRO	c	-1.717	c	-1.750	c	0.560**	not stat.

Variable (level)	ADF Mod	ADF Test statistic	PP Mod	PP Test statistic	KPSS Mod	KPSS Test statistic	Classification
EXR_SLOROW	c	-0.892	c,t	-2.076	c	0.913***	not stat.
EXR_SLOSRB	c	-1.318	c,t	-2.129	c	0.882***	not stat.
EXR_SRB	c,t	-3.820**	c,t	-3.704**	c	0.968***	not stat.
EXR_SRBBIH	c,t	-3.545**	c,t	-3.393*	c	0.736**	not stat.
EXR_SRBCRO	c,t	-2.778	c,t	-2.798	c	0.827***	not stat.
EXR_SRBROW	c,t	-4.302***	c,t	-4.216***	c	0.890***	not stat.
EXR_SRBSLO	c,t	-3.642**	c,t	-3.034	c	0.877***	not stat.
FINWEALTH_SLO	c,t	-1.848	c,t	-1.791	c	1.027***	not stat.
G_BIH	c,t	-3.113	c,t	-8.682***	c	0.866***	not stat.
G_CONS_CRO	c,t	-3.258*	c,t	-3.314**	c	0.768***	not stat.
G_CRO	c,t	-2.641	c,t	-2.069	c	0.847***	not stat.
G_OTHEREXP_CRO	c,t	-2.614	c,t	-5.738***	c	0.592**	not stat.
G_SRB	c,t	-3.092	c,t	-6.228***	c	0.890***	not stat.
G_SUBSIDIES_CRO	c,t	-5.635***	c,t	-5.644***	c	0.819***	not stat.
GCONS_BIH	c,t	-1.629	c,t	-7.304***	c	0.786***	not stat.
GDEF_SLO	c	-1.945	c,t	-3.897**	c	1.059***	not stat.
GDP_CRO	c,t	-2.732	c,t	-4.295***	c	0.893***	not stat.
GDP_EXP_BIH	c,t	-3.964**	c,t	-6.378***	c	0.885***	not stat.
GDP_SRB	c,t	-3.352*	c,t	-3.893**	c	0.899***	not stat.
GDPDEF_SLO	c	-1.960	c	-3.004**	c	1.055***	not stat.
GDPN_SLO	c	-1.440	c,t	-3.989**	c	1.057***	not stat.
GDPR_CRO	c	-1.801	c,t	-3.830**	c	0.815***	not stat.
GDPR_EXP_BIH	c	-0.863	c,t	-8.138***	c	0.885***	not stat.

Variable (level)	ADF Mod	ADF Test statistic	PP Mod	PP Test statistic	KPSS Mod	KPSS Test statistic	Classification
GDPR_SLO	c	-1.507	c,t	-4.105***	c	1.032***	not stat.
GDPR_SRB	c,t	-3.372*	c,t	-5.429***	c	0.967***	not stat.
GFCFR_SRB	c,t	-2.522	c,t	-1.849	c	0.796***	not stat.
GINVR_SLO	c	-2.129	c,t	-9.913***	c	1.573***	not stat.
GN_SLO	c,t	-3.738**	c,t	-8.757***	c	1.068***	not stat.
GNFIN_SLO	c	-1.594	c,t	-10.28***	c	1.059***	not stat.
GOV10Y_SLO	c	-1.486	c,t	-4.746***	c	0.900***	not stat.
GOV10YR_SLO	c	-4.190***	*n*	-2.075**	c,t	0.166**	not stat.
GOVCONS_SRB	c	-1.369	c,t	-5.175***	c	0.734**	not stat.
GR_BIH	c	-0.862	c,t	-10.487***	c	1.160***	not stat.
GR_CRO	c,t	-2.248	c,t	-3.830**	c	0.772***	not stat.
GR_SLO	c,t	-2.484	c,t	-9.091***	c	1.062***	not stat.
GR_SRB	c,t	-3.206*	c,t	-6.464***	c	0.774***	not stat.
GRGDPR_SLO	c,t	-3.743**	*n*	-1.956**	c	0.430*	stat.
GRGDPR_SRB	*n*	-1.818	*n*	-4.040***	c,t	0.146*	stat.
GROSS_WAGE_CRO	c,t	-3.427*	c	-1.402	c	0.910***	not stat.
GROSS_WAGER_CRO	c	-1.333	c,t	-1.993	c	0.868***	not stat.
GRYPOT_SLO	*n*	-1.124	*n*	-1.005	c	0.680**	not stat.
GWAGE_BIH	c,t	-1.889	c,t	-1.936	c	0.950***	not stat.
GWAGE_SLO	c	-1.873	c,t	-4.752***	c	1.074***	not stat.
GWAGE_SRB	c,t	-3.013	c,t	-2.698	c	0.882***	not stat.
GWAGER_BIH	c,t	-2.013	c,t	-2.341	c	0.878***	not stat.
GWAGER_SLO	c,t	-2.906	c,t	-10.181***	c	1.021***	not stat.
GWAGER_SRB	c	-1.197	c,t	-2.267	c	0.851***	not stat.

Variable (level)	ADF Mod	ADF Test statistic	PP Mod	PP Test statistic	KPSS Mod	KPSS Test statistic	Classification
HRKDIN	*n*	-3.350***	c,t	-6.292***	c	0.535**	not stat.
HRKEUR	*n*	-0.549	c,t	-3.679**	c	0.705**	not stat.
HRKUSD	*n*	-1.027	c,t	-2.679	c	0.752***	not stat.
I_DEBT_CRO	*n*	-0.013	c,t	-15.625***	c,t	0.169**	not stat.
I_LR_CRO	*n*	-2.636***	*n*	-2.005**	c	0.591**	stat.
I_SR_CRO	*n*	-3.713***	*n*	-2.660***	c	0.558**	stat.
IFIXR_BIH	c,t	-2.496	c,t	-8.910***	c	0.927***	not stat.
IFIXR_CRO	c	-2.178	c,t	-2.948	c	0.706**	not stat.
IGOVDEBT_SLO	*n*	-2.210**	c,t	-11.225***	c	0.500**	not stat.
IL_BIH	c	-2.616*	*n*	-1.814**	c	0.572**	not stat.
IL_DEBT_BIH	c	-2.472	c,t	-14.993***	c,t	0.125*	stat.
IL_DEBT_SRB	c	-3.660***	c,t	-3.975**	c,t	0.149**	not stat.
ILEND_SRB	*n*	-1.883*	*n*	-2.220**	c	0.758***	not stat.
ILREAL_BIH	c	-2.689*	*n*	-1.249	c,t	0.148**	not stat.
IMPDEF_SLO	c,t	-2.597	c,t	-2.264	c	1.065***	not stat.
IMPR_SLO	c,t	-2.996	c,t	-3.052	c	1.008***	not stat.
IMR_BIH	c,t	-3.057	c,t	-5.298***	c	0.534**	not stat.
IMR_BIHROW	c	-2.086	c,t	-8.007***	c	0.418*	stat.
IMR_CRO	c	-1.836	c	-2.044	c	0.616**	not stat.
IMR_CROROW	c	-2.283	c,t	-3.209*	c	0.648**	not stat.
IMR_SLOROW	c,t	-2.905	c,t	-2.850	c	0.811***	not stat.
IMR_SRB	c,t	-3.821**	c,t	-3.821**	c	0.826***	stat.
IMR_SRBROW	c,t	-3.780**	c,t	-3.690**	c	0.779***	stat.
INCOME_SLO	c,t	-2.187	c,t	-3.491**	c	0.838***	not stat.
INCOMER_SLO	c	-4.559***	c	-2.892*	c	0.463**	not stat.

Variable (level)	ADF Mod	ADF Test statistic	PP Mod	PP Test statistic	KPSS Mod	KPSS Test statistic	Classification
INCTAX_CRO	c	-3.239**	c,t	-4.199***	c	0.554**	not stat.
INCTAX_SLO	c	-1.197	c,t	-7.318***	c	0.998***	not stat.
INCTAXCORP_CRO	c	-4.058***	c,t	-4.746***	c	0.629**	not stat.
INCTAXCORP_SLO	c	-1.245	c,t	-6.149***	c	0.777***	not stat.
INCTAXPERS_CRO	*n*	-2.580**	c,t	-6.090***	c	0.802***	not stat.
INCTAXPERS_SLO	c	-1.216	c,t	-10.837***	c	1.057***	not stat.
INFL_BIH	c	-3.936***	*n*	-1.776*	c	0.085	stat.
INFL_CRO	c,t	-4.882***	c	-2.346	c	0.090	stat.
INFL_SLO	c,t	-2.992	*n*	-1.337	c	0.773***	not stat.
INFL_SRB	c	-3.557**	*n*	-1.595	c	0.461*	stat.
INTEREST_BIH	c	-1.518	c,t	-15.322***	c	0.119	stat.
INTEREST_CRO	c,t	0.570	c,t	-14.788***	c	1.265***	not stat.
INTEREST_SLO	c,t	-1.244	c,t	-9.729***	c	0.799***	not stat.
INTEREST_SRB	c,t	-3.190	c,t	-3.159	c	0.441*	not stat.
INVENTR_BIH	*n*	-1.081	c,t	-7.149***	c,t	0.134*	stat.
INVENTR_CRO	c	-1.971	c,t	-7.730***	c,t	0.134*	stat.
INVENTR_SLO	c	-2.959**	c,t	-5.533***	c	0.423*	stat.
INVENTR_SRB	c	-5.757***	c,t	-6.568***	c	0.673**	not stat.
INVESTR_BIH	c,t	-2.207	c,t	-11.894***	c,t	0.203**	not stat.
INVESTR_CRO	c	-1.515	c,t	-5.906***	c,t	0.255***	not stat.
INVR_SLO	c	-2.159	c	-2.190	c	0.757***	not stat.
IR_LR_CRO	*n*	-0.969	*n*	-1.314	c,t	0.162	not stat.
IS_BIH	*n*	-2.418**	*n*	-2.988***		0.645**	not stat.
KMDIN	*n*	-4.014***	c	-8.998***	c	0.505**	not stat.
KMHRK	c	-2.170	c	-2.906*	c	0.593**	not stat.

Variable (level)	ADF Mod	ADF Test statistic	PP Mod	PP Test statistic	KPSS Mod	KPSS Test statistic	Classification
KMUSD	c,t	-3.319*	c,t	-2.419	c	0.746***	not stat.
LFORCE_ADJ_BIH	c	-1.597	c	-1.510	c	0.581**	not stat.
LFORCE_BIH	c,t	-1.725	c,t	-2.693	c	0.910***	not stat.
LFORCE_CRO	c	-3.492**	c	-3.486**	c,t	0.161**	not stat.
LFORCE_SLO	c,t	-2.769	c,t	-2.792	c,t	0.146**	not stat.
LFORCE_SRB	*n*	-1.390	*n*	-1.362	c,t	0.133*	not stat.
NAIRU_BIH	c	-3.241**	c	-3.534**	c	0.748***	not stat.
NAIRU_CRO	c,t	-5.783***	*n*	-2.407**	c	0.860***	stat.
NAIRU_SLO	c	-3.574***	*n*	-0.930	c	0.856***	not stat.
NAIRU_SRB	c	-3.091**	c	-2.987**	c,t	0.231***	stat.
NBSRATE_SRB	*n*	-1.713*	c	-4.977***	c	0.479**	not stat.
NEER_BIH	c	-2.246	c,t	-2.973	c	0.691**	not stat.
NEER_CRO	c	-3.308**	c,t	-2.540	c	0.788***	not stat.
NEER_SRB	*n*	-3.269***	*n*	-10.893***	c,t	0.229***	not stat.
NET_WAGE_CRO	c,t	-2.687	c	-3.060**	c	0.918***	not stat.
NET_WAGER_CRO	c	-2.493	c	-2.768*	c	0.873***	not stat.
NWAGE_BIH	c,t	-2.062	c,t	-1.826	c	0.950***	not stat.
NWAGE_SLO	c	-0.994	c,t	-7.797***	c	1.071***	not stat.
NWAGE_SRB	c,t	-2.994	c,t	-2.566	c	0.878***	not stat.
NWAGER_BIH	c,t	-2.221	c,t	-2.458	c	0.883***	not stat.
NWAGER_SLO	c,t	-2.719	c,t	-11.209***	c	0.993***	not stat.
NWAGER_SRB	c,t	-1.949	c	-1.556	c	0.852***	not stat.
OILDIN	c,t	-3.786**	c,t	-3.057	c	1.002***	not stat.
OILEUR	c,t	-3.880**	c,t	-3.013	c	1.006***	not stat.

Variable (level)	ADF Mod	ADF Test statistic	PP Mod	PP Test statistic	KPSS Mod	KPSS Test statistic	Classification
OILHRK	c,t	-3.531^{**}	c,t	-2.800	c	0.860^{***}	not stat.
OILKM	c,t	-3.649^{**}	c,t	-2.878	c	0.888^{***}	not stat.
P_CONSUM_CRO	c,t	-2.575	c,t	-3.289^{*}	c	0.915^{***}	not stat.
P_G_CRO	c,t	-3.367^{*}	c,t	-2.647	c	0.870^{***}	not stat.
P_GDP_CRO	c,t	-2.989	c,t	-4.432^{***}	c	0.912^{***}	not stat.
PARTRATE_BIH	c,t	-2.738	c,t	-2.742	c	0.879^{***}	not stat.
PARTRATE_CRO	c	-4.423^{***}	c	-3.684^{***}	c,t	0.156^{**}	not stat.
PARTRATE_SLO	c	-2.328	c	-2.636^{*}	c,t	0.156^{**}	not stat.
PARTRATE_SRB	*n*	-1.138	*n*	-1.195	c,t	0.149^{**}	not stat.
PENSIONERS_SLO	*n*	1.776	c,t	-4.840^{***}	c	1.065^{***}	not stat.
PENSIONS_SLO	c,t	-2.360	c,t	-14.654^{***}	c	1.070^{***}	not stat.
PGDP_EXP_BIH	c,t	-2.823	c,t	-2.490	c	0.867^{***}	not stat.
PGDP_SRB	c,t	-3.418^{*}	c,t	-2.793	c	0.898^{***}	not stat.
POP1564_SLO	c,t	-3.095	c,t	-2.665	c	1.066^{***}	not stat.
PRINVR_SLO	c	-2.168	c	-2.126	c	0.675^{**}	not stat.
PROD_BIH	c	-1.050	c,t	-9.013^{***}	c	1.045^{***}	not stat.
PROD_CRO	c	-1.293	c,t	-4.251^{***}	c	0.854^{***}	not stat.
PROD_SLO	c,t	-2.855	c,t	-5.168^{***}	c	1.053^{***}	not stat.
PROD_SRB	c,t	-1.578	c,t	-6.122^{***}	c	1.030^{***}	not stat.
REER41_SLO	c,t	-4.290^{***}	c,t	-2.984	c	0.567^{**}	not stat.
REER_BIH	c,t	-4.842^{***}	c	-2.861^{*}	c	0.295	stat.
REER_CRO	c	-2.749^{*}	*n*	-1.216	c	0.759^{***}	not stat.
REER_SRB	c,t	-4.938^{***}	*n*	-0.368	c	0.746^{***}	not stat.
REMIT_BIH	c,t	-2.665	c,t	-5.329^{***}	c	0.659^{**}	not stat.

Variable (level)	ADF Mod	ADF Test statistic	PP Mod	PP Test statistic	KPSS Mod	KPSS Test statistic	Classification
REV_OTHER_CRO	c	-1.535	c,t	-6.960***	c,t	0.121*	stat.
REVOTHER_BIH	c	-1.793	c,t	-5.096***	c	0.724**	not stat.
REVREST_SLO	c	-1.002	c,t	-8.738***	c	1.058***	not stat.
REVREST_SRB	c	-1.081	c,t	-5.291***	c	0.761***	not stat.
REVTOTAL_BIH	c,t	-2.548	c,t	-4.946***	c	0.815***	not stat.
SLO3M	c	-2.734*	*n*	-1.919*	c	0.552**	not stat.
SOCBENEFIT_SRB	c,t	-1.886	c,t	-4.713***	c	0.742***	not stat.
SOCCOMP_SLO	c,t	-2.110	c,t	-6.369***	c	1.053***	not stat.
SOCCONTR_BIH	c,t	-2.373	c,t	-4.002**	c	0.800***	not stat.
SOCCONTR_SRB	c,t	-2.097	c,t	-4.354***	c	0.736**	not stat.
SOCCONTREMP_BIH	c,t	-2.179	c,t	-5.122***	c	0.818***	not stat.
SOCEMP_SLO	c,t	-2.193	c,t	-8.368***	c	1.068***	not stat.
SOCIALCONT_CRO	c	-1.971	c	-1.690	c	0.792***	not stat.
SOCTOTAL_SLO	c,t	-2.149	c,t	-7.748***	c	1.064***	not stat.
SUBSIDIES_BIH	c,t	-2.149	c,t	-8.362***	c	0.943***	not stat.
SUBSIDIES_SRB	c,t	-3.971**	c,t	-6.931***	c	0.698**	stat.
TAX_OTHER_CRO	c	-2.448	c	-2.482	c	0.459*	not stat.
TAX_VAT_CRO	c	-1.182	c,t	-5.045***	c	0.858***	not stat.
TAXCORP_SRB	c	-1.245	c,t	-4.990***	c	0.614**	not stat.
TAXINC_SRB	c,t	-2.474	c,t	-4.871***	c	0.717**	not stat.
TAXINCOME_BIH	c	6.309	c,t	-3.807**	c,t	0.221***	not stat.
TAXVAT_BIH	c,t	-2.944	c,t	-4.395***	c	0.793***	not stat.
TAXWEDGE_CRO	c,t	-2.184	c,t	-2.942	c	0.879***	not stat.
TOTALEXP_CRO	c,t	-5.375***	c,t	-5.366***	c	0.900***	stat.

Variable (level)	ADF Mod	ADF Test statistic	PP Mod	PP Test statistic	KPSS Mod	KPSS Test statistic	Classification
TOTALREV_CRO	c	-1.293	c,t	-3.780**	c	0.861***	not stat.
TRANSFERS_BIH	c	-1.881	c,t	-4.536***	c	0.776***	not stat.
TRENDEMP_BIH	c,t	-2.831	c,t	-2.747	c	0.811***	not stat.
TRENDEMP_CRO	c	-2.716*	c	-2.952**	c	0.688**	not stat.
TRENDEMP_SLO	c	-1.736	c	-0.992	c	0.893***	not stat.
TRENDEMP_SRB	*n*	-2.190**	*n*	-2.210**	c	0.759***	stat.
TRENDTFP_BIH	c	-2.452	c	-1.414	c	0.882***	not stat.
TRENDTFP_CRO	c	-2.613*	c	-4.057***	c	0.830***	not stat.
TRENDTFP_SLO	*n*	-1.985**	c	-4.630***	c	0.957***	not stat.
TRENDTFP_SRB	c,t	-3.808**	c,t	-2.898	c	0.862***	not stat.
UCC_BIH	c	-2.689*	*n*	-1.096	c,t	0.148**	not stat.
UCC_SLO	c	-4.169***	c	-2.833*	c,t	0.166**	not stat.
UCC_SRB	*n*	-3.249***	*n*	-3.019***	c,t	0.126*	stat.
ULC_CRO	c,t	-2.540	c,t	-4.979***	c	0.841***	not stat.
ULC_SLO	c,t	-2.467	c,t	-4.500***	c	1.041***	not stat.
ULC_SRB	c,t	-2.051	c,t	-1.962	c	0.875***	not stat.
UN_ADJ_BIH	c	-1.530	c	-1.902	c,t	0.148**	not stat.
UN_BIH	c	-1.062	c	-1.076	c	0.843***	not stat.
UN_CRO	*n*	-0.969	c,t	-3.212*	c	0.680**	not stat.
UN_SLO	c,t	-2.559	*n*	-0.468	c	0.674**	not stat.
UN_SRB	c	-2.260	c	-1.438	c,t	0.177**	not stat.
UNBENEFIT_SLO	c	-0.175	c,t	-1.252	c	0.645**	not stat.
UR_ADJ_BIH	c	-1.531	c	-1.938	c	0.136*	not stat.
UR_BIH	c	-1.980	*n*	-1.886	c	0.499**	not stat.

Variable (level)	ADF Mod	ADF Test statistic	PP Mod	PP Test statistic	KPSS Mod	KPSS Test statistic	Classification
UR_CRO	*n*	-0.937	c,t	-3.198*	c	0.686**	not stat.
UR_SLO	c	-1.597	*n*	-0.478	c	0.704**	not stat.
UR_SRB	c	-1.877	c	-1.876	c	0.668**	not stat.
UTIL_BIH	c	-1.719	c,t	-12.274***	c,t	0.162**	not stat.
UTIL_CRO	c	-2.969**	c,t	-6.568***	c,t	0.500***	not stat.
UTIL_SA_BIH	*n*	-0.510	c,t	-8.838***	c,t	0.306***	not stat.
UTIL_SLO	c	-4.455***	c,t	-7.246***	c,t	0.076	stat.
UTIL_SRB	c	-3.893***	c,t	-13.986***	c,t	0.228***	stat.
VAT_SLO	c	-1.192	c,t	-10.470***	c	1.039***	not stat.
VAT_SRB	c,t	-3.334*	c,t	-3.334*	c	0.724**	not stat.
WEDGE_BIH	c,t	-1.738	c,t	-1.774	c	0.944***	not stat.
WEDGE_SLO	c	-1.341	c,t	-13.023***	c	1.076***	not stat.
YD_BIH	c,t	-3.113	c,t	-6.422***	c	0.806***	not stat.
YD_CRO	c,t	-2.922	c,t	-4.723***	c	0.902***	not stat.
YD_SRB	c,t	-3.107	c,t	-6.921***	c	0.756***	not stat.
YDR_BIH	c	-1.533	c,t	-7.910***	c	0.800***	not stat.
YDR_CRO	c,t	-2.052	c,t	-4.502***	c	0.859***	not stat.
YDR_SRB	c	-1.455	c,t	-4.913***	c	0.731**	not stat.
YPOT_BIH	c	-0.628	c,t	-1.313	c	0.847***	not stat.
YPOT_CRO	*n*	-3.249***	c	-2.951**	c	0.867***	stat.
YPOT_SLO	c	-1.940	c	-2.120	c	1.048***	not stat.
YPOT_SRB	c,t	-2.649	c,t	-2.633	c	0.824***	not stat.
DEBTADJ_SLO	c	-3.285***	c,t	-17.31***	c,t	0.387***	stat.
DELTA_DEBT_CRO	c	-6.571***	c,t	-6.502***	c,t	0.082	stat.
DELTADEBT_SRB	*n*	-4.328***	c,t	-4.361***	c,t	0.152**	stat.

Variable (level)	ADF Mod	ADF Test statistic	PP Mod	PP Test statistic	KPSS Mod	KPSS Test statistic	Classification
EUR10Y	c	-3.573***	c,t	-2.807	c	0.756***	not stat.
EUR3M	*n*	-2.041**	*n*	-1.921*	c	0.643**	not stat.
EURUSD	c,t	-2.598	c	-1.211	c	0.520**	not stat.
G_TRANSFER_CRO	c,t	-2.505	c,t	-2.294	c	0.874***	not stat.
GINVN_SLO	*n*	-1.635*	c,t	-9.694***	c	1.095***	not stat.
OIL	c,t	-4.160***	c,t	-2.580	c	0.984***	not stat.
PENSIONERS1549_SLO	*n*	-2.733***	c,t	-3.924***	c	0.996***	stat.
PENSIONERS50_SLO	c	-4.334***	c	-2.558	c	0.753***	not stat.
PENSIONERS51_SLO	c	-2.655*	c	-1.270	c	0.798***	not stat.
PENSIONERS52_SLO	c	-1.936	c	-1.160	c	0.843***	not stat.
PENSIONERS53_SLO	c,t	-1.762	c,t	-1.779	c	0.880***	not stat.
PENSIONERS54_SLO	c,t	-2.008	c,t	-2.116	c	0.894***	not stat.
PENSIONERS55_SLO	c,t	-3.218	c,t	-2.112	c	0.862***	not stat.
PENSIONERS56_SLO	c,t	-1.663	c,t	-1.966	c	0.822***	not stat.
PENSIONERS57_SLO	c,t	-1.620	c,t	-1.844	c	0.779***	not stat.
PENSIONERS58_SLO	c,t	-0.986	c,t	-1.755	c,t	0.204**	not stat.
PENSIONERS59_SLO	c,t	-2.191	c,t	-1.646	c,t	0.191**	not stat.
PENSIONERS60_SLO	c,t	-2.165	c,t	-1.534	c,t	0.169**	not stat.
PENSIONERS61_SLO	c	-0.470	c	-1.899	c,t	0.131*	not stat.
PENSIONERS62_SLO	c	-1.680	c	-1.466	c,t	0.084	not stat.
PENSIONERS63_SLO	c	-5.462***	c	-1.991	c,t	0.054	stat.
PENSIONERS64_SLO	c	-6.466***	c	-6.662***	c,t	0.093	stat.
PENSIONERS65_SLO	c	-3.144**	c	-6.585***	c,t	0.169**	stat.

Variable (level)	ADF Mod	ADF Test statistic	PP Mod	PP Test statistic	KPSS Mod	KPSS Test statistic	Classification
PENSIONERS66_SLO	c	-1.603	c	-10.251***	c,t	0.160**	not stat.
PENSIONERS67_SLO	c	-1.461	c	-3.021**	c	0.458*	stat.
PENSIONERS68_SLO	c	-1.352	c	-1.595	c	0.589**	not stat.
PENSIONERS69_SLO	c	-1.327	c,t	-3.681**	c	0.652**	not stat.
PENSIONERS70PLUS_SLO	c	-0.416	c,t	-6.361***	c	1.075***	not stat.
POP1549_SLO	*n*	-2.131**	*n*	-2.589***	c	1.005***	stat.
POP50_SLO	c	-4.326***	c	-2.557	c	0.753***	not stat.
POP51_SLO	c	-2.681*	c,t	-1.650	c	0.797***	not stat.
POP52_SLO	c,t	-1.983	c,t	-1.829	c	0.847***	not stat.
POP53_SLO	c,t	-1.925	c,t	-1.880	c	0.873***	not stat.
POP54_SLO	c,t	-2.565	c,t	-2.118	c	0.891***	not stat.
POP55_SLO	c,t	-2.330	c,t	-2.121	c	0.861***	not stat.
POP56_SLO	c,t	-2.240	c,t	-1.949	c	0.827***	not stat.
POP57_SLO	c,t	-2.053	c,t	-1.879	c	0.776***	not stat.
POP58_SLO	c,t	-1.608	c,t	-1.678	c	0.688**	not stat.
POP59_SLO	c,t	-1.813	c,t	-1.579	c	0.583**	not stat.
POP60_SLO	c,t	-1.467	c,t	-1.445	c	0.466**	not stat.
POP61_SLO	c,t	-2.355	c,t	-1.236	c,t	0.133*	not stat.
POP62_SLO	c	-2.997**	c,t	-1.571	c	0.116	stat.
POP63_SLO	c	-3.747***	c,t	-1.769	c	0.054	stat.
POP64_SLO	c	-3.51**	c,t	-2.189	c	0.150	stat.
POP_BIH	c	-2.426	c	-6.409***	c,t	0.229***	not stat.
POP_CRO	*n*	-1.111	c	-3.793***	c	0.602**	not stat.
POP_SRB	*n*	-2.629***	*n*	-7.908***	c	0.953***	stat.
PUBINVEST_BIH	*n*	0.715	c	-8.932***	c	1.102***	not stat.

Variable (level)	Mod	ADF Test statistic	Mod	PP Test statistic	Mod	KPSS Test statistic	Classification
REPRATE_SLO	*n*	-2.545**	c,t	-13.053***	c	1.142***	stat.
RESTTRANSFERS_SLO	c,t	-2.512	c,t	-20.951***	c	1.071***	not stat.
SITEUR	c	-3.654***	c	-5.850***	c	0.917***	stat.
WTRADE	c,t	-3.818***	c,t	-2.507	c	1.064***	not stat.

*Notes: ADF: Augmented Dickey-Fuller test; PP: Phillips-Perron test; KPSS: Kwiatkowski, Phillips, Schmidt and Shin test. *, **, *** means that the null hypothesis (ADF and Phillips-Perron: no stationarity of the series; KPSS: stationarity of the series) can be rejected at the 10, 5 and 1 percent level of significance respectively.*

In the "Mod" column, the specification of the test model is shown, i.e. either without constant and trend (n), only constant (c) or constant and trend (c,t).

In the "classification" column, the variables are classified as either stationary or non-stationary when this is indicated by at least two of the unit root tests.

Table 16: Results of unit root tests for the model variables (first differences)

Variable (1st diff)	ADF Mod	ADF Test statistic	PP Mod	PP Test statistic	KPSS Mod	KPSS Test statistic	Classi-fication
AVPENSION_SLO	c,t	-22.609***	c	-31.774***	c	0.190	not stat.
AVUNBENEFIT_SLO	*n*	-8.901***	c	-9.934***	c	0.235	stat.
BALANCE_BIH	*n*	-2.777***	c	-22.293***	c	0.167	stat.
BALANCE_CURR_BIH	c,t	-18.16***	c	-19.136***	c	0.158	stat.
BALANCE_CURR_RATIO_BIH	*n*	-3.106***	c	-18.996***	c	0.165	stat.
BALANCE_SRB	*n*	-7.615***	c	-23.971***	c	0.277	stat.
BALANCEGDP_SLO	*n*	-11.089***	c	-23.316***	c	0.117	stat.
BALANCEN_SLO	*n*	-9.854***	c	-20.971***	c	0.111	stat.
BALANCERATIO_BIH	*n*	-2.835***	c	-22.197***	c	0.159	stat.
BALANCERATIO_SRB	*n*	-4.585***	c	-5.965***	c	0.099	stat.
BUD_BALANCE_CRO	*n*	-9.729***	c	-15.862***	c,t	0.135*	stat.
BUD_RATIO_CRO	*n*	-9.395***	c	-16.429***	c,t	0.133*	stat.
CAGDP_SLO	*n*	-10.553***	c	-33.448***	c,t	0.167**	stat.
CAN_SLO	*n*	-4.599***	c	-22.015***	c,t	0.157**	stat.
CAPITALSTOCK_CRO	*n*	-1.433	*n*	-1.742*	c,t	0.169**	not stat.
CAPR_BIH	c	-2.003	c	-12.286***	c,t	0.217***	not stat.
CAPR_SLO	*n*	-0.995	c	-2.944**	c,t	0.157**	not stat.
CAPR_SRB	c,t	-2.110	*n*	-0.398	c	0.752***	not stat.
CDEF_SLO	c	-2.369	c	-8.808***	c	0.349*	stat.
CN_SLO	*n*	-1.471	c	-24.512***	c	0.124	stat.
COMP_EMP_BIH	*n*	-2.344**	c	-6.507***	c	0.178	stat.

Variable (1st diff)	ADF Mod	ADF Test statistic	PP Mod	PP Test statistic	KPSS Mod	KPSS Test statistic	Classi-fication
CONS_BIH	*n*	-1.413	c	-19.370***	c,t	0.199**	not stat.
CONS_SRB	c	-8.358***	c	-14.150***	c,t	0.152**	stat.
CONSR_BIH	c	-2.352	c	-20.667***	c,t	0.229***	not stat.
CONSR_SRB	c,t	-13.223***	c	-24.146***	c	0.148	stat.
CONSUM_CRO	*n*	-1.671*	c	-25.240***	c	0.382*	stat.
CONSUMR_CRO	*n*	-1.699*	c	-23.776***	c	0.455*	stat.
CPI_BIH	*n*	-4.212***	c	-4.750***	c	0.086	stat.
CPI_CRO	c	-6.135***	c	-5.969***	c	0.087	stat.
CPI_SLO	c,t	-3.282*	c	-7.882***	c	0.576**	not stat.
CPI_SRB	c	-4.719***	c	-4.665***	c	0.115	stat.
CR_SLO	c	-4.301***	c	-32.419***	c	0.189	stat.
DEBT_BIH	c	-4.940***	c	-5.111***	c	0.375*	stat.
DEBT_CRO	c	-4.834***	c	-4.928***	c	0.168	stat.
DEBT_RATIO_CRO	c	-4.301***	*n*	-4.233***	c,t	0.160**	stat.
DEBT_SLO	c	-7.968***	*n*	-6.983***	c	0.464**	stat.
DEBT_SRB	*n*	-3.041***	*n*	-2.950***	c,t	0.160**	stat.
DEBTGDP_SLO	c	-7.335***	*n*	-6.965***	c,t	0.184**	stat.
DEBTRATIO_BIH	c,t	-5.075***	*n*	-4.570***	c,t	0.152**	stat.
DEBTRATIO_SRB	*n*	-2.321**	*n*	-2.731***	c,t	0.146**	stat.
DELTADEBT_BIH	*n*	-8.694***	c	-15.692***	c,t	0.023	stat.
DEMAND_SLO	*n*	-2.765***	c	-24.521***	c,t	0.093	stat.

Variable (1st diff)	ADF Mod	ADF Test statistic	PP Mod	PP Test statistic	KPSS Mod	KPSS Test statistic	Classi-fication
DEMANDR_BIH	*n*	-2.404**	c	-24.233***	c, t	0.098	stat.
DEMANDR_CRO	*n*	-2.333**	c	-7.284***	c, t	0.135*	stat.
DEMANDR_SRB	*n*	-3.166***	c	-16.792***	c, t	0.135*	stat.
DINEUR	*n*	-6.918***	c	-7.413***	c, t	0.057	stat.
DINUSD	*n*	-6.846***	c	-6.973***	c, t	0.072	stat.
EMP_ADJ_BIH	*n*	-7.559***	c	-6.586***	c, t	0.120*	stat.
EMP_BIH	*n*	-7.384***	c	-7.193***	c, t	0.129*	stat.
EMP_CRO	*n*	-8.519***	c	-10.216***	c, t	0.183**	stat.
EMP_SLO	*n*	-2.781***	c	-8.110***	c, t	0.142*	stat.
EMP_SRB	*n*	-6.154***	c	-6.469***	c, t	0.124*	stat.
EXPDEF_SLO	*n*	-2.336**	c	-6.727***	c, t	0.046	stat.
EXPOTHER_BIH	*n*	-14.807***	c	-19.436***	c, t	0.159**	stat.
EXPREST_SLO	c	-19.866***	c	-36.330***	c, t	0.085	stat.
EXPREST_SRB	c	-9.894***	c	-17.278***	c, t	0.194**	stat.
EXPTOTAL_BIH	*n*	-2.104**	c	-28.624***	c, t	0.093	stat.

Variable (1st diff)	ADF		PP		KPSS		
	Mod	Test statistic	Mod	Test statistic	Mod	Test statistic	Classi-fication
EXR_BIH	c	-3.220**	c	-9.259***	c, t	0.098	stat.
EXR_BIHCRO	*n*	-1.904*	c	-8.107***	c, t	0.108	stat.
EXR_BIHROW	*n*	-2.416**	c	-8.756***	c, t	0.125*	stat.
EXR_BIHSLO	*n*	-2.179**	c	-8.240***	c, t	0.444***	stat.
EXR_BIHSRB	*n*	-2.556**	c	-11.084***	c, t	0.138*	stat.
EXR_CRO	*n*	-2.913***	c	-14.937***	c, t	0.106	stat.
EXR_CROBIH	*n*	-3.445***	c	-13.784***	c, t	0.106	stat.
EXR_CROROW	*n*	-3.513***	c	-15.121***	c, t	0.105	stat.
EXR_CROSLO	*n*	-2.759***	c	-15.498***	c, t	0.103	stat.
EXR_CROSRB	*n*	-3.254***	c	-18.901***	c	0.409*	stat.
EXR_SLO	*n*	-3.484***	c	-7.895***	c	0.075	stat.
EXR_SLOBIH	*n*	-3.947***	c	-12.99***	c, t	0.277***	stat.
EXR_SLOCRO	*n*	-6.202***	c	-6.154***	c, t	0.076	stat.
EXR_SLOROW	*n*	-3.087***	c	-6.416***	c, t	0.057	stat.
EXR_SLOSRB	c	-6.543***	c	-6.530***	c, t	0.052	stat.
EXR_SRB	c	-7.362***	c	-13.134***	c, t	0.500***	stat.

Variable (1st diff)	ADF		PP		KPSS		
	Mod	Test statistic	Mod	Test statistic	Mod	Test statistic	Classi-fication
EXR_SRBBIH	c	-6.458***	c	-15.445***	c, t	0.168**	stat.
EXR_SRBCRO	c	-6.657***	c	-13.501***	c, t	0.314***	stat.
EXR_SRBROW	c	-6.952***	c	-19.691***	c, t	0.479***	stat.
EXR_SRBSLO	c	-6.384***	c	-8.373***	c, t	0.147**	stat.
FINWEALTH_SLO	c	-4.993***	c	-4.982***	c, t	0.141*	stat.
G_BIH	c	-15.745***	c	-40.541***	c, t	0.082	stat.
G_CONS_CRO	c	-9.449***	c	-9.819***	c, t	0.432***	stat.
G_CRO	*n*	-1.483	c	-10.316***	c, t	0.278***	not stat.
G_OTHEREXP_CRO	*n*	-11.673***	c	-21.109***	c, t	0.119*	stat.
G_SRB	c,t	-5.750***	c	-22.930***	c, t	0.101	stat.
G_SUBSIDIES_CRO	*n*	-8.917***	c	-23.333***	c, t	0.479***	stat.
GCONS_BIH	*n*	-3.043***	c	-30.803***	c, t	0.088	stat.
GDEF_SLO	*n*	-1.309	c	-17.087***	c	0.405*	stat.
GDP_CRO	*n*	-1.007	c	-8.957***	c, t	0.177**	not stat.
GDP_EXP_BIH	*n*	-1.442	c	-21.574***	c	0.132	stat.
GDP_SRB	c	-2.780*	c	-11.874***	c	0.395*	stat.
GDPDEF_SLO	c	-2.194	c	-9.376***	c	0.429*	stat.
GDPN_SLO	*n*	-1.641*	c	-14.221***	c	0.211	stat.

Variable (1st diff)	ADF Mod	ADF Test statistic	PP Mod	PP Test statistic	KPSS Mod	KPSS Test statistic	Classi-fication
GDPR_CRO	c	-17.403***	c	-7.825***	c,t	0.180**	stat.
GDPR_EXP_BIH	*n*	-2.121**	c	-18.547***	c	0.108	stat.
GDPR_SLO	*n*	-2.509**	c	-17.976***	c	0.246	stat.
GDPR_SRB	*n*	-1.664*	c	-16.041***	c	0.119	stat.
GFCFR_SRB	*n*	-2.262**	c	-7.822***	c	0.123	stat.
GINVR_SLO	*n*	-1.022	c	-28.838***	c	0.087	stat.
GN_SLO	c	-2.605*	c	-29.581***	c	0.104	stat.
GNFIN_SLO	*n*	-2.086**	c	-43.199***	c	0.136	stat.
GOV10Y_SLO	*n*	-12.010***	c	-11.403***	c	0.433*	stat.
GOV10YR_SLO	*n*	-6.047***	c	-5.974***	c	0.135	stat.
GOVCONS_SRB	c,t	-10.070***	c	-19.112***	c,t	0.143*	stat.
GR_BIH	c,t	-18.326***	c	-51.037***	c,t	0.082	stat.
GR_CRO	c,t	-6.539***	c	-14.581***	c,t	0.139*	stat.
GR_SLO	*n*	-0.954	c	-30.254***	c,t	0.086	stat.
GR_SRB	*n*	-3.221***	c	-21.554***	c,t	0.101	stat.
GRGDPR_SLO	*n*	-5.376***	c	-7.526***	c,t	0.035	stat.
GRGDPR_SRB	*n*	-6.138***	c	-9.169***	c,t	0.057	stat.
GROSS_WAGE_CRO	*n*	-1.172	c	-11.392***	c,t	0.500***	not stat.
GROSS_WAGER_CRO	*n*	-1.812*	c	-12.045***	c,t	0.162**	not stat.
GRYPOT_SLO	*n*	-7.363***	c	-7.459***	c,t	0.061	stat.

Variable (1st diff)	ADF		PP		KPSS		
	Mod	Test statistic	Mod	Test statistic	Mod	Test statistic	Classification
GWAGE_BIH	*n*	-4.689***	c	-4.807***	c,t	0.096	stat.
GWAGE_SLO	c	-3.815***	c	-17.640***	c,t	0.094	stat.
GWAGE_SRB	c	-2.165	c	-11.007***	c,t	0.500***	not stat.
GWAGER_BIH	c	-5.983***	c	-5.992***	c,t	0.080	stat.
GWAGER_SLO	c,t	-24.681***	c	-24.183***	c,t	0.210**	stat.
GWAGER_SRB	*n*	-2.247**	c	-10.359***	c,t	0.176**	stat.
HRKDIN	*n*	-6.756***	c	-6.868***	c,t	0.115	stat.
HRKEUR	*n*	-8.447***	c	-12.123***	c,t	0.191**	stat.
HRKUSD	*n*	-2.694***	c	-5.160***	c,t	0.161**	stat.
I_DEBT_CRO	*n*	-37.885***	c	-37.367***	c,t	0.100	stat.
I_LR_CRO	c,t	-6.430***	c	-6.009***	c	0.442*	stat.
I_SR_CRO	c,t	-7.716***	c	-6.247***	c	0.593**	stat.
IFIXR_BIH	*n*	-3.143***	c	-26.684***	c,t	0.258***	not stat.
IFIXR_CRO	*n*	-1.832*	c	-9.404***	c,t	0.135*	stat.
IGOVDEBT_SLO	*n*	-43.373***	c	-37.960***	c,t	0.098	stat.
IL_BIH	*n*	-7.705***	c	-8.244***	c,t	0.295***	stat.

Variable (1st diff)	ADF Mod	ADF Test statistic	PP Mod	PP Test statistic	KPSS Mod	KPSS Test statistic	Classi-fication
IL_DEBT_BIH	*n*	-16.132***	c	-54.976***	c, t	0.104	stat.
IL_DEBT_SRB	*n*	-5.858***	c	-13.754***	c, t	0.171**	stat.
ILEND_SRB	*n*	-4.237***	*n*	-4.243***	c, t	0.047	stat.
ILREAL_BIH	*n*	-4.001***	*n*	-4.031***	c, t	0.042	stat.
IMPDEF_SLO	*n*	-5.585***	c	-6.737***	c, t	0.040	stat.
IMPR_SLO	*n*	-2.617***	c	-11.558***	c, t	0.416***	stat.
IMR_BIH	*n*	-2.642***	c	-15.132***	c, t	0.207**	stat.
IMR_BIHROW	*n*	-7.321***	c	-55.600***	c, t	0.158**	stat.
IMR_CRO	*n*	-2.758***	c	-11.075***	c, t	0.142*	stat.
IMR_CROROW	*n*	-2.166**	c	-14.042***	c, t	0.112	stat.
IMR_SLOROW	*n*	-2.560**	c	-11.588***	c, t	0.408***	stat.
IMR_SRB	*n*	-9.827***	c	-12.710***	c, t	0.236***	stat.
IMR_SRBROW	*n*	-9.735***	c	-14.914***	c, t	0.470***	stat.
INCOME_SLO	*n*	-9.315***	c	-9.388***	c, t	0.060	stat.
INCOMER_SLO	*n*	-6.474***	c	-6.476***	c, t	0.054	stat.

Variable (1st diff)	ADF		PP		KPSS		
	Mod	Test statistic	Mod	Test statistic	Mod	Test statistic	Classification
INCTAX_CRO	*n*	-3.234***	c	-15.551***	c, t	0.116	stat.
INCTAX_SLO	*n*	-10.454***	c	-29.888***	c, t	0.081	stat.
INCTAXCORP_CRO	*n*	-1.483	c	-16.160***	c, t	0.116	stat.
INCTAXCORP_SLO	*n*	-13.271***	c	-22.484***	c, t	0.103	stat.
INCTAXPERS_CRO	*n*	-3.742***	c	-18.103***	c, t	0.179**	stat.
INCTAXPERS_SLO	*n*	-8.412***	c	-51.729***	c, t	0.069	stat.
INFL_BIH	*n*	-5.959***	c	-3.920***	c, t	0.037	stat.
INFL_CRO	*n*	-4.437***	c	-5.547***	c, t	0.053	stat.
INFL_SLO	*n*	-5.613***	c	-5.651***	c, t	0.044	stat.
INFL_SRB	*n*	-3.799***	*n*	-3.811***	c, t	0.054	stat.
INTEREST_BIH	*n*	-17.506***	c	-86.080***	c, t	0.103	stat.
INTEREST_CRO	*n*	-3.174***	c	-36.942***	c, t	0.090	stat.
INTEREST_SLO	*n*	-5.634***	c	-22.999***	c, t	0.091	stat.
INTEREST_SRB	*n*	-7.808***	c	-14.807***	c, t	0.207**	stat.
INVENTR_BIH	*n*	-25.993***	c	-18.101***	c, t	0.212**	stat.

Variable (1st diff)	Mod	ADF Test statistic	Mod	PP Test statistic	Mod	KPSS Test statistic	Classification
INVENTR_CRO	*n*	-3.153***	c	-14.953***	c, t	0.098	stat.
INVENTR_SLO	*n*	-3.904***	c	-18.957***	c, t	0.135*	stat.
INVENTR_SRB	*n*	-8.440***	c	-23.504***	c, t	0.142*	stat.
INVESTR_BIH	*n*	-29.335***	c	-20.879***	c, t	0.109	stat.
INVESTR_CRO	*n*	-3.303***	c	-20.657***	c, t	0.220***	stat.
INVR_SLO	*n*	-2.492**	c	-12.803***	c, t	0.107	stat.
IR_LR_CRO	*n*	-4.188***	c	-5.948***	c, t	0.047	stat.
IS_BIH	*n*	-3.322***	*n*	-3.129***	c	0.405*	stat.
KMDIN	*n*	-3.871***	c	-7.100***	c	0.288	stat.
KMHRK	*n*	-8.355***	c	-7.542***	c, t	0.296***	stat.
KMUSD	*n*	-2.449**	c	-5.576***	c, t	0.151**	stat.
LFORCE_ADJ_BIH	*n*	-6.759***	c	-6.732***	c, t	0.104	stat.
LFORCE_BIH	*n*	-7.382***	c	-11.011***	c, t	0.309***	stat.
LFORCE_CRO	*n*	-6.626***	c	-8.201***	c, t	0.500***	stat.
LFORCE_SLO	*n*	-3.174***	c	-10.767***	c, t	0.097	stat.
LFORCE_SRB	*n*	-6.464***	c	-6.607***	c, t	0.141*	stat.
NAIRU_BIH	*n*	-1.594	*n*	-1.280	c	0.627**	not stat.

Variable (1st diff)	ADF		PP		KPSS		
	Mod	Test statistic	Mod	Test statistic	Mod	Test statistic	Classi-fication
NAIRU_CRO	*n*	-2.389**	*n*	-0.740	c, t	0.230***	not stat.
NAIRU_SLO	*n*	-2.310**	*n*	-0.005	c, t	0.257***	not stat.
NAIRU_SRB	*n*	-1.777*	*n*	-1.072	c, t	0.154**	not stat.
NBSRATE_SRB	*n*	-6.653***	c	-6.588***	c, t	0.142*	stat.
NEER_BIH	*n*	-4.807***	c	-6.244***	c, t	0.109	stat.
NEER_CRO	c,t	-4.450***	c	-6.453***	c, t	0.181**	stat.
NEER_SRB	c,t	-8.141***	c	-7.586***	c	0.484**	stat.
NET_WAGE_CRO	c	-3.366**	c	-11.691***	c, t	0.277***	stat.
NET_WAGER_CRO	c,t	-7.614***	c	-12.162***	c, t	0.154**	stat.
NWAGE_BIH	c,t	-5.395***	c	-5.721***	c, t	0.112	stat.
NWAGE_SLO	c,t	-14.08***	c	-30.236***	c, t	0.108	stat.
NWAGE_SRB	c	-2.086	c	-10.442***	c, t	0.180**	not stat.
NWAGER_BIH	*n*	-5.656***	c	-7.848***	c, t	0.086	stat.
NWAGER_SLO	*n*	-13.283***	c	-45.207***	c, t	0.100	stat.
NWAGER_SRB	*n*	-2.021**	c	-8.443***	c, t	0.500***	stat.
OILDIN	*n*	-5.509***	c	-5.605***	c, t	0.047	stat.

Variable (1st diff)	ADF		PP		KPSS		
	Mod	Test statistic	Mod	Test statistic	Mod	Test statistic	Classi-fication
OILEUR	n	-6.804***	c	-6.280***	c,t	0.047	stat.
OILHRK	n	-5.594***	c	-5.326***	c,t	0.062	stat.
OILKM	n	-5.951***	c	-5.578***	c,t	0.070	stat.
P_CONSUM_CRO	c	-3.890***	c	-10.011***	c,t	0.448***	stat.
P_G_CRO	c,t	-6.852***	c	-11.582***	c,t	0.186**	stat.
P_GDP_CRO	n	-7.645***	c	-10.968***	c,t	0.138*	stat.
PARTRATE_BIH	n	-7.481***	c	-10.051***	c,t	0.500***	stat.
PARTRATE_CRO	n	-5.790***	c	-7.652***	c,t	0.155**	stat.
PARTRATE_SLO	n	-3.457***	c	-10.858***	c,t	0.13*	stat.
PARTRATE_SRB	n	-6.271***	c	-6.360***	c,t	0.161**	stat.
PENSIONERS_SLO	c,t	-4.933***	c	-15.023***	c	0.421*	stat.
PENSIONS_SLO	c,t	-25.252***	c	-34.476***	c	0.092	stat.
PGDP_EXP_BIH	n	-2.127**	c	-7.962***	c,t	0.500***	stat.
PGDP_SRB	c	-2.466	c	-6.728***	c,t	0.091	stat.
POP1564_SLO	c,t	-6.179***	c	-4.760***	c,t	0.046	stat.
PRINVR_SLO	n	-2.849***	c	-8.914***	c,t	0.128*	stat.

Variable (1st diff)	ADF		PP		KPSS		
	Mod	Test statistic	Mod	Test statistic	Mod	Test statistic	Classi-fication
PROD_BIH	*n*	-2.618***	c	-17.600***	c, t	0.101	stat.
PROD_CRO	*n*	-14.262***	c	-8.899***	c, t	0.137*	stat.
PROD_SLO	*n*	-2.135**	c	-20.060***	c, t	0.091	stat.
PROD_SRB	c,t	-4.000**	c	-16.951***	c, t	0.110	stat.
REER41_SLO	*n*	-6.625***	c	-6.641***	c, t	0.068	stat.
REER_BIH	*n*	-4.078***	c	-12.167***	c, t	0.500***	stat.
REER_CRO	*n*	-0.760	c	-6.229***	c, t	0.226***	not stat.
REER_SRB	*n*	-1.762*	*n*	-3.887***	c, t	0.114	stat.
REMIT_BIH	*n*	-2.308**	c	-15.116***	c, t	0.194**	stat.
REV_OTHER_CRO	*n*	-3.701***	c	-34.232***	c, t	0.252***	stat.
REVOTHER_BIH	c	-10.113***	c	-15.002***	c, t	0.177**	stat.
REVREST_SLO	c	-18.145***	c	-31.055***	c, t	0.083	stat.
REVREST_SRB	c	-10.441***	c	-10.692***	c, t	0.192**	stat.
REVTOTAL_BIH	c	-2.404	c	-15.133***	c, t	0.159**	not stat.
SLO3M	c	-5.789***	c	-5.777***	c, t	0.059	stat.

Variable (1st diff)	ADF		PP		KPSS		
	Mod	Test statistic	Mod	Test statistic	Mod	Test statistic	Classi-fication
SOCBENEFIT_SRB	c	-2.679*	c	-19.112***	c,t	0.138*	stat.
SOCCOMP_SLO	c	-2.720*	c	-25.114***	c,t	0.098	stat.
SOCCONTR_BIH	c	-2.704*	c	-14.057***	c,t	0.172**	not stat.
SOCCONTR_SRB	c	-1.957	c	-15.712***	c,t	0.132*	stat.
SOCCONTREMP_BIH	c	-3.202**	c	-17.934***	c	0.377*	stat.
SOCEMP_SLO	c	-2.642*	c	-30.839***	c	0.135	stat.
SOCIALCONT_CRO	*n*	-2.875***	c	-6.867***	c	0.259	stat.
SOCTOTAL_SLO	c	-2.656*	c	-31.147***	c	0.102	stat.
SUBSIDIES_BIH	*n*	-15.028***	c	-23.333***	c,t	0.198**	stat.
SUBSIDIES_SRB	*n*	-6.791***	c	-22.813***	c,t	0.230***	stat.
TAX_OTHER_CRO	*n*	-7.138***	c	-7.058***	c,t	0.054	stat.
TAX_VAT_CRO	*n*	-2.797***	c	-10.841***	c,t	0.166**	stat.
TAXCORP_SRB	*n*	-1.749*	c	-11.914***	c,t	0.123*	stat.
TAXINC_SRB	c,t	-4.254**	c	-29.865***	c,t	0.242***	not stat.
TAXINCOME_BIH	c,t	-0.878	c	-11.699***	c,t	0.195**	not stat.
TAXVAT_BIH	*n*	-1.336	c	-12.641***	c,t	0.140*	stat.
TAXWEDGE_CRO	*n*	-1.649*	c	-11.709***	c,t	0.272***	not stat.

Variable (1st diff)	ADF		PP		KPSS		
	Mod	Test statistic	Mod	Test statistic	Mod	Test statistic	Classification
TOTALEXP_CRO	c	-8.831***	c	-21.139***	c,t	0.176**	not stat.
TOTALREV_CRO	c,t	-2.869	c	-12.670***	c,t	0.184**	not stat.
TRANSFERS_BIH	*n*	-1.112	c	-16.380***	c,t	0.159**	not stat.
TRENDEMP_BIH	*n*	-7.653***	c	-9.479***	c,t	0.419***	stat.
TRENDEMP_CRO	*n*	-6.588***	c	-7.917***	c,t	0.500***	stat.
TRENDEMP_SLO	*n*	-2.166**	c	-9.215***	c,t	0.202**	stat.
TRENDEMP_SRB	*n*	-6.441***	c	-6.858***	c,t	0.118	stat.
TRENDTFP_BIH	*n*	-1.211	*n*	-0.706	c,t	0.195**	not stat.
TRENDTFP_CRO	*n*	-1.773*	*n*	-1.471	c	0.829***	not stat.
TRENDTFP_SLO	c,t	-4.294***	*n*	-2.052	c	0.871***	not stat.
TRENDTFP_SRB	c	-5.027***	c	-2.349	c,t	0.235***	not stat.
UCC_BIH	*n*	-4.001***	*n*	-4.031***	c,t	0.042	stat.
UCC_SLO	*n*	-6.095***	c	-6.022***	c,t	0.031	stat.
UCC_SRB	*n*	-6.551***	c	-9.090***	c,t	0.500***	stat.
ULC_CRO	*n*	-3.171***	c	-12.065***	c,t	0.132*	stat.
ULC_SLO	c	-3.085**	c	-12.467***	c,t	0.073	stat.

Variable (1st diff)	ADF Mod	ADF Test statistic	PP Mod	PP Test statistic	KPSS Mod	KPSS Test statistic	Classification
ULC_SRB	*n*	-1.313	c	-6.967***	c, t	0.152**	not stat.
UN_ADJ_BIH	*n*	-5.736***	c	-5.794***	c, t	0.069	stat.
UN_BIH	*n*	-4.485***	c	-4.871***	c, t	0.083	stat.
UN_CRO	*n*	-3.148***	c	-7.488***	c, t	0.173**	stat.
UN_SLO	*n*	-2.665***	c	-5.668***	c, t	0.152**	stat.
UN_SRB	*n*	-2.316**	c	-6.396***	c	0.397*	stat.
UNBENEFIT_SLO	*n*	-8.118***	c	-8.307***	c	0.239	stat.
UR_ADJ_BIH	*n*	-5.664***	c	-5.635***	c	0.110	stat.
UR_BIH	*n*	-4.970***	c	-5.012***	c	0.122	stat.
UR_CRO	*n*	-2.785***	c	-7.588***	c, t	0.155**	stat.
UR_SLO	*n*	-2.688***	c	-5.829***	c, t	0.165**	stat.
UR_SRB	*n*	-6.284***	c	-6.400***	c, t	0.068	stat.
UTIL_BIH	*n*	-47.464***	c	-18.577***	c, t	0.104	stat.
UTIL_CRO	*n*	-17.970***	c	-13.531***	c, t	0.227***	stat.
UTIL_SA_BIH	*n*	-18.902***	c	-17.003***	c, t	0.100	stat.
UTIL_SLO	*n*	-4.282***	c	-29.929***	c, t	0.084	stat.
UTIL_SRB	*n*	-3.576***	c	-21.045***	c, t	0.114	stat.
VAT_SLO	*n*	-17.168***	c	-36.240***	c, t	0.082	stat.

Variable (1st diff)	ADF Mod	ADF Test statistic	PP Mod	PP Test statistic	KPSS Mod	KPSS Test statistic	Classi-fication
VAT_SRB	*n*	-7.225***	c	-10.467***	c	0.277***	stat.
WEDGE_BIH	c	-6.673***	c	-6.682***	c, t	0.064	stat.
WEDGE_SLO	c	-15.905***	c	-47.893***	c, t	0.071	stat.
YD_BIH	*n*	-1.248	c	-15.838***	c, t	0.107	stat.
YD_CRO	c	-2.549	c	-9.865***	c, t	0.178**	not stat.
YD_SRB	c	-2.911*	c	-13.869***	c, t	0.160**	not stat.
YDR_BIH	*n*	-1.431	c	-16.791***	c, t	0.108	stat.
YDR_CRO	*n*	-1.654*	c	-10.617***	c, t	0.216**	not stat.
YDR_SRB	*n*	-1.600	c	-12.649***	c, t	0.126*	stat.
YPOT_BIH	c,t	-5.519***	c	-5.589***	c, t	0.151**	stat.
YPOT_CRO	c,t	-6.526***	c	-5.632***	c	0.709**	stat.
YPOT_SLO	*n*	-1.011	c	-4.086***	c	0.489**	not stat.
YPOT_SRB	*n*	-4.280***	c	-5.453***	c, t	0.248***	stat.
DEBTADJ_SLO	*n*	-9.480***	c	-50.09***	c, t	0.127*	stat.
DELTA_DEBT_CRO	*n*	-8.767***	c	-29.974***	c, t	0.474***	stat.
DELTADEBT_SRB	*n*	-8.818***	c	-22.783***	c, t	0.500***	stat.
EUR10Y	*n*	-5.344***	c	-5.364***	c, t	0.084	stat.

Variable (1st diff)	ADF Mod	ADF Test statistic	PP Mod	PP Test statistic	KPSS Mod	KPSS Test statistic	Classi-fication
EUR3M	*n*	-4.308***	*n*	-4.358***	c, t	0.057	stat.
EURUSD	*n*	-6.177***	c	-5.772***	c, t	0.106	stat.
G_TRANSFER_CRO	*n*	-7.905***	c	-8.883***	c, t	0.077	stat.
GINVN_SLO	*n*	-0.722	c	-28.185	c, t	0.082	not stat.
OIL	*n*	-7.240***	c	-6.636	c, t	0.103	stat.
PENSIONERS1549_SLO	c,t	-3.906**	c	-11.09***	c, t	0.130*	stat.
PENSIONERS50_SLO	*n*	-3.775***	c	-3.928***	c, t	0.040	stat.
PENSIONERS51_SLO	c,t	-5.988***	c	-3.702***	c, t	0.078	stat.
PENSIONERS52_SLO	*n*	-2.979***	c	-5.067***	c, t	0.097	stat.
PENSIONERS53_SLO	*n*	-2.495**	c	-7.211***	c, t	0.101	stat.
PENSIONERS54_SLO	*n*	-2.664***	c	-4.706***	c, t	0.077	stat.
PENSIONERS55_SLO	*n*	-4.008***	*n*	-3.357***	c, t	0.071	stat.
PENSIONERS56_SLO	*n*	-2.774***	*n*	-6.617***	c, t	0.080	stat.
PENSIONERS57_SLO	*n*	-2.784***	*n*	-5.346***	c, t	0.065	stat.
PENSIONERS58_SLO	*n*	-2.736***	*n*	-5.664***	c, t	0.053	stat.

Variable (1st diff)	ADF Mod	ADF Test statistic	PP Mod	PP Test statistic	KPSS Mod	KPSS Test statistic	Classification
PENSIONERS59_SLO	*n*	-3.896***	*n*	-3.818***	c, t	0.048	stat.
PENSIONERS60_SLO	*n*	-3.906***	*n*	-3.819***	c, t	0.051	stat.
PENSIONERS61_SLO	*n*	-3.846***	*n*	-9.385***	c, t	0.352***	stat.
PENSIONERS62_SLO	*n*	-3.747***	*n*	-6.404***	c, t	0.075	stat.
PENSIONERS63_SLO	*n*	-3.733***	*n*	-3.650***	c, t	0.065	stat.
PENSIONERS64_SLO	*n*	-3.218***	*n*	-17.322***	c, t	0.091	stat.
PENSIONERS65_SLO	*n*	-4.297***	*n*	-19.099***	c, t	0.106	stat.
PENSIONERS66_SLO	*n*	0.078	*n*	-22.098***	c, t	0.091	stat.
PENSIONERS67_SLO	*n*	-3.671***	*n*	-12.282***	c, t	0.135*	stat.
PENSIONERS68_SLO	*n*	-2.514**	*n*	-5.130***	c, t	0.141*	stat.
PENSIONERS69_SLO	*n*	-2.607***	*n*	-11.154***	c, t	0.127*	stat.
PENSIONERS70PLUS_SLO	c	-4.136***	*n*	-7.857	c, t	0.137*	stat.
POP1549_SLO	*n*	-3.450***	c,t	-5.352***	c	0.710**	stat.
POP50_SLO	*n*	-3.766***	*n*	-3.892***	c	0.440*	stat.
POP51_SLO	*n*	-4.290***	*n*	-3.594***	c	0.108	stat.
POP52_SLO	*n*	-2.794***	*n*	-3.261***	c	0.098	stat.
POP53_SLO	*n*	-2.828***	*n*	-3.121***	c	0.106	stat.
POP54_SLO	*n*	-2.764***	*n*	-3.172***	c	0.087	stat.
POP55_SLO	*n*	-2.785***	*n*	-3.293***	c	0.109	stat.
POP56_SLO	*n*	-2.899***	*n*	-3.247***	c	0.107	stat.

Variable (1st diff)	ADF Mod	ADF Test statistic	PP Mod	PP Test statistic	KPSS Mod	KPSS Test statistic	Classi-fication
POP57_SLO	*n*	-2.682***	*n*	-3.143***	c	0.100	stat.
POP58_SLO	*n*	-2.743***	*n*	-3.209***	c	0.188	stat.
POP59_SLO	*n*	-2.640***	*n*	-3.244***	c	0.172	stat.
POP60_SLO	*n*	-2.736***	*n*	-3.131***	c	0.189	stat.
POP61_SLO	*n*	-2.742***	*n*	-3.054***	c	0.211	stat.
POP62_SLO	*n*	-2.626***	*n*	-2.935***	c	0.160	stat.
POP63_SLO	*n*	-2.827***	*n*	-2.972***	c	0.138	stat.
POP64_SLO	*n*	-2.457**	*n*	-2.522***	c	0.156	stat.
POP_BIH	*n*	-7.139***	c	-7.391***	c	0.599**	stat.
POP_CRO	c,t	-0.442	c	-7.124***	c	0.172	stat.
POP_SRB	c	-2.715*	c	-2.763*	c	0.380*	not stat.
PUBINVEST_BIH	c	-20.25***	c	-20.421***	c	0.135	stat.
REPRATE_SLO	c	-28.976***	c	-31.017***	c	0.104	stat.
RESTTRANSFERS _SLO	c	-22.509***	c	-43.124***	c	0.125	stat.
SITEUR	c	-1.996	c	-5.670***	c	0.934***	not stat.
WTRADE	c	-4.984***	*n*	-3.498***	c	0.046	stat.

*Notes: ADF: Augmented Dickey-Fuller test; PP: Phillips-Perron test; KPSS: Kwiatkowski, Phillips, Schmidt and Shin test. *, **, *** means that the null hypothesis (ADF and Phillips-Perron: no stationarity of the series; KPSS: stationarity of the series) can be rejected at the 10, 5 and 1 percent level of significance respectively.*

In the "Mod" column, the specification of the test model is shown, i.e. either without constant and trend (n), only constant (c) or constant and trend (c,t).

In the "classification" column, the variables are classified as either stationary or non-stationary when this is indicated by at least two of the unit root tests.